The Art
of Hating

COMMENTARY

"This timely book focuses on a neglected dark side of our humanity. Its principal contribution is the elaboration of our hatred and a method of using it constructively rather than destructively. Of special interest to therapists is the portion discussing a heretofore taboo topic—the therapist's hatred of the patient and its usefulness in treatment."

—Richard Robertiello, M.D.

"In his intriguing book, Dr. Schoenewolf clearly distinguishes subjective (destructive) hate and objective (constructive) hate in all walks of life. Drawing upon clinical case examples, famous cases in analysis, examples from everyday life and from literature, Dr. Schoenewolf guides the reader in becoming adept at recognizing the signs and indications of subjective hate. His description of subjective hate in the various characterological diagnostic categories is of encyclopedic scope and will be invaluable to the therapist in diagnosing and treating subjective hatred. Dr. Schoenewolf is to be especially commended for describing how the germs of subjective hate may grow within cultural, political, and social movements that often express the loftiest and most idealistic goals and aspirations. He vividly describes subjective hate in all walks of life, including parent–child interactions, love relationships, in the work place, in politics, and in the therapeutic relationship. His examples are bold and intriguing, demonstrating an independence of thought that avoids truisms and stereotyped thinking.

"The reader of this volume will come away having grown in the art of hating and being better able to help his clients to hate constructively. Dr. Schoenewolf convincingly demonstrates that objective hating is an important component of good object relating. This book is highly recommended for all mental health professionals who work with patients with difficulties around aggression and to all persons who are inclined to improve their capacity for bonding by mastering the art of hating."

—Jeffrey Seinfeld, Ph.D.

The Art
of Hating

Gerald Schoenewolf, Ph.D.

JASON ARONSON INC.
Northvale, New Jersey
London

Library of Congress Cataloging-in-Publication Data

Schoenewolf, Gerald.
   The art of hating / Gerald Schoenewolf.
      p.   cm.
   Includes bibliographical references and index.
   ISBN 0-87668-693-5
   1. Hate.   2. Love-hate relationships.   I. Title.
BF575.H3S36   1991   90-45054
152.4--dc20

Manufactured in the United States of America. Jason Aronson Inc. offers books and cassettes.
For information and catalog write to Jason Aronson Inc., 230 Livingston Street, Northvale,
New Jersey 07647.

To Jacob Kirman

Contents

Preface

The world is full of hate, but very few people know how to hate well. Most of us hate in destructive ways. As individuals we routinely act out hateful feelings—from jealousy to loathing to bitterness to contempt to disgust to irritation to rage—with hardly a backward glance. We are concerned with the immediate need to protect ourselves, to be right, to teach a lesson, to gain an advantage, to defeat an opponent, or to revenge oneself against an enemy. In the process we hurt others and ourselves, and create a climate of animosity and distrust. As groups we express our hate in ways that lead to religious crusades, racial bias, national strife, wars, and the threatened extinction of our planet through nuclear holocaust, environmental pollution, and overpopulation. Yet there is relatively little alarm raised among the general populace, as the final permutation of destructive hate is apathy.

Hating is an art. As with any art, its mastery takes practice and discipline. It's as easy to hate badly as it is to do a bad painting, forget a piano lesson, or fail an examination. To hate well, we must be able to distinguish between our objective and subjective hate, willing to risk verbalizing the objective hate and determined to ride out the consequences of verbalizing it. Objective hating resolves the conflicts that breed hate and transforms hate into its alternate feeling state, love. Objective hating affirms life, whereas subjective hating affirms destruction and death.

In a sense, this book is an answer to the many books such as Erich Fromm's *The Art of Loving* (1956), which exhort us to love one another while neglecting to adequately consider the equally important necessity for us to hate one another. It is fine and perhaps even noble to preach the art of loving, but it is difficult, if not impossible, to practice that art unless one has also mastered the art of hating. You cannot have one without the other.

Love and hate are inextricably bound; to love is to hate, and to hate is to love. When love wanders, hate springs up in its place. Subjective hate shows itself in therapy as a resistance to therapeutic progress and an aversion to the establishment of a genuine relationship. In daily life, various forms of subjective hate are expressed by individuals and groups. These include characterological, perverse, political, cultural, sexual, and parent–child hate. The art of hating can be used to counter all these as well as the ever-present menace of global hate. The question is whether the talent for artistic hating is inherited or acquired, and whether we as individuals and as a planet can learn to hate well before it is too late.

This book avoids psychoanalytic jargon as much as possible since it attempts to communicate with the widest range of people. Its aim is to fill a gap in the literature and address some of the pressing issues we face today. Subjective hating lies beneath many of the psychological, social, and physiological ills that plague humanity, and objective hating offers a potential cure for those ills. Living well, they say, is the best revenge; hating well is even better.

Disclaimers and Acknowledgments

The case histories from my own pratice included in this book have been fictionalized and do not represent actual cases but approximations based on experiences with a number of individuals of a similar type. They are presented not as scientific proofs, but as illustrations of my thesis. However, I do wish to thank my patients for supplying me with the research for this book.

I also wish to thank, whole-heartedly, the following for their advice, assistance, and support: Jason Aronson, M.D., David Belgray, Ph.D., Jerome Levin, Ph.D., Jacob Kirman, Ph.D., Paul Avila Mayer, M.S.W., Bonita K. Ullman, M.S.W., Alexander Bernstein, C.Psy., Abigail Hirsch, M.S.W., Martin Naidoff, M.S.W., Mary R. Remito, M.S.W., E. Jane Alford, and Leah Schoenewolf.

1

Love and Hate: An Overview

THE NATURE OF LOVE AND HATE

What is love? What is hate? Many have tried to define them, but no definition seems good enough. Many have tried to explain them, but no explanation seems deep enough. Perhaps no definition or explanation will ever be good or deep enough, for we humans have a tendency to keep terms such as "love" and "hate" undefined and unexplained. When we love or hate, we do not want to analyze it, fearful that analysis of these intense emotions might take away from their pleasure. Yet, by not analyzing them, they remain in the realm of the subjective; they take control of us, usually with bad consequences.

Freud's (1930) explanation of love and hate linked them to sexual and death drives that he believed to be a part of our natural endowment. Love is brought about by gratification of the sexual drive. "Man's discovery that sexual love afforded him with the strongest experiences of satisfaction, and in fact provided him with the prototype of all happiness, must have suggested to him that he should . . . make genital eroticism the central point of his life" (p. 102). Hate grows from the aggression that is an offshoot of the death drive. "The inclination to aggression is an original, self-subsisting instinctual disposition. It constitutes the greatest impediment to civilization" (p. 120). Freud saw existence as a struggle between reproduction (the instinct of life) and death (the instinct of aggression and destruction), and held out the hope that the former could prevail over the latter.

Eibl-Eibsfeldt (1970), an ethologist whose perspective is representative of his field, also posited a dual drive theory, but saw things a bit differently than Freud. Instead of a drive for sex, he spoke of a drive for bonding, and instead of a death drive with an aggressive derivative, he perceived an aggressive drive for territoriality and self-preservation. Having studied many human cultures as well as groups of higher vertebrates, he concluded that aggression is universal. "Cultural differences certainly exist in human aggression. But convincing proof that a human group is wholly lacking in aggressive behavior has so far never been produced" (p. 73). He believed our aggressive drive can be modified by our drive for bonding and, like Freud, pointed out that although the aggressive drive is innate, its intensity can be influenced by environmental circumstances.

Many variations of these two views have been advanced over the years, and there is a general consensus among psychoanalysts that some combination of bonding and aggressive drives exists. Harlowe (1958) verified the existence of a bonding drive in monkeys by conducting an experiment in which he rigged up two surrogate mothers for a group of monkey infants separated from their mothers at birth. One surrogate was made of wire and had a bottle of milk; the other was made of terrycloth but did not have milk. The infant monkeys quickly satisfied their primary needs with the wire mother, then made more extended physical contact with the terrycloth mother. Harlowe thus interpreted that the drive for physical contact was more important than the drive to satisfy primary needs. Spitz (1965) provided an illustration of the interplay of the bonding and aggressive drives, as well as the environment's influence on them, studying ninety-one infants in a foundling home who had been separated from their mothers after the age of 3 months and fed by a succession of nurses. Thirty-four of the infants died by the second year, and Spitz noticed a pattern. Upon first being separated from their mothers, they would cry and cling angrily to whatever nurse was feeding them (aggression turned outward); then they would go through a phase of anaclitic depression, lying sullenly in their cribs (aggression turned inward); then motor retardation would set in; and finally marasmus and death. Bowlby (1979) detected a similar pattern in his studies of children in British nurseries who were mourning the loss of their parents during World War I. These studies show how essential human bonding is for life, and how aggression and self-destruction erupt as a defense against the loss of bonding.

Kardiner (1954) looked at the societal dimension of this process by observing how an abrupt change in the cultural values of a society resulted in an increase in aggression. He studied a primitive tribe in which there was a change in the way rice was cultivated. Before the change, the community as a whole cultivated and distributed food. When it was decreed that all individuals were responsible for their own subsistence, there was an aggressive scramble to acquire the uncultivated wet valleys and a subsequent increase in criminality. "People became hostile to one another, feared one another, envied one another and became ruthless in dealing with one another" (p. 172).

According to these theorists, when we are in harmony with others either as individuals or as groups—an infant's attachment with its mother being the prototype of such harmony—our aggressive drive is put to the service of that harmony. When that harmonic balance is disturbed, we try to get it back be becoming more aggressive; but when it is severely disturbed over a period of time, that aggression becomes destructive to others and ourselves. This view also accords with Eastern philosophical concepts of harmony. Whereas Spitz spoke of the fusion of the sexual and aggressive drives, the Chinese sage, Lao Tzu, wrote of the harmony between man's aggressiveness and woman's softness: "One who has man's wings and a woman's also is a womb of the world" (Bynner 1944, p. 42).

Love, then, may be defined as the pleasure associated with attachment, sexual intimacy, or bonding with other people, and hate may be defined as the pain and aggression associated with separation. Love is characterized by feelings of gratitude and contentment, as when an infant has just been fed, or lovers have just had sex, or a town has just had a good meeting. Hate is characterized by feelings of betrayal or anger, as when a baby does not get fed, when lovers quarrel, when a town splits into factions, or when a world goes to war.

OBJECTIVE AND SUBJECTIVE LOVE

Fromm (1956) further refines the definition of love by making a distinction between subjective and objective love, explaining that objective love requires primarily the overcoming of one's narcissism. "The opposite pole to narcissism is objectivity; it is the faculty to see people and things *as they are*, objectively, and to be able to separate this *objective* picture from a picture which is formed by one's desires or fears" (p. 99).

Fromm (1956) links narcissistic, or subjective, love to the dreams of omniscience and omnipotence all children have during infancy, and which narcissistic individuals carry with them throughout their lives. "The insane person or the dreamer fails *completely* in having an objective view of the world outside; but all of us are more or less insane, or more or less asleep; all of us have an unobjective view of the world, one which is distorted by our narcissistic orientation" (p. 100). Objective love, on the other hand, is reasonable, and those who love objectively tend to be humble. "To be objective, to use one's reason, is possible only if one has achieved an attitude of humility, if one has emerged from the dreams of omniscience and omnipotence which one has as a child" (p. 101).

As examples of narcissistic love, Fromm cites the kinds of parents who experience their children's behavior in terms of how it reflects on them, being always concerned about whether they are obedient, give them pleasure, and are a credit to them; husbands who perceive their wives as domineering because they themselves have not separated from their mothers and blow even the slightest demands by their wives out of proportion; and wives who think their husbands are weak or stupid because they do not live up to their childhood fantasies of the white knight. Conversely, objectively loving parents are interested in what their child feels and thinks by and for herself; husbands relate to their wives as beings who are distinctly different from their own mothers; and wives do not allow their childhood fantasies to distort the reality, nor interfere with the pleasure, of their marriage. Practicing the art of loving, Fromm emphasizes, calls for discipline, concentration, patience, the courage to take risks, and a supreme concern with the mastery of that art.

Fromm's distinction between objective and subjective love parallels a distinction made in regard to patients in psychoanalysis—a distinction between the transference relationship and the real relationship. The more severely disturbed an individual is, the more subjectively he relates to the analyst; the more subject the relationship, the more the patient transfers people from his past onto the analyst and does not see the analyst for who he really is; the greater the transference, the less genuine the relationship; the less genuine the relationship, the less objective. Hence, in a successful analytic experience, the relationship between the patient and analyst gradually becomes less and less subjective and more and more objective and real.

Transference is not simply an aspect of psychoanalytic therapy, however, but is found in everyday life as well. According to Freud (1925), it is "a universal phenomenon of the human mind ... and in fact dominates the whole of each person's relations to his human environment" (p. 42). An element of all transference is narcissism—an impairment in the capacity to love. In neurotics, narcissism is less severe, while in borderlines and psychotics it is more severe. The more severe people's narcissism is, the more disturbed their transference will be and the more subjective their form of loving.

Objective loving requires what is referred to as mature object relations. When Freud and subsequent analysts allude to the sphere of object relations, they refer to the entire spectrum of relationships between the individual and the people and things in the environment. Kernberg (1976), who expanded on object relations theory, wrote of the barriers that keep people from falling and staying in love, outlining a continuum of object relations from the most subjective to the most objective. The continuum goes from psychotics, who have "an almost total incapacity for establishing genital and tender relations with any other human being," to moderately narcissistic personalities whose relations are "characterized by sexual promiscuity," to borderline characters who show "primitive idealization of the love object (with clinging infantile dependency on it) and some capacity for genital gratification," to neurotics who have the ability to establish "stable and deep object relations without the capacity for full sexual gratification," to normal individuals who attain "the capacity for tenderness and a stable, deep object relation" (p. 186). What Kernberg is suggesting is that the more deeply an individual relates to an object, the more objective is that individual's form of loving.

There is no shortage of writings on the topic of love, nor on the associated topics of bonding, sex, and narcissism. Many have pondered the meaning of love, and many others have attempted to describe the art of loving; but the writings about hate and aggression are far less numerous and more recent.

OBJECTIVE AND SUBJECTIVE HATE

Winnicott was the first to distinguish between subjective and objective hate. In his classic paper, "Hate in the Countertransference" (1949), he defined two types of countertransference reactions. Subjective countertransference feelings were associated with unresolved issues from the analyst's own past, while objective countertransference stemmed from "the analyst's love and hate in reaction to the actual personality and behavior of the patient based on objective observation" (p. 195). If an analyst was to be able to analyze psychotics or antisocial individuals, Winnicott contended, "he must be able to be so thoroughly aware of the countertransference that he can sort out and study his *objective* reactions to the patient. These will include hate" (p. 195). The analyst's main task was to maintain objectivity, "a special case of this is to hate the patient objectively" (p. 196).

Winnicott described how an orphan boy who had briefly lived with him and his wife had aroused intense feelings of hate. This boy, like many deeply disturbed patients, had a need to induce intense feelings of hate as part of what Winnicott saw as a maturational process. In order to advance that process, it was necessary for Winnicott to let the patient know about the hate. "If the patient seeks objective or justified hate, he must be able to reach it, else he cannot feel he can reach objective love" (Winnicott 1949, p. 199). Ferenczi (1931) had made this same point eighteen years earlier. Both felt that it was an error to show love to a patient who was inducing hate, because the patient would know it was a lie. "Should the analyst show love," Winnicott explained, "he will surely at the same moment kill the patient" (p. 199).

The way Winnicott dealt with his hate of the orphan boy, who was prone to destructive fits of temper, was to take him "by bodily strength" and put him outside the front door, no matter what the weather was like nor if it was day or night. There was a special bell the boy could ring, and he knew that if he rang it he would be readmitted and nothing would be said about his fit. Each time Winnicott put him outside, he told the boy he hated him for what he had just done. It was easy for Winnicott to say this, he explained, because it was true. Moreover, saying this was important not only for the boy's therapeutic progress but also because it enabled Winnicott (1949) to continue working with him "without losing my temper and without every now and again murdering him" (p. 200).

Winnicott suggests that not only should analysts learn to hate their patients objectively, but also mothers should learn to hate their infants. He lists numerous reasons why mothers should hate their babies, among them: The baby is a danger to her body during pregnancey and birth; the baby hurts her by sucking and chewing on her nipples; the baby is ruthless, treating her as a slave; the baby has to be loved unconditionally, even his excretions; the baby's love is "cupboard love," so that having gotten what he wants, he discards her; the baby has no idea how much she sacrifices for him, and especially cannot "allow for her hate;" the baby suspiciously refuses her food, but eats well with his aunt; and the baby sexually excites her but she cannot act out her feelings.

Winnicott describes objective hating by mothers as a capacity to hate without "paying the child out, " as, for example, by singing certain nursery rhymes which the child cannot understand, such as "Rockabye baby, on the tree top,/When the wind blows the cradle will rock, /When the bough breaks the cradle will fall,/Down will come baby, cradle and all." By singing such rhymes, Winnicott (1949) suggests, mothers will be able to release pent up hate without actually hurting the child, and it also spares them from reacting to the child's hateful behavior with false sentiments. "It seems to me doubtful whether a human child, as he develops is capable of tolerating the full extent of his own hate in a sentimental environment. He needs hate to hate" (p. 202).

What Winnicott was saying, in other words, was that analysts (and mothers) were likely to experience two kinds of hate towards their patients (and babies), corresponding to the two types of countertransference. Objective hate was justified by a patient's hateful behavior, while subjective hate was unjustified by the patient's behavior but stemmed from unresolved issues in the analyst's past (he had, say, a hateful father). The first task of the analyst, according to Winnicott, was to figure out whether the hate he felt was subjective or objective. If it was subjective, it should be analyzed; if necessary, the analyst should go back into analysis himself. If it was objective, he might simply use it to help him understand the nature of the transference (what role was the patient putting him into?), or he might need to verbalize it to the patient in order to help get him past a maturational block. He might also need to verbalize the feelings so as to resolve his intense countertransference reaction (as Winnicott did with the orphan boy) and continue functioning constructively.

Although Winnicott was the first to use the terms "objective" and "subjective" in terms of countertransference, he was not the first to advocate using countertransference feelings as tools to understand the patient, or verbalizing them to the patient when necessary. Ferenczi (1931), as noted earlier, was the first to suggest verbalizing hate and other emotions, and he was later echoed by Little (1951), Gitelson (1952), Searles (1958), Racker (1968), Jacobson (1971), and Spotnitz (1976), to name but a few.

Racker did not come right out and advocate the expression of hate to patients, but he did not rule it out either. Primarily he showed therapists how to objectify their hate and other feelings and use them as a tool to understand patients. He suggested that analysts ask themselves: Why have I fallen into this position now? Is the patient treating me as though I were his mother? His father? His brother? Or is this a reversal in which he identifies with his father or mother and I become the naughty child? Do my feelings indicate that he needs my love or hate? Do they indicate that he wants to triumph over me, or that he wants me to punish, criticize, or demean him? Racker's point was that a therapist cannot understand a patient through his intellect alone, but must also have an emotional awareness of what is happening in the therapy office, which would provide him with a better sense of how to treat the patient.

Spotnitz, following in the footsteps of Winnicott and Racker, also distinguished between objective and subjective countertransference. More than any other analyst before him, he laid particular stress on understanding and using the patient's hateful behavior toward him, and he devised a systematic method of objectively hating the patient back. One of his primary interventions is "the toxoid response," a way of giving the patient a dose of his own medicine.

Like Winnicott, Spotnitz believed that certain patients, particularly those who are more narcissistic, need to have their hate reflected back to them. He called this a maturational communication, and its most dramatic form was the toxoid response. An example of how Spotnitz reflected a patient's hate can be found in his case history about Fred. Fred, a sociopathic young man, would occasionally threaten Spotnitz during the course of his treatment, and Spotnitz found himself feeling angry after such threats and other provocative behavior. He analyzed his anger and decided that it was objective rather than subjective, then determined to mirror Fred's anger at the next occasion. When, a few sessions later, Fred threatened to bash Spotnitz's head in if Spotnitz did not stop "stalling," Spotnitz retorted, "No you won't, because I'll bash yours in before you can get off the couch" (Spotnitz 1976, p. 55).

Spotnitz explains the use of the toxoid response by observing that "in cases of schizophrenia, psychotic depression, and other severe disturbances, one encounters resistances, chiefly preverbal, that do not respond to objective interpretation. Their resolution is thwarted by toxic affects that have interfered with the patient's maturation and functioning" (p. 49). He contends that such resistances only yield to an "emotional working-through process" rather than to customary "working-through on an intellectual basis." With respect to the toxoid response, he compares it to the science of immunology, whereby individuals are injected with a mild case of a disease in order to immunize them against it. When narcissistic patients act out hate, their analysts "catch" that hate—developing a narcissistic countertransference to the patient's narcissistic transference. The analysts then must detoxify themselves through self-analysis, determining whether the hate they feel has been induced by the patient, stems from their own unresolved narcissism, or is a combination of both. Like Winnicott, Spotnitz advises analysts who cannot resolve countertransference feelings to seek help from a supervisor or their own analyst. When they are sure they have objectified the hate and determined it has been wholly induced by the patient, and if they also feel the patient needs to know about the hate in order to get past an impasse, they give the patient back a dose of the hate. Spotnitz explains that the patient "is given verbal injections of the emotions he has induced in the analyst, carefully 'treated' to destroy their toxicity and to stimulate the formation of antibodies. In brief, the induced emotions are employed as a toxoid" (p. 50). Spotnitz cautions that this intervention is not to be used indiscriminately, for it can cause damage to the patient if the analyst has not carefully objectified his hateful response.

The toxoid response is only one of many interventions Spotnitz devised for transforming hate from the subjective to the objective. Other interventions range from questions to commands, from explanations to puzzles, and from out-silencing the patient to out-crazying him. He referred to all the analyst's communications as verbal feedings, and suggested that the analyst time feedings according to a patient's conscious or unconscious requests for contact.

Unfortunately, many analysts do not make this distinction between objective and subjective hate. Indeed, many take a position similar to that of A. Reich (1966), who strongly attacked not only the use of countertransference feelings such as hate in understanding the patient, but particularly their expression to the patient. According to Reich, if an analyst reacts to the patient's behavior with any kind of emotional response, it is simply a symptom of the analyst's psychopathology and indicates that the analyst needs more analysis. As for expressing feelings to a patient, Reich asserts that "such an approach disregards Freud's most important formulation concerning the therapeutic aim of analysis: 'Where id was, there shall ego be.' Therefore, no lasting effect can be expected from these methods" (p. 394). Reich's arguments may be refuted on several grounds. First, she cites Freud as the ultimate authority on this question, concluding that if analysts ignore Freud's dictum of "Where id was, there shall ego be," no lasting effect will be obtained. Why? Simply because Freud said so? Classical analysts often revert to Freud the way Christians revert to the Bible. But Freud himself continually revised his views as he came to a deeper understanding of human behavior. In addition, Reich's belief that an analyst must always remain neutral does not address the contention of Winnicott and Spotnitz that there are times, in working with severely disturbed patients, when an emotional communication by the analyst is necessary to break an impasse. Finally, her notion that all emotional responses by analysts to patients are indications that the analyst has emotional problems is simply absurd. Analysts who share this view are prone to denying any feelings aroused by patients, and will therefore not really be in tune with them, much less be capable of providing them with needed maturational communications. Indeed, this notion that analysts should not have any emotional responses harkens back to a time in the early days of psychoanalysis when it had a strong empirical slant and analysts had to maintain an illusion that they were completely detached and neutral scientists: healthy people simply did not feel hate.

More and more, however, therapists are beginning to realize that healthy people are people who feel and accept the full range of emotions. Moreover, they are capable of making distinctions between subjective and objective feelings of love and hate, and of expressing that love and hate to others in ways that can be helpful in resolving conflicts. In therapy, expressing hate to a patient provides the patient with a needed emotional communication—the need to be related to in a genuine way, but without being overvalued, devalued, rewarded, or punished.

The use of objective hate to resolve an individual's pattern of acting out subjective hate has a correlation in behavioral psychology. Meyer and Chesser (1970) cite experimental evidence showing that standard psychotherapy and behavioral therapy do not work well with certain disorders. "Some disorders . . . may become autonomous as a result of biochemical or structural changes associated with their repetitive occurrence. The relative inefficacy of psychotherapy and systematic desensitization in these conditions, and their response to negative practice or aversion therapy, provides some support for the hypothesis that they are not being maintained by anxiety" (p. 202). In other words, standard psychotherapy or behavioral therapy works with neurotic disorders whose care is anxiety, but not with narcissistic disorders. For these, negative practice (having a patient repeat a form of behavior until he becomes exhausted or satiated) or aversion therapy (arranging it so that he receives some kind of shock each time he performs the behavior) work best. While analytic therapists talk of resolving resistance, behavioralists speak of extinguishing conditioned responses. It amounts to the same thing. And negative practice and aversion therapy are behavioral terms for objective hate.

When Fred told Spotnitz he wanted to bash his head in, he was relating in his typical way, acting out subjective hate. Like all sociopathic personalities, he was attempting to provoke a response from the environment. He wanted an emotional response of hate from Spotnitz, being determined to induce Spotnitz to either yield to his intimidation or kick him out of therapy. Either would have allowed him to escape from his anxiety. Spotnitz tried the classical approach of analyzing these threats, but this did not break the impasse. Fred saw all interpretations as attempts to manipulate. Had the relationship continued in this vein, Fred might have had to temporarily suppress his hate, putting the impasse into an entrenched mode, or he might have had to give vent to his impulse to behave violently. By responding with a counterthreat, Spotnitz (1976) provided Fred with the objective hate he needed at that particular point. Afterward Fred spoke with relief, exclaiming, "You really do hate me as much as I hate you, and you can be even more vicious!" (p. 55)

Spotnitz understood that one of Fred's main problems was that all his life he had been told that he was bad, that his violent impulses were evil, and that he was evil for having them; subsequently he had developed the compulsive need to continually act out such impulses in order to punish those who had told him he was bad, as if to say, "Well, if you think I'm so bad, I'll show you just how bad I can be!" Instead of telling Fred he was bad, Spotnitz mirrored him. By doing so he refrained from squashing, judging, or analyzing the impulses, as others had done. Fred was relieved by this response and felt his hate was understood. "If someone he respected and relied on could accept and verbalize such urges, so could he," Spotnitz notes (1976, p. 55). After a while Fred learned to accept these urges and they lost their compulsive, destructive quality. Spotnitz was able to return to standard analytic technique. Objective hate had resolved subjective hate.

Can the methods employed by analysts such as Winnicott, Racker, and Spotnitz be used by nonanalysts in their relations with themselves and others? Can ordinary citizens learn to understand their own subjective hate and master the art of hating objectively in order to facilitate progress in their personal and professional relationships? This book contends that they can.

THE RELATIONSHIP BETWEEN LOVE AND HATE

"What the world needs now is love, sweet love..." goes the first line of a popular song. This sentiment has been expressed in countless songs, movies, television shows, and books. I disagree with this notion. What the world needs now is not love. It needs hate—objective hate.

You cannot live on love alone. This popular yearning for "love, sweet love" represents a kind of magical thinking, a childish wish for boundless love without any disruptions of hate. Only infants during the first weeks of life can have love without hate—only they receive love unconditionally (and even they do not always receive it).

Yet we constantly come up against this sentiment, a sentiment which, in actuality, is an expression of narcissism and subjective hate. For example, a man comes home from war, and he is bombarded with sweet love by his wife, children, and friends. Yet it does not help him. Haunted by memories and nightmares, he cannot work, cannot sleep, and cannot make love to his wife. He babbles on and on about war, particularly about a time when he was wounded and lost an arm. He complains endlessly about being a cripple, and recalls how he starred on his high school football team. His wife and friends do not want to hear this endless babbling and complaining; their message to him is, "Everything's going to be all right. Our love will make you better. Why don't you just put all that behind you and get on with your life?" The man is not consoled by their love, and he cannot put "all that" behind him. Why? Because he is not getting what he needs in order to progress to the stage of putting all that behind. He needs to be able to verbalize his hate about what has happened to him, his hate for the enemy who did this to him, his envy toward those soldiers more fortunate than he, and his resentment toward his wife and friends for so blithely telling him to forget about it and enjoy what he has now. His wife, children, and friends need to verbalize their hate for what has happened to him, their disgust for the stump that has to substitute for his arm, and their resentment about his endless babbling and complaining. The objective verbalization of this hate will allow for the transition into the next stage of mourning—sadness about the loss of the arm and all it represents—and into the ultimate stage of gratitude and rebonding between the soldier, his wife, and his friends.

If the man's wife and friends insist on telling him to put it all behind him and move on, they will keep him stuck in this dysfunctional state of being. Unconsciously, his complaints are attacks on them, designed to arouse their guilt and pity. Unconsciously they will perceive them as attacks and will retaliate by responding unempathically—belittling his complaints, trying to make him feel guilty in turn. It is a case of his subjective hate meeting their subjective hate; it is an impasse. Only if one party or the other can rise above this subjectivity will the impasse be broken. If he somehow gains insight into the effect his constant complaining is having on his wife and friends, sees that it is not getting him what he wants, and learns to verbalize his hate objectively, he can break the impasse himself. Of if his wife and friends can rise above their subjective hate and respond as outlined above, they can break it. Such impasses are common to all relationships between individuals and between groups.

Subjective hate is the chief problem of human existence. Subjective hate invariably gets acted out in a destructive way. Most people live by the proverb, "That which you don't know won't hurt you," but just the reverse is true; it is precisely what you do not know that will hurt you. A great many, if not all, of the dilemmas that face individuals, as well as the social problems that face humanity, stem from hate that has been denied, attributed to others, rationalized, and in other ways subjectively experienced and expressed.

As Fromm points out, the opposite of love is not hate, but apathy. When all our efforts to hate objectively or subjectively fall short, we sink into an apathetic state. We wish to die. Such was the case with Spitz's abandoned babies, and such is often the case with those who suffer from schizophrenia.

Suttie (1935) saw hate as a plea for love: when that plea is not heeded it becomes the source of all human misery. "All 'good' and human happiness depend upon personal relationships of a harmoniously responsive character and ... all evil and unhappiness spring from the inadequacy of these relations" (p. 127). Both love and hate are forms of caring and living. To hate somebody is to express an intense need for them that has been frustrated. When the soldier kept babbling and complaining about his lost arm, he was pleading for love. When Fred threatened to bash Spotnitz's head in, he was pleading for love. When a baby screams and has a fit, this is a plea for love. They are not pleading for the popular notion of "love, sweet love," but rather for a particular kind of emotional reaction, a genuine response that is both loving and hating at the same time.

Objective hate and objective love are one.

2

Hate as Resistance in Therapy

RESISTANCE

In order to hate well, we must first learn how we hate badly; that is, we must learn all about subjective hating. A prototype of subjective hating is the way patients resist therapy. All resistance to therapy is, directly or indirectly, an expression of hate.

People who enter therapy share one thing in common: they all have problems with intimacy. They are unable to bond effectively with other people because during their childhoods they did not learn how to form healthy bonds. For whatever reasons, their caretakers were unable to supply them with the kind of environment they needed, and their drive for bonding was frustrated. They suffer—in therapy and in life—from an excess of aggression, a reaction to the early environmental fault; it is sometimes directed outward to the environment and sometimes inward at the self; it is sometimes obvious and sometimes disguised. This excess of aggression turns into hate and ignites a resistance to therapy and to all forms of genuine bonding.

Two brief examples of resistance in therapy come to mind—one that is rather striking, and one more subtle.

A man walked into my office for an initial consultation, picked up a chair, and moved it close to mine. He sat staring into my eyes for a moment, his face only inches away. There was a slight grin in the corners of his mouth.

"You're the twelfth therapist I've seen," he told me. "I hope you don't turn out like the others."

"What were the others like?" I asked.

"Honestly? Jerks," he said. "Pompous jerks. They pretended to be neutral and unbiased, but I found that not only were they *not* neutral but they were arrogant as well. Quite frankly, I've been to some of the top therapists in New York. Not one of them really understood me." He glared into my eyes probingly, suspiciously. It was the glare of a paranoiac. He had already decided I was out to get him, and he was studying the glint of my eyes for any trace of hate. As he studied me I found myself feeling hateful—miffed at being so abruptly challenged—and I had to keep looking away as he went on a diatribe about his life, about how he had gone from job to job because his bosses were usually inferiors who sooner or later felt jealous of his superior intellect and would either fire him or force him to quit, and how he had recently married a woman whose many declarations of love did not calm his suspicions that she was seeing other men. He could not find anybody who was trustworthy, he said, and looked at me even more pointedly. "All of the therapists I've gone to were liars," he said, "but I could always see right through their facades." He paused and looked at me, the grin on his face a bit wider. "So, tell me," he asked. "Do you think you can help me?"

"Suppose I said I could? What would that mean to you?" I asked.

"Don't give me any of your psychoanalytic crap. Answer the question." His grin had turned accusatory.

I felt a wave of anger rise up in me, and I had an impulse to do violence to his upper body. I held these feelings in check, recognized them to be countertransference feelings induced by the patient, and waited for them to subside. After a moment I asked, "What kind of answer did you want from me?" I purposely raised my voice a bit, letting him see the anger he had aroused. It took him aback, but not enough.

"Just tell me the truth," he said impatiently.

"The truth is that there's no guarantee I can help you."

"That's what they all say."

"It seems that whatever I say is going to be wrong."

"I think this is a good time to stop." He grinned knowingly and made a show of putting my chair back where he had gotten it. "It's quite clear where you're coming from," he said as he went to the door. "And you're not going to have a chance to play your games with me." He walked out of my office without paying the consultation fee.

This man's resistance was enormous. His desire for therapy—that is, for bonding—had been completely derailed by his hate for me. He hated me before he even walked through the door, quite obviously and consciously. He had decided in advance that I was another therapist who pretended to know things, a liar, and a jerk. He had already typecast me and there was no way I could get out of it. His mission was to seek and destroy male authority figures—primarily therapists, but also bosses and others. He was not interested in knowing me as a human being or learning from me; he was bent on degrading, defeating, and abandoning me, as he had done with eleven previous therapists. It may well be that he had been degraded, defeated, and abandoned in his childhood.

The patient had transferred a hated figure from his past onto me—perhaps his father, his mother, an uncle, or an older brother or sister who had abused him. This instant transference brought with it an instant resistance to therapy and to me. From his point of view, he had to defeat me before I defeated him. Having experienced earlier authority figures as deceitful, he imagined I was going to play games with him. Having found his childhood caretakers to be arrogant and abusive, he imagined I would be so. Actually, *he* was arrogant and abusive toward me, and *he* was playing the games. But he was a long way from being able to look at that. Maybe after another twelve therapists this repeating pattern would run out of steam. Then, if a therapist said to him, "It seems that whatever I say is wrong," a ray of light would enter his brain and he would be ready to start therapy. Until then the repeating pattern of resistance to therapy and hate for all therapists would continue.

The second example of resistance concerns a young woman who seemed to be the perfect patient. She was tall and attractive with rosy cheeks and a pleasant smile—the kind of person people generally think of as wholesome. From the moment she entered my office she was friendly and cooperative. I suggested she lie on the couch so as to get deeper into her thoughts, and she did so without hesitation. I asked her to bring in dreams and she brought in gobs of them. I gave her interpretations of the dreams and she smiled joyfully and exclaimed, "I never thought of that before. It's so true!" Yet, despite this overtly cooperative attitude I did not have positive feelings about her. Instead I felt anxious about what was to come, the way one feels during the calm before a storm.

One day she decided not to lie down on the couch. She sat facing me with a thoughtful expression in her eyes. She was dressed differently, clad in a white summer dress with a low-neckline, and was wearing a dark red shade of lipstick. "I have something I want to tell you. I think I'm falling in love with you," she said, blushing.

Her declaration of love did not arouse tenderness in me, but rather more anxiety. "Why don't you lie down and we'll discuss it," I suggested.

"Why can't we talk face to face like normal people?"

"What do you mean by 'normal people'?"

"I don't know . . . never mind. I'll lie back if that's what you think is best." She smiled cheerily, as though what had just happened did not matter.

"So, you think you're falling in love with me?" I pressed on.

"Yes."

"What does that mean exactly?"

"What does it mean?"

"Yes. Like, does it mean you want to run away with me to Rio?"

"No."

"Does it mean you want to marry me and have my children?"

"I don't know," she blushed. "It's not important."

She fell silent for a while, then changed the subject. Once again she became the pleasant, dutiful patient, recalling several recent dreams.

A month later she again sat up. "I don't know what to do. I feel so . . . in love with you." Again I asked her to lie down and talk about it. She did so with more reluctance than the first time, and once more refused to analyze it. After several months of this she began to come late for her sessions, cancel frequently, and fall silent for minutes at a time. Then she began to talk about wanting to move to another town and about not being able to afford therapy.

What was really going on? It would appear, initially, that this patient had simply fallen in love with me, had felt spurned by me, and had then stopped cooperating. However, when we were able to resolve her resistance and analyze this early phase in the treatment, it became apparent that there was much more to it than that.

This young woman had a great deal of hate and resentment toward men, which we traced back to a mother who also had this kind of unconscious resentment, and to a father who demanded complete allegiance from his daughter, an allegiance which required her to be dutiful and compliant and forbade her from displaying any outward aggression toward him, lest he disapprove of her. Subsequently, the patient built up a lot of hate and resentment for her father that could never be expressed directly and which had to be kept unconscious. Because she harbored unconscious hostile thoughts toward him, and later to other men, she also unconsciously feared he and other men had the same thoughts about her. Having learned to defend against this fear by being pleasant and seductive with her father, she did likewise with other men. She had had many affairs at the time she began therapy with me, and in no instance had an affair lasted more than a year. Soon after her initial sexual encounter with a man, she would find herself feeling bored with him, then contemptuous, particularly if he expressed tenderness to her. Before long she would drop him.

When she entered treatment with me, she began repeating the same pattern. Both her seeming cooperation and her profession of love were, in reality, expressions of resistance and hate: they were lies. Her unconscious hostility toward her father and men made it impossible for her to truly give herself to a man, or to the process of therapy, which represented another way of giving herself to a man. Truly surrendering to an experience of intimacy with a man was associated by her, in some back lot of her mind, with annihilating the man or being annihilated by him. It meant reactivating infantile fears and hatred of her father.

As the analysis progressed, she got in touch with her deep-seated resentment of her father, envy of his masculinity, loathing of his sexuality and his penis, and anger about the apparent privileges his masculinity afforded him. She also discovered anger at her mother for not standing up to her father. All this hate got transferred to me in therapy. Hence my response to her apparent love was anxiety, not love. From the beginning I sensed an unreal quality to it. Had I responded to her seduction I would have ended up like all the other men she had gone out with—the object of her contempt. By not responding and, instead, analyzing her resistance, I helped her to understand this pattern and break it.

These are but two examples of resistance in therapy. Variations of resistance are as numerous as the kinds of people who inhabit this planet, and they are just as numerous outside as inside the therapy office. Resistances apply to all kinds of relationships—therapy and otherwise.

THE HISTORY OF RESISTANCE ANALYSIS

Freud first spoke of resistance in *Studies in Hysteria* (Breuer and Freud 1895), when he described his efforts to help patients remember traumatic events from their pasts. "By means of my psychical work I had to overcome a psychical force in the patients which was opposed to the pathogenic ideas becoming conscious (being remembered)" (p. 268). Later, he broadened his definition of resistance, calling it "whatever interrupts the progress of analytic work" (Freud 1900, p. 517). Then, toward the end of his life, he added that "resistance prevents any change from taking place" (Freud 1937, p. 252).

Fenichel (1945) details various types of resistant behavior in therapy. Common forms include silence, endless superficial babbling, frequent lateness, frequent canceling of sessions, and frequent protests that the therapy costs too much. Patients may forget important events from the day before, or something that has already been discussed in the therapy. They may be critical of the therapist or feel generally antagonistic and ill at ease. They may wish to talk only of present problems and avoid looking at the past, or they may want to talk only of the past and not link the past with the present. They may be too intellectual, avoiding an understanding of their emotions, or they may be too emotional, avoiding an objective understanding of themselves. They may have what Fenichel called a "hidden" resistance, agreeing with everything the therapist says, but still make no progress because unconsciously they are telling themselves, "That would all be very fine if it were true, but I don't know if it is true." They may constantly try to refute the theoretical validity of psychoanalysis instead of seeking clarification in their own life. Or they may "become enthusiastic supporters of psychoanalysis in order to avoid applying it to themselves" (p. 29). Fenichel divides resistances into two types: acute resistances, which are easier to handle, and which defend against the analysis of a particular topic, such as one's parents, one's obesity, or one's indirect aggression; and character resistances, which are harder to handle, and which are made up of prevailing attitudes that serve to maintain a patient's repressions. These attitudes come into play in therapy and are exhibited toward the therapist; they "must first be broken down before the repressions can be resolved" (p. 29).

Wilhelm Reich (1933) was among the first to note that resistance was generally related to unexpressed aggression. He chastised his colleagues for unconsciously training their patients to be polite, contending that when patients were positive and cooperative, analysts responded positively, but when they were critical, analysts were silent. "It may be more agreeable to treat a polite patient than it is to treat an impolite, highly outspoken patient who might, for example, tell the analyst straight off that he is too young or too old, hasn't a beautifully furnished apartment or has an ugly wife, is not very bright or looks too Jewish, acts like a neurotic, should be in analysis himself" (p. 32). Indeed, in Reich's day many analyses ended prematurely because they dealt only with surface symptoms and not with the deeper layers of resistance which stemmed from the patients' hate.

Reich developed a method he called character analysis, which advocated that analysts draw out a patient's negative transference by confronting through interpretation or other means the characterological resistance. In other words, Reich believed the patient's hate was expressed through his very personality, and hence an analyst had to confront aspects of the patient's personality to get at the resistance. He listed four typical kinds of patients: passive-feminine and hysterical patients who have converted their hate into the opposite and are always "obsequious, obtrusively friendly, implicitly trustful, in short, the good patients; compulsive patients who have converted their hate into "being polite at all costs" and are always "rigidly conventional and correct"; compulsive and hysterics whose emotions are paralyzed and are characterized by "an exaggerated but blocked aggressiveness"; and narcissistic patients who defend against their aggression by depersonalizing—usually by numbing themselves from the neck downward—and play-acting that they are having other feelings while secretly chuckling "at everything and everybody, a chuckle which becomes a torture to the patient himself" (pp. 34–35).

Winnicott (1950), noting that aggression is "part of the primitive expression of love, " sees resistance as stemming from unfused aggression. When the love drive is frustrated, hate gets split off from love, bringing about emotional or physical illness. "In illness a patient may display activities and aggressiveness not fully meant" (p. 205). Thus unfused, aggression makes itself felt in all kinds of relationships, he asserts, but "it is very common to find large quantities of unfused aggression complicating the psychopathology of an individual who is being analyzed" (p. 214).

Kernberg (1975) and Spotnitz (1985), like Reich, believe that a therapist should focus, first and foremost, on the hate—as manifested by the character resistances. Kernberg, however, primarily utilizes confrontation through interpretation. The character resistances need to be confronted, Kernberg contends, especially in work with borderline patients, because of their extreme distrust of the therapist and their tendency to "bite the hand that feeds them." Spotnitz uses an array of interventions to confront, and sometimes provoke or attack, a patient's character resistances.

At the deepest level, resistance always represents the expression of subjective hate. It may also represent many other things, according to the framework in which one views it; for example, psychoanalysts from the classical tradition might say that resistance represents anything from which the ego has to defend itself, including castration fear, penis envy, oral cravings for dependence, fears of reengulfment by the mother, fears of the loss of grandiose delusions, and so on. It is my theory, however, that such defenses have invariably been brought into play due to a flaw in the bonding process, and that hate underpins all these resistances, even if they are related to envy, fear, or need; for in every case in which a defense against an envy, fear, or need emerges as resistance, upon deeper inspection one also finds aggression that has been induced through some form of frustration during a particular phase of development.

For example, if a child has a clinging mother, such a mother will frustrate a child's natural drive for independence, particularly during certain phases of development. There is a critical phase dubbed by Mahler (1968) as the "separation-individuation phase" during which an infant separates from the mother, first through crawling, then walking, then through opposing the Mother commands. (This last stage has been referred to as "the terrible twos" by popular writers.) If during this phase a mother, due to a narcissistic need to keep the child dependent on her or obedient to her authority, squashes all the child's attempts to separate by preventing her from walking away from her, or spanking her every time she says "no," the child will develop a certain kind of character. The child will feel frustrated by her mother's clinging behavior and will fight for her independence. If the mother allows her to fight but nevertheless continues to cling, the little girl may develop an overtly aggressive and stubbornly defiant character. If her mother not only stifles her drive for independence but also suppresses her aggression, she may develop a masochistic character. In any case, the child learns to act out some form of subjective hate in response to the mother's expression of subjective hate (the clinging and squashing behavior).

Later, in her relationships in general, and in her relationship to her therapist in particular, the effects of the frustration of her quest for independence will emerge as resistances to genuine communication and intimacy with loved ones and with the therapist. She will fear that if she surrenders to the therapy process, the therapist, like her mother in infancy, will try to make her dependent on him and squash her. Deep down she will resent and hate him, as she once did her mother.

Resistance in therapy (and in relationships in general) represents a defense against the reactivation of infantile envy, fear, and need, and the struggles associated with them. At the same time, on a more basic level, it is an acting out of the subjective hate first engendered by caretakers during infancy.

RESISTANCE AND ACTING OUT

Freud (1914a) first used the term *acting out* and related it to resistance in his paper, "Remembering, Repeating, and Working Through." In it he wrote that "the patient does not *remember* anything of what he has forgotten and repressed, but acts it out. He reproduces it not as a memory but as an action; he *repeats* it, without, of course, knowing that he is repeating it" (p. 150). He added, "The greater the resistance, the more extensively will acting out (repetition) replace remembering" (p. 151). Freud noticed that patients had repeating patterns of behavior, a phenomenon he called "repetition compulsion" and linked with the death drive. In therapy, the repetition compulsion became evident in the way Freud's patients behaved toward him. He realized they were repeating a form of overly defensive behavior they had first developed in childhood, and this behavior had almost nothing to do with how he was responding to them.

Since Freud, the concept of acting out has been redefined, enlarged, and narrowed. In the beginning it was used to describe the behavior of neurotics reacting to the frustrations of the analytic procedure; then it was broadened to include all forms of irrational, impulsive, delinquent, or perverse behavior. Eventually the term found its way into popular usage, and became synonymous with "acting up." In the process, the subtle distinction between "acting out" and "acting up" was lost. Acting up refers solely to overtly antisocial or criminal behavior, while acting out refers to all ways of expressing feelings through behavior. Hence, murder or rape are forms of acting up as well as acting out, while frequent tardiness or forgetfulness cannot be viewed as acting up, but may be seen as acting out.

Acting out is not the only way in which resistance to bonding is expressed, but it is the most prevalent way. Resistance may also take the form of a physical illness, as when a patient loses his voice due to an unconscious conflict about something that he has said or is afraid to say, or develops a hearing problem because of what he hears or does not want to hear. This is referred to as somatizing, rather than acting out. It is equally destructive to bonding.

The behavior of the paranoid man described in the beginning of this chapter is an example of acting out. Instead of remembering that as a child he had been persecuted by his father or mother and had not been able to successfully defend himself against that persecution, he acted out this memory with me and other therapists. He stormed into my office and moved my chair without my permission. He glared into my eyes. He put me on the defensive. He accused me of playing games with him. This may be the way he would like to have defended himself with his parents, or it may have been the way they treated him, and he now identifies with them and persecutes therapists, who become symbolic stand-ins for his split-off child self.

The behavior of the seductive young woman is another example. When she sat up instead of lying on the couch and attempted to lure me into a romantic relationship, she was reliving a past memory rather than recalling it. She was acting as though I were her stern, oppressive father, rather than remembering how he was and how she felt about him.

Why do people act out? (Or, to use the paranoid man's term, why do they "play games?") Boesky (1982), struggling with this question, refers to Freud's (1912) explanation that acting out occurs when the patient's transference to the therapist becomes too hostile or too intense. He adds, "Viewed from the angle of defense, clinical experience easily confirms that the shift to action serves to avoid unpleasant affects evoked by emerging transference fantasies in the 'here and now'" (p. 48). In other words, in Freud's and Boesky's opinion, acting out happens when a patient is threatened by emerging feelings such as sexual or aggressive impulses toward the therapist. This explains how, but not why a patient acts out his feelings.

I would put it more schematically. Patients—and people in general—act out rather than remember and verbalize because they feel threatened by intimacy and the prospect of bonding with another person. They assume that verbalizing their feelings will make them vulnerable to psychological or physical danger. As children, they learn not to verbalize their feelings. Indeed, many of their tantrums happen before they are even able to talk, and when they occur after they have learned to talk, children are often throttled when they attempt to verbalize their feelings and express objective hate to their parents.

It is probable that if the paranoid man had attempted to verbalize his feelings to his childhood persecutors—his mother and father, let us say—they would have denied abusing him. Had he been able to say to them, "You're mistreating me and I don't like it!" they would have replied, "You're getting just what you deserve!" Such a child will learn that it is not beneficial to acknowledge or verbalize things. It is best just to "beat the other person to the punch." He believes that only fools verbalize their feelings.

Similarly, the compliant and seductive young woman would not have been able to verbalize her feelings of hate for her stern and oppressive father, for had she done so he would probably have expressed dismay at her misperception of things and disapproval of her for verbalizing it. She learned to keep such feelings to herself, to be compliant and seductive, and to express the hate in indirect ways—namely by the seduction and abandonment of men in her adult life.

Parents who hate subjectively produce children who hate subjectively. Parents who are resistant to bonding will produce children who are resistant to bonding. Parents who act out rather than verbalize feelings will produce children who act out rather than verbalize feelings. Children of subjectively hateful and resistant parents will not be allowed to verbalize their thoughts and feelings. They will not learn to express objective hate or to experience trust, gratitude, genuine tenderness, and the security of healthy bonding. The traumatic frustrations resulting from their parents' subjective hate causes them to become stuck in a repeating pattern, one which was originally developed to defend themselves from self-destruction but which, in adulthood, prevents them from achieving adequate bonding and mires them in the very self-destructive pattern they wish to avoid.

Resistance in therapy is, as I have said, a prototype of the resistance that is common to all relationships. Unless one has had a perfect upbringing, one will have a degree of resistance to bonding, and that resistance will be expressed one way or another, usually through a form of acting out and sometimes through the somatizing of feelings. The under-belly of all resistance is subjective hate, and the ultimate goal of subjective hate is control, destruction, and death.

3

Characterological Forms of Hate

People express subjective hate in characteristic ways. In psychoanalysis we have names for these characterological forms of hating: character defenses and resistances. All character types have typical methods of defending against presumed threats and resisting genuine communication with others and with themselves. These characterological defenses and resistances are learned in early childhood.

Reich (1933), who pioneered the study of character, believed that every character type represents both a defense against the outer world and a defense against repressed inner drives. Personalities are formed, he contended, as a result of identification with caretakers in infancy and according to how and when the drive for bonding meets its most crucial frustration. However, constitution also plays a role; recent research on infant behavior such as that conducted by Stern (1977) suggests that certain basic personality features may be part of our genetic make-up, since they are present from birth, and research with identical twins separated at birth and reared in different environments has established a genetic link with some forms of schizophrenia and manic-depression (Kolb 1977).

Be that as it may, one's capacity for bonding or the way one pathologically defends against bonding—and therefore expresses subjective hate—is primarily derived from how one is loved or hated during infancy and childhood. Even infants with cranky dispositions can be nurtured toward healthy functioning by good parenting, and psychoanalytic research has shown that even in schizophrenia or depression there is invariably an environmental factor (Laing and Esterson 1964, Lidz et al. 1965).

Below is a partial list of character types, along with schematic descriptions of how they form and how they express subjective hate. Most of us fall under one or more of these categories.

HYSTERIA

Hysteria was the first emotional disorder studied by psychoanalysis, but it has been known since ancient times. It was pandemic at certain periods of time, especially during the Middle Ages and the Victorian Era—both periods of extreme sexual repression. Hysterics are generally women, but on occasion they can be men, usually homosexual men who have a strong identification with their hysterical mothers. They are prone to acting out as well as somatizing their hate.

Genesis

Freud noted early in his career that "hysterical patients suffer from reminiscences" (1910, p. 19), meaning they suffer from repressed memories of the frustration of their sexuality in infancy. Fairbairn (1941) building on Freud's theory, suggested that the basis of hysteria was a rejection of the female sexual organs. Fenichel (1945) found a rejection of the male sexual organ, specifically "a wish to bite off and incorporate the penis" so as to gain revenge "on the man who possesses the envied organ" (p. 229).

They are usually quite attractive as little girls, and are made to feel guilty about their infantile sexual feelings. The mother, generally hysterical herself, transmits to the little girl negative feelings about femininity and sexuality and acts out competitive feelings by intruding on the little girl's relationship with the father. The father contributes to the dilemma by either condemning the little girl's sexual feelings or responding in a covertly or overtly sexual manner. As a result, the little girl builds up a resentment toward both the mother and father and has ambivalent feelings about her femininity and sexuality. Parents of hysterics are generally intolerant of any direct expression of aggression, so the child has to resort to the subjective expression of hate. Hysterical mothers model hysterical behavior.

Hysterical Hate

Hysterics act out hate in a variety of ways. Having been shamed sexually as children, they become compulsively flirtatious as adults while denying that they are doing so. They tease men, but are shocked if a man claims he was led on. The most hateful kind will tease a boss or other authority figure and then, when the boss makes an advance, cruelly reject him. If he gets angry at having been led on and tells her so, she may sue him for sexual harassment, rape, or the like, loudly proclaiming her innocence. Indeed, the more guilty she is of leading the man on, the more vigorously she will attempt to pin all the blame on him. Her hatred of men has to do with feelings of inferiority about her femininity and resentment toward men—who are seen as superior or as having a superior status—and fear of her sexuality. Feelings of sexual attraction for men reactivate Oedipus conflicts and the fear of competing with mother. The hysteric runs from men to prove her lack of interest in her father (for whom all men become symbols); and toward women as a way of appeasing mother (for whom all women become symbols).

Their relationships with both men and women are frought with anxiety and ambivalence. They are unconscious of their seductive and provocative behavior and their hate toward men, which they project onto men; hence they are intensely fearful of the hate they assume men feel for them. This fear often takes the form of an obsessive fear of male sexuality—of rape, sexual molestation, and sadism.

Hysterics fear honest communication with both men and women, as well as with their children, always anxious that they will be confronted with their hateful (seductive, provocative) behavior—the behavior for which they were shamed as children; hence they use guilt-induction, shaming, blaming, threats of leaving, and fits of temper to suppress real relating. Through their hysterical outbursts and other behaviors they often make it seem as though they are being victimized, while in fact it is they who are often victimizing those around them.

In times past hysterics were prone to somatizing their hate through hysterical illnesses such as becoming suddenly paralyzed or blind even though physicians could find nothing structurally wrong with them. Through such illnesses they were able to avoid conflict and manipulate those around them. Nowadays hysterics are more likely to somatize their hate by getting headaches and severe menstrual cramps, or developing cysts or cancers, particularly in their female organs (Alexander 1950; Baker 1967; Wilson and Mintz 1989). Those who had smothering parents may also develop asthma or anorexia. Such illnesses are an expression of their unconscious ambivalence about sexuality and bonding, often aimed specifically at those around them whom they make responsible for their conflicts. A wife may express hate for her husband, for example, by developing headaches or vaginismus whenever he wants sex or, in extreme cases, by developing cysts in her breasts or uterus, or other problems which require an hysterectomy. If she resents being a mother, she may develop ovarian cancer or another form of illness that will render her sterile. (Often, it also renders her dead; which supports the idea that hysterics would rather die than be confronted with the reality of their subjective hating.)

Examples

Portraits of hysterics abound, as their attractiveness, overt sexuality, and temperamental behavior lend themselves to drama. Examples in literature include Cleopatra in *Antony and Cleopatra*, Blanche Dubois in *A Streetcar Named Desire*, Scarlett O'Hara in *Gone With the Wind*, and Becky Sharp in *Vanity Fair*, and the heroines of *Anna Karenina* and *Lady Chatterly's Lover*. The operas *Carmen* and *Madame Butterfly* also provide interesting portraits of hysterics—the former a borderline hysteric who drives a man into killing her, the latter an example of how much hysterics can use denial to defend against reality (the fact that her lover will never return), along with its tragic results. In movies, Godard's *Breathless* and Wertmuller's *Swept Away* provide fascinating characterizations of hysterics using intellectual and phallic-aggressive defenses to control men.

PHALLIC AGGRESSION

Phallic-aggressives have historically been males, but recently one sees more and more phallic-aggressive females—sometimes referred to in the literature as masculine-aggressives or phallic women. It was Reich (1933) who first described this character type and, coincidentally, was himself a phallic-aggressive. Athletic and attractive, phallic men are prone to being womanizers (they are sometimes referred to in popular literature as "Don Juans"). Phallic women are confident, physically vigorous, and often intellectual. Phallics of both genders are openly aggressive, proud, and outgoing. They always anticipate an attack (whether or not one is forthcoming), and therefore generally attack first.

Genesis

Phallics are fixated at the oedipal stage of development, a stage between the ages of 3 to 6 when boys become phallic-narcissistic. During this period boys become infatuated with the magical things their penises can do (urinate, become erect), and with the good sensations they bring. Girls also become infatuated with penises, and imagine that they have one or that they will get one. Phallics have a close-binding relationship with the parent of the opposite sex, often one with a sexualized undertone. However during the phallic stage this parent in some way frustrates, demeans, or denies the child's sexuality. Mothers of phallics, because of unresolved penis envy, often cannot tolerate the kind of exhibitionism that boys are prone to at this age, and behave rejectingly. Fathers of girl phallics, because of unresolved castration fear, cannot tolerate a daughter's sexual aggression and curiosity about their penises, and also behave rejectingly and scornfully. As adults, phallics remain narcissistically attached to their genitals and have a compulsive need to prove their sexual prowess. They cultivate an aggressive, arrogant attitude as a defense against the possibility of being sexually humiliated, as they were during the phallic stage. Mildly neurotic phallics tend to be leaders; those with more psychopathology may end up as serial rapists.

PHALLIC-AGGRESSIVE HATE

In their relationship with both men and women, phallics must always be dominant, and they generally have contempt, sometimes disguised as humor, for those around them. Phallic men use sex to degrade women by piercing them with their "powerful" penis and destroying them. They wish to obtain "genital revenge," as W. Reich (1933) puts it, humiliating all women the way they once felt humiliated by their mothers. Phallics can be equally degrading toward other men, always fearing that other men will attempt to knock them from their position of power. Because of their deep-seated fear of castration, they do not let anybody, male or female, get very close to them. They have a compulsive need for sex and will often have intercourse with more than one woman a day. They are usually driven personalities, which makes them successful in their careers, their compulsive drive being a displacement of the compulsive sexuality and another way of compensating for the ever-present fear of sexual humiliation and emasculation. They are also perfectionistic (Lowen 1983).

The French novelist, Georges Simenon is an example of a phallic-aggressive. A compulsive writer who turned out several hundred books, he is said to have written most of his books in a week or two. Whenever he completed a book, he would need to have sex with two or more women in succession. In his obituary, it was estimated that he had "known" 10,000 women during his lifetime.

Phallic women, through identification with their fathers, imagine that they have penises or fantasize about taking penises from the men around them. They are dominating with both men and women. If they are married, they choose a weak man whom they can dominate, and they try to feminize him, figuratively taking away his penis and incorporating it within themselves. They take vengeance on men by psychologically castrating them. They are aggressively competitive, always trying to cut men down, generally by using their intellect to outsmart them. Like the phallic male, their aggression is a defense against the fear of being cut down themselves.

Phallic women use feminism as a vehicle for controlling and degrading men. Many feminist leaders are phallic. They use their shrewdness and their aggressiveness to intimidate men into giving them special treatment while being openly hostile to them. For example, a phallic woman may write an obviously inadequate doctoral thesis, but her doctoral committee of men will be enraptured by it out of fear that she will lambaste them for being sexists if they find fault with it. Phallics are often lesbians, and their clitorises become their phalluses; they cannot allow themselves to have vaginal orgasms, for this to them represents surrender to the male and it is a reminder of their lack of a penis. Also like phallic men, they cannot allow anybody to get very close to them. The arrogance and aggression of both male and female phallics generally precludes genuine communication and bonding, yet they are often less neurotic than other types.

Examples

Phallic-aggressive males, like hysterics, have been abundantly portrayed in the arts. Works of literature with portraits of phallics include *Tom Jones*, the *Memoirs* of Casanova, Robert Jordan in *For Whom the Bell Tolls* (with its famous scene in which the lovers feel the ground move during orgasm due to the potency of their love-making), and Stanley in *A Streetcar Named Desire*. In fiction and in movies, Ian Fleming's famous secret service agent, James Bond, represents an idealized version of a phallic, as do numerous other protagonists of that genre. Henry Miller's *Tropic of Cancer* is an illustration of a phallic with an oral-dependent feature to his personality (he is always bragging about his sexual exploits while sponging off everybody). Orson Welles's movie, *Citizen Kane*, is a tragic portrait of a phallic with obsessive-compulsive features. His final memory of a sled with the name "Rosebud" on it is symbolic of his fixation to the trauma of losing his mother and his childhood and, on a deeper level, may represent his fear of the loss of his phallus, for which he spent his life compensating.

Literary examples of female phallic-aggressives are not as numerous. Kate in *The Taming of the Shrew* is one. The mother in *The World According to Garp* is another. Martha in *Who's Afraid of Virginia Woolf* is a portrait of a pushy, intellectualizing, deceitful wife. The opera *Turandot* tells of a frigid, stubborn, and vengeful woman who has her suitors beheaded, until she is "thawed" by a determined applicant.

OBSESSIVE COMPULSION

This character type is noted for caution, orderliness, stubbornness, and stinginess, as well as for obsessions with certain rituals, things, or people. Obsessive-compulsives may be of either sex. They are noted for planning their whole lives ahead of time, with a great attention to detail; any change of plans is felt as a great threat to self-esteem. Because of their attention to detail, many—such as Freud—become psychoanalysts or scholars or technicians, but few become artists. They cannot give very much, but must hold on to everything.

Genesis

Obsessive compulsion is a defense against soiling. Abraham (1921) pointed out, and subsequent psychoanalytic research has proved, that obsessives are generally given harsh or premature toilet training. He cites, for example, a case of a mother who quickly became pregnant again after having her first child, so she was in a hurry to train the first-born to use the potty. At only 3 months of age, he was hardly ready. Hence it took him a long time to learn, and his mother showed much impatience and anger with him. As a consequence the child became fixated at this stage, and spent the rest of his life defending against losing control and incurring the wrath of those around him (who become symbolic of his toilet-training mother).

Compulsives not only learn to hold in their feces, but everything else as well, including their love and hate. They have a fear of spontaneity, which to them, according to Shapiro (1965), portends going crazy, or, on another level, losing complete control of their bowels. This harkens back to the toilet-training stage, when they were made to feel that something was radically wrong with them because they wanted to play, as all infants do, and could not master the toilet as quickly as their caretaker wanted. Their inability to do what the parent thinks they should do results in a traumatic shock to the ego, the repetition of which much be avoided at all costs from that point on.

Obsessive-Compulsive Hate

Obsessive-compulsives act out hate through defiance, stinginess, and the domination of others with their obsessive-compulsive rituals. Freud (1905), writing about the mother of one of his patients, alludes to obsessive-compulsive domination when he describes Dora's mother as a woman whose days were spent in "cleaning the house with its furniture and utensils and in keeping them clean—to such an extent as to make it impossible to use or enjoy them" (p. 28). In their personal relationships they are depriving of their loving or hating feelings as well as of their money, time, and the like. On their jobs they defy their bosses by procrastinating and missing deadlines. They are not outright rebellious, but quietly stubborn and passive-aggressive. Their underlying unconscious aim is to get back at their caretakers for demanding so much of them in early childhood, and making their lives miserable. It's as though they were saying to everybody, "You think I'm slow to master things? I'll show you how slow I can really be!"

As a defense against letting go, they collect things: money, cars, houses, art, house supplies. A typical compulsive will see a bargain on paper towels at the supermarket and buy a year's supply, so as not to run out of them when they are needed. Yet if you ask him or her to give you a roll, the answer will likely be "no." While they stubbornly hold back from those close to them, they may at the same time become obsessed with some cause, belief, idea, or movie personality from afar. These obsessions with "things" is a defense against bonding, which for compulsives is frought with fears of having impossible demands placed on them. Their obsessions also at times cause them to drive themselves, as when they are obsessed with solving a problem or making money, and in such instances they tend to somatize their hate. Baker (1967) and Alexander (1950) describe how such characters keep their bodies in a state of chronic tension so that their body chemistry changes, veins and arteries constrict and harden, and they develop gastrointestinal problems, strokes, or heart attacks.

Often compulsive's have rituals they must go through several times each day, such as washing their hands (or in the case of Dora's mother, cleaning the house and utensils). These rituals are enactments of hate not only because they inconvenience others, but because they give the compulsive a feeling of superiority over others (i.e., they are more clean) and an attitude of moral self-righteousness toward others. Compulsives often tend to be religious.

Examples

Classic examples of obsessive-compulsives include the character of Scrooge in *A Christmas Carol*, Fogg in *Around the World in 80 Days*, and Captain Ahab in *Moby Dick*, whose stubborn defiance toward the realities of life and obsession with hunting down and killing a white whale might be seen as prototypical of the compulsive's behavior. Through his obsession for the white whale (which perhaps came to represent his quest for revenge on the mother who controlled him in infancy), he avoided genuine bonding with humans in his current life. In movies, as previously mentioned, *Citizen Kane* evinces a phallic with obsessive-compulsive features. His compulsivity is evident both in his penchant for collecting things (at the end of the movie his cellar is brimming with junk), as well as in his obsession with making his wife an opera singer, despite her protests and her lack of ability. (This obsession with making her do something she had no innate capacity for may have been an unconscious reversal of what had been done to him as a child.) Another movie, Truffaut's *The Story of Adele H.*, is about an hysteric with obsessive-compulsive features who develops an obsession for a soldier with tragic consequences.

MASOCHISM

The masochist is an individual who is constantly whining. Masochists are prone to see themselves as martyrs and victims, and they derive a sense of moral superiority through their victimization. Hence they have a need to get people to victimize them so that they can continue to maintain their position of superiority. Masochists can be of either sex, and tend to be physically awkward and socially clumsy. They generally have a frown on their faces and give the impression of always being in pain. They defend against feelings of inferiority by provoking people to mistreat them; this provides them with an excuse for their inferior feelings. Due to deep-seated conflicts with respect to asserting themselves, they cannot get what they want from people in healthy ways; therefore they resort to bribing "love" or provoking hate.

Genesis

Children generally become masochistic when their caretaker in early childhood is sadistic. (They become sadistic when their caretaker is masochistic; but this is rare.) The caretaker's sadism reaches its height during the toilet-training stage, when the caretaker uses cruelty and humiliation to enforce the training. Further cruelty and humiliation is administered during the phallic stage, when the child is sexually humiliated. W. Reich (1933) observes that parents of masochists are often in conflict, the father being harsh and distant and the mother permissive and seductive. Panken (1973), echoing Reich, notes that fathers of masochists are "angry, critical, or undermining" while "markedly inadequate and threatened by the mother," and that mothers of masochists are "phallic, seductive, overwhelming, or castrating" and tend to be martyrs who are "contemptuous of their husbands and rejecting their feminine role" (p. 91). Sadistic parents literally "add insult to injury"; they not only injure the child with their humiliating treatment, they also deny they are doing anything wrong and attempt to make the child feel guilty for complaining about it. The child thus gets stuck in a complaining mode. Deep down he knows he has been victimized, and he seeks retribution in the only way allowed to him: he punishes those he hates by inciting them to be cruel to him and then wallowing in his victimhood. As an adult the masochist will become involved in a repeating pattern of trying to induce punishment, sympathy, or guilt from others.

Masochist Hate

Reik (1941) described the manner in which masochists express subjective hate as "victory through defeat." Masochistic men will chase after teasing and castrating women. Because of their feelings of low self-esteem they will shower the object of their affections with flowers or gifts, which are perceived by the woman as smothering and arouse her resentment. When the woman rejects a masochistic man, he will go back for more, until the woman completely destroys him. A masochistic woman will get involved with an abusive man, shower him with a clinging kind of affection which is an inverted expression of her hate, and be unable to leave him. Both the masochistic man and woman revel in their victimhood, parading it before their friends and family, proclaiming their martyrdom in order to gain sympathy. However, when friends try to advise them or intervene, they are continually frustrated. Masochists on one hand ask for help, but when you try to give it to them they will dismiss and devalue your help. This is another way they act out subjective hate.

The recurrent themes of masochism are martyrdom and revenge. Masochists seek always to prove to others what victims they are, and are often busily concocting schemes of revenge against those who have wronged them. When they act out these schemes of revenge, they invariably backfire and end up provoking more punishment on themselves. Masochistic women are prone to complaining that women are victimized by men, and they seek ways of getting vengeance against the entire male gender; likewise, masochistic men often feel that women victimize men and their entire focus of attention is diverted to the cause of righting this wrong. Neither the masochistic woman nor the masochistic man is open to seeing that both men and women victimize each other. They have a need to see themselves, and their gender, as innocent martyrs.

In general masochists tend to act out hate by provoking hate and punishment from others. They derive a sense of power at being able to provoke others, and feel it a moral victory when they are abused, although, in their own minds, they have tried their best to fight this abuse. The more charming masochists will use self-deprecating humor rather than complaining to express their feelings of victimhood, and they sometimes become comedians and writers. In their jokes and their writings they portray those they hate as villains and themselves as innocent victims.

Because they are in a state of chronic tension, due to the feeling of always being victimized and always longing for revenge, masochists somatize their hate through asthmatic attacks, gastrointestinal problems, rheumatism, arthritis, back problems, heart conditions, skin diseases, hemorrhoids, cysts, cancer, and a host of other maladies (Alexander 1959, Monro 1972). These diseases are also used by them to gain sympathy for their plight.

Examples

In literature, the novel *Candide* provides a prime example of a masochist. Candide wanders around from country to country, finding only cruelty, and chases after a woman who alternately lies to him, ridicules him, deceives him, and incites him to murder. As he wanders, he concocts an elaborate philosophy in which he depicts himself as an innocent in a corrupt world. Other portraits of masochists include Philip in *Of Human Bondage*, Holden Caulfield in *Catcher in the Rye*, the antihero of *Notes from the Underground*, *Gulliver's Travels*, and *Billy Budd*. The children's story *Cinderella* shows how losing a beloved father and being left in the hands of a cruel stepmother and stepsisters can foster a masochistic orientation in a girl and depicts a typical masochistic belief system that pain is enobling. Feminist novels such as *Diary of a Mad Housewife* about long-suffering women victimized by a world of villainous, sexist men, reflect a masochistic theme, as do movies of the same genre. Nearly all the movies of Charlie Chaplin and, more recently, the Woody Allen films, are depictions of masochistic men utilizing self-disparaging humor to gain sympathy and show their enemies in a bad light. The theme of "victory through defeat" is woven heavily into their plots. Allen's *Annie Hall* is about a relationship between a masochistic man and a masochistic woman, both of whom disparage themselves and use clowning to deflect aggression. Masochists often project their self-disparagement, as when Allen (quoting Groucho Marx) says in one of his movies, "I wouldn't want to join a club that would have me as a member."

PASSIVITY

Passive characters are those whose aggression has been rendered completely passive, along with their sexuality. On the surface they appear to be sweet, compliant, and modest. Their speech and gestures are soft and mild. They do not want to offend. Male passives tend to be "good boys" even as adults, always striving to do what is right. They are good "company men" in the corporate world, and take the passive-feminine role in relationships with women. Female passives are "good girls" who are always pleasant, and always passive in their relationships with men and women. Reich and Baker found the passive (or passive-feminine) character only among men, but in my research I have also encountered women of that type; they are somewhat rare in Western society, but more common in Oriental cultures.

Genesis

Passive males generally have mothers who show particular interest in them until they reach the phallic stage, at which point, as Baker (1967) puts it, passive boys are "slapped down severely by the mother" (p. 128). Baker found that passives are primarily fixated in the anal stage, but Brody (1964) in a study of two passive boys, noted that their mothers had resented the role of child-rearing and were so anxious to get back to their vocations that they neglected them from early in the nursing stage. Mothers of passives are generally hysterics or phallic-aggressives who are dominating and castrating. Their "slapping down" is not so much a teasing humiliation such as the phallic-aggressive male receives, but a complete repudiation of male sexuality and aggression, which causes the passive to defend against such impulses by becoming a good boy who gives off no outward signs of either. The passive female usually has a father and/or mother who likewise completely shuts down the daughter's sexuality and aggression and molds her into a good girl.

Passive Hate

Passives act out subjective hate in more subtle ways than any other character types. Because they cannot allow themselves to be overtly hateful,
their aggression is always passive aggressive. They wish to avoid conflicts
at all costs, since in their relationships with their parents they were the
losers of all conflicts (Mother or Father was always right). A passive may
appear to be a perfect gentleman yet drive his wife into a rage. He will
express all the correct sentiments and do all the right things, in and out
of bed, but on a subtle level he will deny her what she wants most, a
genuine response to her as a human being and as a woman. He will go
through the motions beautifully, but underneath will be a secret, contemptuous defiance that will induce her to castigate him as a nerd or
weakling. This in turn will cause him to become even more subtly defiant. The same process holds true for a passive female in her relationships
with men. She will appear to be a dutiful wife and mother, yet drive her
husband crazy with her evasiveness, dottiness, or indecisiveness.

Passives appear sweet and loving, but in actuality they are quite
depriving of their affection. This is upsetting and unnerving to their
spouses and the people around them, who are usually taken in by their
outward manner. Passives are quite skilled at tuning in on what other
people want of them, and pretending to give it to them; but their giving
is merely surface compliance. It is merely a pose, and underneath the
pose is contempt for the person so taken in, which comes out in subtle
ways. Their very agreeableness becomes a major source of irritation. If
you ask a passive what movie he wants to see, he will say, "What movie
would you like to see?" You can never pin him down or find out what he
really wants, because he is always afraid something he says might be used
to start an argument with him. If his wife becomes infuriated he will be
impeccably apologetic and say, "I love you, my dear, and I just want you
to be happy." This, of course, will infuriate her even more, as it is just
another evasion. He never loses his temper while she always does, and
that arouses guilt about her being so angry at him while he is being so
nice. Likewise, men married to passive women often find themselves becoming upset and at times violent. Some "battered women" passives
induce violence by being annoyingly sweet or stupid. They are masters at
"killing with kindness." Those in relationships with passives cannot fig-

ure out what is making them so angry.

Because of their fear of expressing direct hate or love, passives never achieve genuine bonding, yet they often appear to have happy marriages and harmonious relationships with their bosses, co-workers, and friends. They will use alcohol or drugs to release or soothe their hate (Baker, 1967), and will somatize their hate through colds, flus, fevers, and more severe illnesses such as heart disease or cancer, which they use to gain sympathy or control. Winnicott (1965) tells of a father who lay bedridden with cancer for ten years, making servants of his wife and children. "Nothing can be done because cancer sits supreme at the head of the father's bed, grinning and omnipotent" (p. 77).

Examples

Thurber's short story, "The Secret Life of Walter Mitty," also made into a movie, shows a passive who is dominated by his wife and acts out hate by being absent-minded when it comes to carrying out her orders to buy dog food; his fantasy life of heroism is more important to him than his real life. Camus' *The Stranger* is another literary portrait of a passive trying his best to avoid conflicts but getting into them anyway. Sidekicks such as Dr. Watson in the Sherlock Holmes detective novels are examples of passives who become dependent on a phallic-aggressive man or woman, through whom they live vicariously. Sometimes, when they attach themselves to someone of the same sex, there is a latent or actual homosexual element, a sexual surrender to an idealized phallic-aggressive, who behaves as the passive would secretly like to behave.

The fathers portrayed in the movies *Ordinary People* and *Rebel Without a Cause* are passive types, both seeking always to keep the peace in their families, to appease their wives, and to avoid conflict. Fellini's *La Strada* is a poignant rendering of a passive woman who idealizes a phallic-aggressive man, with tragic consequences. Elaine May's *A New Leaf* characterizes a passive woman of the slightly dotty variety, whose dottiness serves, in a passive-aggressive way, to undermine her opportunistic suitor. The character, Edith, on the classic television series, *All in the Family*, also uses dottiness to cover up her passive-aggressive undermining and psychological castration of her husband, Archie Bunker.

PARANOIA

Paranoids are almost totally unable to recognize that their problems come from within themselves, but rather see them as all coming from an outside world of injustice and persecution. But unlike masochists, who have a similar outlook, paranoids do not wallow in suffering, but are more likely to either act out hostility toward others before it is done to them (as did my paranoid patient in Chapter 2), or to retreat from reality, rationalizing that people want to persecute them because of their greatness, saintliness, or the like. They tend to be suspicious of everybody and everything, irritable, stubborn, resentful of authority, and unable to trust anyone enough to achieve genuine bonding.

Genesis

Paranoids are noted for their piercing eyes, and they generally have mothers who have piercing eyes. Their primary fixation point is in the symbiotic stage—the earliest months of life—when they feel almost totally merged with their mother, but receive a double message from her having to do with a murderous expression in her eyes as she feeds them (Mahler 1968). Parents of paranoids are generally paranoid themselves. They will persecute a child, usually through psychological means, and, at the same time, due to their paranoid view, firmly believe that when their child complains he is actually persecuting them. This cruel treatment begins from birth, so that paranoids never form a trusting bond. Freud (1918a), studying a paranoid named Dr. Schreber, who believed he was the daughter of God, decided that paranoids were individuals who had strong homosexual impulses but whose superegos were opposed to such impulses; they defended against this fear by projecting it onto others ("*They* think I'm a homosexual, up to something dirty"). Indeed, this fear of homosexual impulses is often an ingredient in male paranoids, but not in females, who are less likely to view homosexuality as ego-alien; however, with females there is regularly a complete disowning of their penis envy and corresponding irrational fear of the penis (Stoller 1968).

Paranoid Hate

Paranoids can be ruthless in the way they act out subjective hate. If they become convinced you are their enemy, they will spare nothing in destroying you. Terrified of self-annihilation, they attempt to attack impetuously while rationalizing their hostility behind a delusional system. Some paranoids become political or religious leaders, attracting a following of passives and hysterics who look for someone upon whom to attach themselves and from whom they may obtain permission for acting out pent-up aggression. Such was the case during the McCarthy era in the United States, when Senator Joe McCarthy became paranoid about communism and for a time convinced a whole nation to hunt for "commies" and "pinkos" who he thought were about to annihilate the country. The same phenomenon occurred in Hitler's Germany, where Jews were perceived as a threat and persecuted, and in Stalin's Russia, where "decadent capitalists" and other enemies of Marxism were persecuted.

Paranoids are absolutely convinced that their way of seeing things is right, and they become hostile to anybody who opposes that view. They will use whatever means necessary to destroy any opposing view, believing that any criticism is a threat to their very existence.

One form of paranoia is the litigious variety; because of deep-seated feelings that they have been wronged, paranoids are quick to initiate ill-advised legal actions. This is an attempt to prove that they are right and superior and to obtain vengeance on those whom they perceive as wrong. If they stumble on a sidewalk outside of a store, they are likely to suspect that the store's owner maliciously put a crack in the sidewalk, and they will not hesitate to sue the store for damages.

In their relations with the opposite sex, they tend to be suspicious and vindictive. They may develop a fixed idea, which nobody will be able to shake, that a certain prominent person of the opposite sex is in love with them. They will pester this person with love letters, telephone calls, and visits until the prominent person has to legally restrain them. When they do have relationships, they tend to be jealous and suspicious of their mates, continually accusing them of being unfaithful. Male paranoids often see all women as potential seductresses or sluts out to destroy them. Female paranoids sometimes see all men as con-artists and rapists. They become crusading radicals who cannot tolerate anybody with an opposing view, and who vigorously persecute those who do.

Paranoids, more than any other type, tend to be not only guarded and acutely aware of their surroundings, but also acutely aware of their own bodies. For that reason they are often hypochondriacal, imagining that they have all sorts of physical illnesses. Often they actually cause themselves to have such illnesses by unconsciously focusing their attention on some part of their bodies until that part becomes irritated, infected, or cancerous—as when somebody keeps picking at a scab. I once had a male patient who had a chronic fear of being kicked in the testicles—stemming from a relationship with a harsh and punitive father. This hate for his father and its associated fear of father-figures caused him to constantly tense up his groin area in anticipation of being kicked. Consequently he developed cancer in one of his testes and had to have it removed. Likewise, females with hate for men and fears of being raped will develop physical problems in their reproductive organs. In these and other ways they somatize their hate.

Examples

In the world of literature, Kafka's *The Trial* is a paranoid nightmare about Joseph K., who is put on trial for some crime, although he is never told what. Nor is he ever really tried. However, in the end he is led to a quarry and stabbed in the heart. Kafka's *Metamorphosis*, in which a man is transformed into a bug, provides a detailed description of a paranoid delusion as a defense against castration fear. In movies, Travis in *Taxi Driver* is an example of a paranoid man, who sees New York City as a persecutory object, full of evil (a projection of his inner torment). He develops a paranoid attraction for a young woman, who he imagines is in love with him, and envisions himself as her savior. Another movie, *Fatal Attraction*, is a portrait of a woman with strong paranoid features, and *Carrie*, which was both a novel and a movie, represents a paranoid fantasy about a girl having superhuman powers which she uses to destroy her persecutors. *Psycho*, however, may contain the best characterization of a paranoid ever portrayed on a screen. Many works of gothic romance and horror have strong elements of paranoia.

IMPULSIVITY

Impulsive characters tend to be addicts of one variety or another. Sometimes they are alcoholics or drug addicts. Sometimes they are addicted to food. Sometimes they are addicted to gambling. They are called oral-receptive types in the psychoanalytic literature, because they impulsively run after oral satisfactions. These characters cannot tolerate frustration; whatever they need, they must have immediately. They are more bonded to their addictions than to people, and will often lie, cheat, or steal in order to feed them. They are unrealistically optimistic and fully expect the world to provide for them without their giving out any effort. They can be of either sex.

Genesis

Impulsives generally have mothers who breed oral dependence. In specific, during the nursing stage such mothers will rush forth with their breast or bottle any time the infant expresses the slightest discomfort. This pattern continues throughout infancy and early childhood; such children are never required to postpone gratification. Mothers of impulsives are always hovering close by, doing everything for their children, so that they never learn to do the normal things for themselves. Children of such mothers often idealize them and are not permitted to express any criticism. They develop a deeply ambivalent relationship toward the mother, grateful for this spoiling, but unconsciously enraged at the stifling of their independence. As adults they have the same kind of ambivalence toward their spouses, as well as to their addictions. They crave the security which the addiction gives them, yet fear and loathe its power over them; therefore they must act quickly, impulsively. As Fenichel (1945) puts it, "Any tension is felt as hunger was felt by the infant, that is, as a threat to their very existence" (p. 368).

Impulsive Hate

Impulsives live precariously, always running from what they presume will be self-annihilation. They must constantly pacify their unconscious rage, which they experience as a threat to their existence. The eruption of this rage, which they have learned to repress since infancy, would mean for them the loss of their mother's love and her milk. Other people are not persons to them, merely deliverers or frustrators of supplies. Those who deliver are given token appreciation; those who frustrate are violently hated.

Impulsives act out subjective hate by using people to assist them in their addictions. Typically, they will have a spouse upon whom they will become dependent in an infantile way. This spouse will attempt to save them from their addictions and will meet repeated frustrations. The impulsive will pretend to want to stop the addiction and will enlist the spouse's aid, but as soon as the spouse believes that the impulsivity is going to stop, a new binge begins.

Some impulsives can become belligerent and sociopathic while under the influence of alcohol or other drugs. Alcohol releases their inhibitions and dulls their consciences, permitting the expression of the long-repressed infantile rage with regard to their stifled independence. Hence the rage at the passive's mother gets displaced onto the spouse, friends, or co-workers.

Impulsives tend to be either selfish or indiscriminately generous, as though they were saying, "I will give nothing because nobody gave anything to me," or "I give to anybody to show I'm more generous than my parents were to me." Although they are spoiled as infants, impulsives come to experience their parents as depriving, because at some point later on when the parents belatedly try to push the impulsive toward independence, the impulsive clings and demands more and more supplies.

Although impulsives do not generally feel their addictions nor their behavior is bad, unconsciously they harbor much guilt about their selfish, exploitative, and sociopathic behavior. Some go through cycles where they seek atonement by being unconsciously accident-prone. ("Don't be angry at me; can't you see I've broken my arm?") Others manage to suffer one financial reverse after another.

Alexander (1950) has noted that it is a variant of the impulsive type, the "oral-aggressive," who is most prone to developing stomach ulcers. Because of a chronic need to be fed, the stomach's juices are always flowing, bringing about chronic acidity. Eventually this leads to gastritis, ulcers, and at times even cancer. The oral craving also causes tobacco and marijuana addictions, which produce heart diseases and cancer of the lungs. It is well known that chronic alcoholism damages the liver, while the injection of nearly all drugs diminishes brain cells, affects the circulatory system, inflames the kidneys, produces birth defects during pregnancy, and has numerous other side effects.

Examples

Dr. Jekyll and Mr. Hyde, while purportedly about a scientist who invents a drug that transforms his personality, is in actuality a good depiction of the belligerent type of alcoholic, who is mild-mannered and sweet when sober but sociopathic when drunk. More recently, Frankie in *Man with the Golden Arm* is a poignant characterization of a heroin addict and gambler. *The Sun Also Rises* captures the impulsive, alcoholic fog of the so-called "lost generation," *On the Road* is a romanticized account of the impulsive wanderings of the "beat generation," and *The Tropic of Cancer* represents Henry Miller's phallic-aggressive brand of impulsivity in Paris. The Odets play, *The Country Girl*, offers a portrait of a relationship between an alcoholic and his mother-surrogate wife, showing how each influences the other's behavior. The movie *The Days of Wine and Roses* is a grim depiction of a relationship between two alcoholics, and Fellini's *La Dolce Vita* shows an impulsive character with passive features drifting from party to party among the Italian rich, always searching for some immediate gratification, unable to settle down, get in touch with his feelings, and write his novel.

BORDERLINE CHARACTEROLOGY

The borderline might be seen as an impulsive with paranoid and depressive features. Kernberg (1976) described such individuals as having an excess of aggression, which causes them to be moody and hyperactive. Indeed, a better name for them might be hyperactives. While healthy people can usually see that there is good and bad in everybody (except in times of extreme duress), borderlines see people in absolute terms, due to a defense mechanism called splitting. In actuality, they split off their own considerable aggression and project it onto certain others, allowing themselves to maintain the delusion that they are all good while certain others are all bad. A. Reich (1950) refers to "as if" personalities who behave in this way. They can go from idealizing you to villainizing you in moments, and they can become quite abusive if they decide you are a "bad guy." Borderlines are more often female than male (in contrast to sociopaths, who are usually male).

Genesis

Research on multiple personalities, a category of borderline, shows that in 97 percent of the cases they have been sexually or physically abused before the age of 6 (O'Regan, 1985). Kernberg (1976) and Masterson (1981) place the major fixation point for borderlines during the rapprochement subphase—between 6 months and 2 years of age—when children must grapple, among other things, with separation from mother. Masterson suggests that mothers of borderlines withdraw their support rather than extend it for the child when he or she experiments with separating from her. "His/her very surge of individuation, which brings with it a greater need for the mother's support, actually induces withdrawal of that support, i.e., the vital process in which he/she is engaged produces the withdrawal that arrests that process and results in the abandonment depression" (p. 133). Borderlines get stuck in this stage, continually experimenting with going toward and leaving the people in their lives, testing to see whether they will accept them (as their mothers did not) in spite of such fluctuations. Like 2-year-olds, they are sensitive to any slight, quick to change moods, volatile, vindictive, and fickle.

Borderline Hate

While paranoids see the world as replete with potential persecutors, borderlines see it as lurking with abusers or abandoners. The slightest gesture on your part can cause them to either abuse you or run from you. One borderline patient idealized me for some months, bringing me presents, proclaiming her gratitude, admiring my therapeutic skill, before suddenly announcing one day that she had decided to cut down to once a week. I listened as she explained that she felt better and had money problems (usual excuses for retreating from therapy). I said only, "If that's what you think is best, then perhaps you should." The following week she burst into my office to inform me she had had it with my "looks." She said she was quitting that day because I had betrayed her, and I should have known not to look at her "that way," after what she had told me about her brother, who had abused her and who she claimed had also looked at her "that way." Before I could say a word she had stormed out. Nor would she answer my phone calls. It was a complete reversal; I had gone from being the good Daddy she had always searched for to a completely evil person, like her older brother, to be castigated and dumped. Such are the vicissitudes of borderline hate.

Borderlines are extremely touchy individuals and it is hard to know quite what is going to set them off or how to relate to them. They are truly "as if" people, always acting, never in touch with their real feelings. Even they themselves generally do not know what they are feeling, until their feelings erupt from them. For that reason their relationships tend to be turbulent and short-lived.

Borderlines bond with others whom they perceive as allies against a common enemy. Borderline women will ally themselves with other "sisters" against men, and then look for opportunities to put men in their place. Borderline men will ally themselves with other men against the threatening female. Borderline blacks may ally themselves against white people and see all whites as racists. Borderline employees will ally themselves against the bosses or the union or "stupid" co-workers who go along with the "evil system." They do not bond in an objective, loving way, but in order to form a consensus that justifies their subjective hate. As such, their bonds are not true friendships.

They will engage in sex as a means of obtaining temporary bonding. As in everything else, they tend to go from extreme to extreme: either they are promiscuous, flying from partner to partner with hardly any discrimination, or they go without sex for long periods of time. In essence, they remain fixated at the rapprochement stage, not yet ready for objective love or sexuality.

Borderlines can become violent to others and to themselves. Not being in touch with their feelings, they have little control over them. Generally they will be violent with those weaker than themselves, such as children. Others will mutilate themselves by cutting their arms with a razor, burning themselves with cigarettes, or biting their fingernails down to the quick, actions designed to calm their hate and appease the evil forces of the world (representative of their parents of early childhood). Like hysterics, they use histrionics and acting out in order to manipulate people. Like the masochist's provocation, their acting out is in actuality a plea for help. Unfortunately, if help comes, they usually cannot trust anybody enough to accept it.

Examples

The previously mentioned *Dr. Jekyll and Mr. Hyde* might be seen as an example of a borderline character with a split personality, except borderlines do not need drugs to transform them; instead they use a form of autohypnosis. Zola's *Nana* is a somewhat overblown description of a borderline prostitute during the Second Empire (many prostitutes are borderline and impulsive personalities). Southern's *Candy* satirizes the "dumb blonde" type of borderline who is sexually promiscuous to defend against hate and to avoid real intimacy. The opera *Carmen* shows a borderline hysteric who seduces, enslaves, and destroys her lover, while the play and opera, *Salome*, illustrates how a borderline woman first idealizes a man and then, when he spurns her, quickly disparages him and has him beheaded. The film *The Blue Angel* portrays a masochistic college professor's destruction by a borderline nightclub singer, *Pretty Poison* describes a borderline woman's seduction and sinister influence on a paranoid young man, and *Fatal Attraction* depicts a borderline with sociopathic features obsessed with a married man, who throws herself at him sexually, then attempts to emotionally bribe him through suicidal attempts and, when that does not work, to wreck his marriage and murder him and his wife.

SOCIOPATHIC CHARACTEROLOGY

Sociopaths are a variant of the borderline personality. However, while borderlines tend to be abusive within the bounds of the law and to act out in ways that are more overtly self-destructive, such as cutting or burning themselves, sociopaths tend to act out subjective hate against society by committing crimes. They are supreme con artists, skilled at winning people's confidences and then betraying them by committing some atrocious deed (stealing, raping, killing). Sociopaths have no conscience, nor do they feel any remorse about their crimes, due to deep feelings of betrayal, abandonment, and bitterness that preclude empathy or sympathy.

Genesis

Lindner, Miller, and Winnicott, in studies of sociopathic personalities, have shown how extreme deprivation leads to antisocial tendencies. In one case, a boy was given up for adoption by his mother at about the age of three, and then went from orphanage to foster home to reformatory school, enduring cruelty upon cruelty, finally ending up as a murderer (Lindner 1955). In another case a boy and his sister were raised by a cruel, physically abusive father and a weak, negligent mother. When the father was gone, which was frequent, the mother paid no attention to her children, even when she passed by their beds and saw that they were engaged in sexual intercourse. This boy also ended up as a criminal (Lindner 1944). In another case, a boy spent the first year of life in a hospital, then was adopted by a mother who locked him in a cellar, bathed him until he was nineteen, and threw butcher knives at him and beat him with coat hangers when he was "naughty"; as a young man he viciously murdered a number of children (Miller 1983). Another boy began stealing things and was kicked out of elementary school, a reaction to an abandonment by his mother at the age of two (Winnicott 1953). Research with lower animals also corroborates that deprivation leads to antisocial tendencies (Melzach and Scott 1957, Harlow and Harlow 1962).

Sociopathic Hate

The many ways in which sociopaths act out subjective hate are well known, and include all the crimes one reads about in the daily newspaper or sees on the nightly television news. Sociopaths hate in the most obvious ways. Because of their neglected and cruel childhoods, they have contempt for society and its values. They tend to be isolated individuals who at times will ally themselves with other sociopaths for a common purpose (to rob a bank), but who in reality do not trust anybody, particularly anybody who tries to win their trust. Therefore they achieve only the barest minimum of bonding.

Sexually, sociopaths are usually impotent and often practice some form of perverse sexuality, if any at all. Their crimes have a sexual meaning: stealing represents sexual violation; murdering, sexual conquest; drug trafficking, forbidden masturbation.

Because they seldom hold on to any aggression, sociopaths are not known to somatize their hate. They are noted for having an unusually large toleration for pain (being insensitive), which is probably linked to their lack of social contact in childhood. They are not to be confused, however, with professional criminal types such as those in the Mafia, who, like soldiers in a war, are responding to a special cultural situation and value system in which criminal behavior is officially sanctioned.

Examples

Examples of sociopaths are plentiful, as the history of humankind is replete with criminals and with a literary fascination with them. Dostoyevsky's *Crime and Punishment* provides one of the best portraits of a sociopath, although it is a bit romanticized and the protagonist shows remorse, which most sociopaths do not. More recently, Capote's *In Cold Blood* is a realistic characterization of two sociopaths that delves into their deprived upbringings. The movie, *Rebel Without a Cause*, is a touching, though somewhat sentimental, look at teenage delinquency, and

Cool Hand Luke captures the stubborn defiance of authority that characterizes sociopaths. Godard's *Breathless* contains an excellent portrait of a relationship between a sociopath and an hysteric, and Malick's *Badlands* is perhaps one of the finest, grimmest, and most accurate descriptions of a criminal on the run (with his passive girlfriend). There are, of course, a plethora of movies about cops and robbers, but not many of them contain realistic characterizations of the criminal personality. Why the tendency to glamorize and romanticize criminals? It's probably connected with the pent-up aggression toward authority figures (parents) which afflicts all character types. The criminal who successfully robs a bank does something that many of us fantasize doing.

NARCISSISM

What is striking about narcissists is that they treat you as though you are not there. People are not people to narcissists; they are things to be used for self-aggrandizement. As a lion uses an antelope to quench his hunger with no regard for the feelings of the antelope, so a narcissist uses other people with no regard for their feelings. As Lowen (1983) put it, "Narcissists are more concerned with how they appear than what they feel" (p. ix). They have an inflated, but fragile, sense of self, and they strive always to put themselves into situations that will support their ego-ideal, while avoiding those that will not. They tend to be proud, vain, ambitious, and always cool. Quite the opposite of borderlines, whose emotionality you feel immediately, narcissists appear to have no emotions. Like the mythological character after which they are named, Narcissus, they are interested only in themselves, and cannot truly empathize with or care about others or the plight of humanity.

Genesis

Freud (1914b) wrote of "a primary narcissism in everyone which may in the long run manifest itself as dominating his object-choice" (p. 68) While Freud stressed a biological predisposition to narcissism, Leowald (1951) and Kohut (1971) examined the nature of the parent–child interaction that leads to narcissism. Narcissists generally have narcissistic parents, who themselves have inflated ego-ideals and are unable to relate realistically with their children. A typical narcissistic mother will train her son from birth onward to admire her as someone who is all-knowing, the best mother and woman in the world; in exchange for this admiration, the son may himself feel special—since he is the favorite of this special woman. A father may do likewise to a daughter. In such instances, when the child becomes an adult his self-esteem will remain dependent upon the mother or father. Often such individuals become homosexual, unable to form a relationship with another member of the opposite sex which would threaten the narcissistic tie with the mother or father.

The reverse also happens: a parent will treat her child as though he or she were the most special, talented, charming, or all-knowing child in the world—even though realistically speaking the child is only average. In this case the child becomes the parent's ego-ideal, representing something which the parent could not attain. When they reach adulthood, such individuals must live out the parent's dream.

Narcissistic Hate

Narcissistic hate stems from rage. Kohut (1971), Miller (1981), Winnicott (1971), and Lowen (1983) have all written about the development of this rage, which arises as a consequence of the narcissist's having to posture a false self to please parents and to hide his or her real self. Loewald (1973) describes the ego-ideal—the false or grandiose self—that narcissists must live up to, a compensation for the underlying rage and feelings of emptiness.

Unless they have been in therapy, they are not at all aware of their rage, which is not in keeping with their inflated self-image. They have been taught to idealize or to be idealized by primary figures in their lives, and to deny their rage and hate. The hate gets displaced on others, who are either exploited as suppliers of narcissistic needs, such as admiration, or kept at a distance.

Because they are proud and vain, narcissists tend to feel humiliated quite easily. For example, a patient of mine who worked as a waiter (but who had ambitions of being a great actor) reported that he felt like killing a customer who had left him a tip he considered too low. "Imagine the nerve of that bitch? Seventy-five cents. It was really insulting." Narcissists see everything in terms of how it reflects on their appearance. They do not often express direct anger but can have fits of rage or hold grudges—

secret, silent grudges that can go on for years—toward those by whom they feel slighted.

In relationships, narcissists tend to link up with those who are like themselves, and they will be equally concerned about the appearance of their mate and of their children. There will be no real caring or empathy for their spouse or children, only a concern with how they make the narcissist look. Thus, the narcissist acts out subjective hate primarily through a complete disregard for the true feelings of others. Ironically, it is this very disregard and obliviousness of others that makes narcissistic personalities attractive. They can be quite seductive and charming and are often charismatic and popular. They use this to exploit those around them.

Because of their preoccupation with themselves, they somatize their hate through hypochondria and problems with their external appearance. For example, they may develop pimples or warts, or they may lose hair due to the chronic tension of overconcern with that part of their anatomy.

Examples

The queen in the children's story, "Snow White," is the very prototype of a narcissistic personality when she asks her mirror, "who is the fairest creature of all?" And her rage, when the mirror does not tell her what she wants to hear, is also typically narcissistic. *Pride and Prejudice* provides a humorous portrait of a man who defends against fear of intimacy by being haughty and disdainful toward those around him—until his narcissistic pride is melted by the love of a perhaps equally proud woman. Blanche in *A Streetcar Named Desire* is an example of an hysteric with strong narcissistic features. Her constant nagging to have her sister and others tell her how good she looks is one of the many ways in which she exploits people into becoming suppliers of her narcissistic needs. *The Great Gatsby* depicts a young man whose attempt to live up to his grandiose expectations ends in disaster. The novel and movie, *Room at the Top*, shows the rise and fall of an opportunistic womanizer; the movie *Network* depicts a narcissistic and beautiful television executive and her exploitation of her colleagues; and *Wall Street* is an etching of a narcissistic man for whom money and power are a substitute for love and bonding.

DEPRESSION

Depressed people are people who hate themselves. They are brooders who blame themselves for everything. In a sense, they are also narcissists who have been totally unable to attain their ego-ideal. They range from neurotic to psychotic, the latter being so full of self-hate they can no longer function. A variant of the depressed personality is the manic-depressive, who swings from a deep depression to a hyperactive state in which he flies from his depression to achieve a maniacal sense of well-being.

Genesis

Bowlby (1979), perhaps more than any other analyst, demonstrated a link between depression and the loss of a parent or other important relation in childhood. According to him, depressed people are stuck in a stage of mourning—the angry, self-recriminative stage—and are unable to get out of it. Sometimes the depression is the result of the actual loss of a parent, sibling, or thing (i.e., an arm), while in other cases it is the result of emotional abandonment. For example, if a mother experiences postpartum depression and has a wish to murder her child, those feelings will be transmitted to the child, who, feeling hated and abandoned, will hate himself and abandon himself (that is, be unable to care for himself). As an adult, he will be quick to feel abandoned and hated.

Depressive Hate

Depressives act out subjective hate by keeping everybody at a distance and withholding their feelings. They complain and complain but do not let anybody help them. Anybody who tries to help will be severely frustrated. They sit around brooding about life's unfairness, envious of the good fortunes of others.

Depressives are rigid, self-righteous, and moralistic—a defense against their guilt. They have an inordinate need for the love and approval they lacked as infants, and usually marry a spouse who becomes a surrogate caretaker or for whom they become a surrogate parent, doing for another what they would like done to themselves. Yet no amount of caring will be enough for them, and their caretakers will invariably be made to feel just as inadequate as the depressive.

They tend to be flooded by feelings of rage, sadness, low self-esteem, hopelessness, and guilt. Because they expend so much energy holding in their feelings, they are immoblized by fatigue, loss of appetite, constipation, and insomnia. They are often agitated by fears of impoverishment (symbolic abandonment), and their self-reproaches sometimes extend to suicidal thinking and on occasion suicidal acts. Baker (1967) speculates that chronic depressive bitterness leads to gall bladder disease.

Mintz (1980) describes a patient who had an alternating sequence of ulcerative colitis, asthma, depression, self-destructive acting out, migraines, noninfectious monoarthritis of the knee, angioneurotic edema, eczema, and nasorhinitis.

Examples

The most notable example of a depressive personality in the literature is *Hamlet*, who broods his way through life, pushing everybody away, contemplating suicide. Hamsun's *Pan* characterizes a depressed man who retreats to a cabin in the woods to obsess about a past love, and eventually provokes a hunter into shooting him. The novel and the movie, *Sophie's Choice*, depicts a woman suffering from chronic depression over her role in the death of her children in a concentration camp.

SCHIZOPHRENIA

Schizophrenia represents the severest form of hate being taken out on the self. Schizophrenics withdraw from life and from their hate. They live in a delusional, fairy tale world, unable to accept or cope with reality.

Genesis

Twin studies aside, many psychoanalysts feel that schizophrenics are fixated at a point right after birth. Reich (1933) believed that there was an initial trauma within the first ten days. Mahler (1968), studying infantile psychosis, observed that parents of autistic children were almost totally neglectful of them from birth onward, except for supplying rudimentary needs such as nursing and changing diapers, while at the same time being physically abusive. Lidz and colleagues (1965) as well as Laing and Esterson (1964) in studies of the families of schizophrenics, found that relationships in such families were extremely pathogenic. In short, the schizophrenic is born in the most toxic of environments and is traumatized from the beginning of life—if not during gestation.

Schizophrenic Hate

Schizophrenics see hate everywhere and withdraw from it. They are terrified of people, acutely aware of other people's unconscious hate. On a deeper level they are also aware of their own hate, and withdraw from others to protect them from it (Spotnitz 1976). They are so terrified of hate that they split themselves off from their feelings. For that reason, they misinterpret what they see in the world, and their own judgment, thought, and speech become impaired.

Schizophrenics barely breathe (Baker 1967). It is as though they are afraid to breathe, as though they got a message from their environment that they did not have the right to live. They usually remain in a state of childlike dependence, unable to care for themselves or anybody else. Like children, they tend to believe in magic, parapsychology, and mysticism, harboring delusions of omnipotence and omniscience. Their rage is considerable, and at times—such as when a catatonic explodes—they can be demented and dangerous. They will let nobody near them.

Schizophrenics somatize their hate through hypochondriasis and an assortment of physically destructive behaviors that surpass those of borderlines. These include smearing feces on themselves, pulling out their hair, or peeling off skin. They are also prone to diseases of various organs, which Meng and Stern (1955) called "organ psychoses."

Examples

Plath's *The Bell Jar* and Greenberg's *I Never Promised You a Rose Garden* are poignant accounts by patients suffering from schizophrenia. Both have also been made into movies. Another book made into a movie, *Lilith*, provides a sinister portrait of a schizophrenic woman and the powerful effect she has on a male therapist, who becomes entranced by her and goes crazy himself. A psychiatrist's novel about two schizophrenics, *Lisa and David*, made into the film *David and Lisa*, is a touching story of how a young man and woman helped each other find sanity. The movie *Frances* provides a chilling portrait of the descent into madness of movie star Frances Farmer, who was eventually given a lobotomy. The book and movie, *Lust for Life*, depicts the schizophrenic breakdown of the painter Vincent Van Gogh.

CONCLUSION

The twelve character types described here do not exhaust the list of possibilities. Indeed, most people are mixed types, and the combinations of mixtures are numerous. However, this list demonstrates the range of psychopathology from the neurotic to the psychotic, and shows how subjective hate in one form or another—behavior that distances rather than binds, destroys rather than builds—stands in the way of effective bonding, emotional and mental health, and contentment. To one degree or another, these character types resist the kind of honest communication and genuine intimacy that would resolve their subjective hate, and the tension that underpins it. Hence, in numerous ways, they kill themselves too soon.

4

Perverse Forms of Hate

Perverse expressions of subjective hate are generally prevalent in societies that are declining; perversity and decadence rose sharply during the last years of both the Greek and Roman empires. This points up Kardiner's (1954) observation, noted in Chapter 1, about the relationship between traumatic social change and perverse and criminal behavior. In particular, it appears that perversity is a reaction to a decline in social order and, on a smaller scale, to a decline in family order. It occurs in families where one or both parents have a perverse attitude toward sexuality, and they in turn unconsciously induce perverse sexuality or a perverse attitude toward sexuality in their children.

Psychoanalytic literature attributes perversity mainly to males, and has noted a particular family constellation that breeds perverse sexuality. Stoller (1968), who spent his life studying gender problems, found that in nearly every case of perversion there was a castrating mother and a weak or absent father. Mothers of transvestites, for example, were usually women who bore unconscious animosity toward men and strived to make their boys into little girls. "There is one consistent fact in the history of adult male transvestites," he writes. "This is the mothers' need to feminize their little boys. These mothers have an unusually strong envy of males which expresses itself in this rather subtle way" (p. 183). Fathers of tranvestites, when they are around at all, are often passive co-conspirators and therefore unable to save the boy from the mother's castrating behavior or to model a healthy heterosexual masculinity.

In general, all male perversions, according to Fenichel (1945), are the result of severe castration anxiety. When perverts reach the phallic stage and begin, as all boys do, playing with their penises and exhibiting them with pride, a mother who has unconscious or conscious animosity toward men and toward male sexuality will shame or humiliate the boy to the point where he retreats from the normal heterosexual expression of his sexuality, back to some form of infantile sexuality. "The pervert, when disturbed in his genital sexuality by castration fear, regresses to that component of his infantile sexuality which once in childhood had given him a feeling of security or at least of reassurance against fear, and whose gratification was experienced with special intensity because of this denial or reassurance" (p. 327). The kind of denial Fenichel is referring to is denial of the knowledge that his mother is penisless. According to psychoanalytic research, upon discovering that some people do not have penises, boys feels guilty and afraid. Elsewhere, I have used the term *phallic guilt* (Schoenewolf 1989b) to describe the feelings boys develop about having a penis since their mothers and other women do not; this guilt and castration fear is heightened if the boy senses a sexual animosity in his mother about his penis, as Fenichel points out, causing him to regress back to infantile perversity.

Fenichel believes that infants are natural perverts; to be more exact, they are polymorphously perverse, and can have sexual feelings in all parts of their bodies from their heads to their toes. They can also have sexual feelings for a range of objects—including males, females, dogs, cats, or inanimate things, and they can have perverse fantasies about all those objects and more, which Klein (1932) so thoroughly studied and described during her research with children. These fantasies involve such things as feces and urine, and contain scenes of infantile notions of rape, sodomy, or murder. According to Fenichel, we all have the capacity to be perverts, since we have all gone through this initial polymorphously perverse stage. However, those of us with castrating, exploitive, or passive parents will become fixated at that stage.

Other psychoanalysts are more or less in agreement on this issue, although each stresses a different element of the family constellation. Gillespie (1956) saw perversions as a defense against competing with father for mother's love. He posited that in perversions there is a retreat from the phallic expression of sexuality and assertiveness, which causes the regression back to a preoedipal stage of development.

Socarides (1978, 1979) who, like Stoller, specializes in research on the perversions, developed a unitary theory of the perversions which adds to Stoller's conclusions. Like Stoller, he emphasizes the importance of the child's interaction with his parents. In specific, he focuses on the rapprochement subphase of development (from about 15 months until 3 years of age). In his view, mothers of perverts are generally overattentive and close-binding, while the fathers are usually hostile and rejecting. He believes that the child's sexual orientation hinges on whether he is able to separate from his mother and form an adequate identification with his father. "At the center of all these conditions [perversions] lies the basic nuclear fear, that is, the fear of merging with, and the inability to separate from, the mother" (Socarides 1979, p. 185). According to Socarides, perverts have a fear of reengulfment by mother, which harkens back to primitive fantasies that infant children have of being sucked back into their mother's womb.

A study by Bieber and nine associates (1988) that originally concentrated on 106 male homosexuals and a comparison group of 100 male heterosexuals and was later corroborated by the analysis of over 1,000 male homosexuals, came to much the same conclusions. They found that the mothers of homosexuals generally formed a "close-binding-intimate" attachment with their sons which, in 85 percent of the cases, had a sexual quality to it, while the fathers were either indifferent or overtly hostile.

As previously noted, most psychoanalysts attribute perversity mainly to males. It is generally believed that there are more male homosexuals than females, and that other forms of female deviation are rare. Stoller's (1968) explanation of why male perversity is apparently more common than female perversity centers on the fact that it is generally the mother who has the closest relationship with both children in infancy, and hence it is generally her attitude which has the greatest impact on how perverse a child becomes, and which perversion he adopts. In cases where the father is the main caretaker from birth on, a female pervert such as a transsexual, is more likely to develop. He has reported a few such cases. However, the psychoanalytic definition of perversity may be too narrow, perhaps focusing on individual symptoms rather than on the larger societal picture.

If we look at this larger picture, we may see forms of female perversity that are hidden behind a screen of social censorship, protected by a double standard that views men more critically than women. In addition, more women than men are prone to an asexual existence and what Kaplan (1979) calls "inhibited sexual desire," a phenomenon that may be seen as a female equivalent of a perversion. In actuality, then, it appears there may be as many female perverts as male.

For example, there is a double standard with regard to male and female homosexuality. Female homosexuality is usually more acceptable to society than male homosexuality. Females do not see their homosexuality as a problem to the same extent as males and may not be as likely seek help; hence they do not become officially counted as homosexual. In addition, since, as Kaplan notes, females generally have less sexual desire than males, female homosexuality is often of the latent variety. This makes it even less visible. "Homosexuality in women," Freud (1920) asserted, "which is certainly no less common than in men, although much less glaring, has not only been ignored by the law, but has also been neglected by psychoanalytic research" (p. 146).

There is also a double standard regarding male and female exhibitionism. Male exhibitionism is considered a perversion because, in the eyes of society, it is seen as repulsive. Meanwhile a certain amount of female exhibitionism is not only acceptable but has become a fashion trend during many periods of history and in many cultures. Even blatant female exhibitionism (when, say, a woman stands in her window naked or opens her coat to expose herself on the street) is not viewed as repulsive, but merely idiosyncratic. Similarly, women who dress in men's clothes, who become excited by wearing men's jeans or men's underwear, are not called transvestic, for it has become socially acceptable for women to do so. Yet it would appear that a large percentage of women have transvestic tendencies, inordinately more so than men, yet are never thought of as perverts. Men who wear women's clothes are unequivically labeled transvestites and perverts.

What I am pointing out here is that women are allowed much more leeway in how they behave and dress than are men, and this social leeway has an impact upon who is seen as perverted and who feels perverted. In actuality, there is probably a correlation between perverse behaviors by females and by males, since the two sexes continually play off one another; hence, perversity would be more or less equal in each sex. For males, perversity usually involves a substitute form of sexual gratification, while for females it often entails some form of castrating behavior. In males, castration fear is the primary cause of the deviation, while in females penis envy lies at the root. In either case, it represents another way of acting out subjective hate.

In perversions subjective hate is acted out sexually by the avoidance of, submission to, or cruelty toward the opposite sex. Like all forms of subjective hate, it represents a resistance to intimacy and precludes maximum bonding. As Khan (1979) states, "The pervert puts an *impersonal object* between his desire and his accomplice: this *object* can be stereotype fantasy, a gadget or a pornographic image. All three alienate the pervert from himself, as, alas, from the object of his desire" (p. 9). Moreover, perversity does not lead to resolution of hate but maintains the hate and creates a barrier against any future attainment of maximum bonding. If one agrees that the goal of all living matter is to reproduce itself, then heterosexual bonding and reproduction would be the means to that goal, and any other form of sexual activity would be seen as a resistance.

Another indication of the subjective hate that underlies perversity is the fact that for the most part perverts do not seek therapy. Like the addict, the pervert does not think his perversion is a problem, and like the addict, he is afraid the therapist will try to take the perversion away from him or convince him it is morally wrong. Beyond this is a fear of what he will find out about himself and a defiance of all those considered as authorities. Generally, the degree of resistance an individual has toward therapy can be used as a measure not only of his resistance to genuine intimacy but also of his resistance to looking at himself objectively. Healthy people—those who do not need it—have no reluctance in making use of therapy.

However, perversity is not only an enactment of subjective hate; in some cases it also serves as a substitute gratification, providing secondary opportunities for bonding and love, even though such opportunities do not lead to procreation. As such, it can also constitute a necessary adaptation to an unhealthy family environment.

Here is a list of the major perversions and how they serve as vehicles for subjective hate.

HOMOSEXUALITY

With the growth of homosexuality in our society, homosexuals have de-manded that health professionals consider their sexual orientation nor-mal. Consequently, the American Psychiatric Association has removed homosexuality from its classification of psychosexual disorders, replacing it with "ego-dystonic homosexuality." This means that homosexuality is only considered a psychosexual disorder if an individual homosexual thinks his homosexuality is a problem for him. Imagine if this way of classifying psychopathology were extended to other disorders, such as, the borderline personality disorder. Most borderlines—indeed most alco-holics, compulsives, hysterics, phallic-aggressives, and paranoids for that matter—do not see their symptoms as problematic. Coles (1982) ob-serves, "There can be no clearer demonstration of the role of social value judgments in establishing the definition of a mental illness" (p. 48). And Levine (1979) echoes the sentiment, explaining that "the humanist ideol-ogy is now frequently used improperly (however compassionate and gen-uine the intent) to legitimatize sexual deviance as behavior which is as proper, acceptable, normal, and natural as heterosexuality" (p. 329).

Much recent research purports to prove that homosexuals function just as well as heterosexuals, and other research has attempted to show that homosexuality is of genetic origin. However, all such research is inconclusive. For example, some researchers point to a predisposition to homosexuality in certain males who are born with lower levels of testos-terone in the umbilical cord blood and who, from birth on, are less aggressive than the average male (Jacklin et al. 1983). Bieber and associ-ates (1988) note that "there may indeed be a biological factor associated with timidity, but there is no evidence that there are specific biological determinants for homosexuality" (p. xxii). At any rate, whether one con-siders homosexuality perverted or pathological, it nevertheless remains a form of sexuality that does not lead to procreation and therefore, from our perspective, is a deviant form and not maximally life-affirming. One must make a distinction between classification on the basis of sexual orientation on the one hand, and respect for a person regardless of sexual orientation (or his character type, political views, or religious beliefs) on the other hand. To classify homosexuality as a deviation from the norm does not imply disrespect for homosexuals, any more than classifying obsessive-compulsion as a neurosis would imply disrespect for obsessive-compulsives.

With regard to the expression of subjective hate, male and female homosexuals do it in different ways. Males act out hate toward females by avoiding them and by alternately idealizing or disparaging them (a manifestation of their ambivalence toward women). At the same time there is a grudging admiration and resentment of men—particularly "straight" men—not only due to castration fear but also because of penis envy acquired via their identification with their mother. There is often a sadomasochistic component in their personalities; those who are masochistic take the submissive position and those who are sadistic, the dominant position during anal intercourse. Bieber and associates (1988) posit that homosexuals have a fear of competing with men. Having, so to speak, won their mothers away from their fathers, they hesitate to try to win another woman. "The intolerable fear of having a romantic heterosexual relationship with a valued woman has a profoundly inhibiting effect, with the result that women are relinquished as lovers" (p. xxii). Socarides (1979) viewing it from another angle, asserts that homosexuals attempt to achieve "masculinity" through identification with the male sexual partner, which at the same time lessens castration fear towards men (who represent the hostile father of their infancy).

Female homosexuals, like males, have also failed to separate from their mothers or to achieve genuine bonding with a father-figure. McDougall (1970) explains: "The mother is felt to demand that everything be rendered up to her: sexual and affectionate feelings for the father, as well as self-mastery and independence" (p. 210). The daughter, fearing the mother's disapproval, regresses back to a preodipal relationship with the mother in which she idealizes the mother and displaces all her hostility onto her father, who in any case is a passive, hostile, or absent figure. In lesbians, intense penis envy underlies their hate, and as such their hate has an undertone of bitterness and revulsion. They rebel against men (their father) and turn to their sisters (their mother) for love and companionship. Men and fathers are treated with aversion and contempt, their penises seen as weapons that threaten to violate them, while women and mothers are idealized as giving and good.

Because of their feelings of inferiority and envy, some male and female homosexuals tend to act out subjective hate towards heterosexuals by disparaging heterosexual love, the family, and motherhood. This is often done by advocating feminist ideas about the importance of careers outside the home, and the virtues of women's independence, singlehood, and homosexuality.

TRANSVESTISM

Stoller's research into male transvestism shows that the transvestite thinks of himself as a woman with a penis. He has sexual relations with women and even gets married and has children; but when he engages in sex with women, he does so while clad in makeup, long hair, and a dress. In his fantasies, he is a woman with a penis making love to another woman. In particular, he becomes the phallic woman his mother longed to be. However, during love-making he is more excited by his own sense of femininity and his fetishistic attachment to women's clothes than his partner. His greatest pleasure is to prove he can be more feminine than a woman and then suddenly expose his penis to show that he is in actuality a man. Hence he acts out subjective hate by competing with women, showing that he can be more female than they, and shocking them with his penis. In essence he spites them.

For the female transvestite or females with transvestic tendencies, the process is much the same. They spite men by having it both ways, dressing like men but being women. They take pleasure in wearing men's clothes and become fetishistically excited by it. (Recently, a New York designer introduced a line of women's underwear fashioned after men's jockey shorts; it immediately became a bestseller.) They are strongly identified with their fathers, yet angry at them for having penises. They view themselves as men with vaginas, or as women who can "do anything that a man can do." When they have sex with a man, they want to prove they can be more masculine than he, yet be a woman at the same time. They act out their subjective hate by competing with and spiting men, showing them they can have what men have and their female genitals, too.

TRANSSEXUALISM

Like the transvestite, the male transsexual usually has a mother who feminizes him; however, the feminization goes much deeper in that his mother, because of deep envy and animosity toward males, not only treats the boy like a girl but also makes him deeply ashamed and fearful about having a penis. Meanwhile, the boy's father, for whatever reasons, allows this process to go on, and in other cases there is no father or male figure around, as when the mother is a lesbian. As an adult the transsexual acts out subjective hate on himself through self-mutilation (having his penis and testicles removed) and also, through an identification with his mother, by hysterically teasing men. (Stoller found in all of his psychological tests of transsexuals, a hysterical personality.)

The transsexual woman, though more rare, goes through a parallel process, acting out subjective hate through the surgical removal of her female genitalia and becoming more manly than any man, often assuming a "butch" phallic-aggressive personality.

EXHIBITIONISM

The male exhibitionist expresses subjective hate by exposing himself to women. Socarides (1979) asserts that the exhibitionist achieves "masculinity" through this practice. By getting a reaction from a woman to his exposed genitals, he reassures himself he is a man and not a woman, and defends against the fear of homosexuality. Exposing himself also constitutes a repetition compulsion in which, on an unconscious level, he is getting revenge at his mother for disparaging his penis and his manhood. The ways he exposes himself are as infinite as his imagination.

Krafft-Ebing (1932) describes a typical variety—a 37-year-old exhibitionist who would expose himself to children in playgrounds and to girls on the street. Occasionally he would masturbate in front of them. Once he stood outside a house and "rapped with his exposed penis on the window so that the children and servant-girls in the kitchen were forced to see it" (p. 510). Another exhibitionist had an uncontrollable impulse, while in crowds at dusk, "to bare his penis and rub it on the buttocks of a very fat woman" (p. 522). On other occasions this man could not calm himself unless he immersed his genitals in a bowl of milk; he would then serve the milk to customers in his wife's milk shop.

Female exhibitionists are much more numerous than male, but no less destructive. A female who parades down the street in a low-cut or see-through blouse, short dress, or tights that conform to her body and reveal every protrusion and orifice, is exposing herself to men out of spite, just as males do with women. Such females act out subjective hate by sexually tantalizing and taunting men and then scorning any who should try to approach them. The femininist-liberal value system supports their "right" to do this, refusing to understand the basic biological fact that females of all species give off sexual messages that arouse male sexual responses. Hence, they arouse and frustrate men, causing widespread feelings of hate that men must then either displace on others or take out on themselves, furthering the rift between the sexes. Like their male counterparts, female exhibitionists are repeating a compulsion that stems from events during the phallic stage, when all children are exhibitionistic. Fathers defend against sexual feelings toward their daughters by shaming and deriding their innocent sexual exhibitionism, hence fixating them at that stage.

VOYEURISM

The male voyeur, according to Kolb (1977) "obtains his sexual gratification through attempting to repeat visually the anxiety-arousing, yet exciting scenes of early childhood" (p. 624). He has often been exposed to aggressive nudity by his mother and felt threatened by it. As an adult he seeks reassurance that he can view the female body and not be swallowed up by it. There is subjective hate connected with his voyeurism in that he peeps at women who do not want to be seen (just as his mother during his early childhood throws her nude body before him in some sexualized way without concern for his feelings). In addition, he acts out hate by avoiding actual sexual intercourse with women, or by entertaining murderous fantasies about them while watching them. Often voyeurs are also exhibitionists, and will exhibit themselves as they peep.

Male voyeurs may at times also peep at other men. One of my patients had an impulse to masturbate in public men's rooms, where he would peer under the divider at the man masturbating in the next booth. In this way he felt comforted that other men masturbated (and that perhaps even his father, whom he idealized, masturbated). After engaging in such practices, he was always fearful that his wife would find out, as it represented an act of defiance against her (and against his mother).

Female voyeurism is uncommon, possibly due to the fact that from birth onward females are the objects of men's and each other's attention.

FETISHISM

Male fetishists make love with objects such as women's shoes, panties, locks of hair, or earrings. Fenichel's (1945) researches into the fantasies of fetishists, following Freud's example, led him to believe that these objects symbolized penises. The fetishist is fixated at the stage of denial—the stage boys go through upon first discovering the difference in sexual anatomy between males and females. Their fetishistic objects symbolize their mother's penis. Having had mothers who were frightening, fetishists remain frightened of women and, according to Socarides (1979) they also unconsciously yearn to be women and to have babies. Winnicott (1965), among others, sees the fetishistic object as an extension of the transitional object to which children cling while sucking their thumb or sleeping (such as a favorite stuffed animal), that is, as a self-soothing instrument. Khan (1979) emphasizes the self-protective role the fetish plays, comparing it to the acts of obsessive-compulsives who wash their hands several times a day to defend against sexual or aggressive thoughts or impulses.

Male fetishists act out subjective hate by avoiding women and through masochistic fantasies about them. They obtain sexual gratification by masturbating while looking at or touching the fetishistic object, and their fantasies involve being degraded by a phallic woman. Through identification with the aggressor (the phallic woman/mother), they view themselves as a hated object and take out hate upon themselves, which keeps them in an infantile sexual mode. Their drive for bonding and sexuality has been diverted onto an object rather than to another human being.

Krafft-Ebing (1932) tells of a fetishist who went around cutting women's dresses with a knife. He was excited only by silk dresses, and would cut pieces of silk from women's dresses or pull off their sashes as they walked on the streets, then go off and use them to masturbate. Upon being brought before a judge, the man, who was a locksmith, explained his actions by saying that once a woman had thrown him down the stairs and he had hated women ever since. Another man was fond of women's gloves, especially leather gloves that were used and stained by sweat. The first thing he would notice when he met a woman were her gloves. If they were the leather kind he liked, he would sometimes grow excited and have an orgasm on the spot. Other gloves, such as those made of cotton or silk, bored him. When he was alone he would tie leather gloves around his testicles while he masturbated.

With respect to female fetishists, Fenichel (1945) speculates that for them the fetish also symbolizes a penis, a phallic symbol that is "a soothing factor against the emotions connected with the idea of lacking this organ" (p. 344). For some women, dildos serve as fetishes, enabling them to defend against the frightening or revulsive prospect of having an actual man's penis inside them, which to them would represent intercourse with the envied object or the forbidden father and betrayal of the mother who demands absolute allegiance. Such women, caught between the demands of the mother and the sexual pull of the father, retreat from both to a world of auto-eroticism or occasional homosexual experiences. When they do find an occasional homosexual lover, they feel a sense of triumph over their mother, playing their lover against her. Sometimes female fetishists will become attached to a celebrity, and will constantly fantasize about him, while others become excited by a particular book, which they read over and over, or a television series. Although they might not engage in masturbation in connection with these objects, there is a sexualized excitement attached to them of a kind which might ordinarily be attached to a lover. Like the male fetishist, the female's drive for bonding and sexuality is primarily diverted to an object rather than to other human beings.

SEXUAL SADOMASOCHISM

The sexual masochist, like the masochistic character, seeks humiliation and punishment, but in the sexual arena, acting out subjective hate by provoking and aggravating a sadist into behaving hatefully and sexually at the same time. The sadist, meanwhile, acts out hate by being cruel and degrading to the masochist. Often there is a fetishistic quality to sado-masochistic rites, as the participants tend to dress up and utilize various paraphernalia such as black leather straps, high heeled shoes, whips, and the like. Loewenstein (1957)—noting that in these rituals the sadist invariably acts like a cruel parental figure while the masochist generally plays the role of a victimized but seductive child—interprets their rituals as symbolic repetitions of childhood fantasies. In specific they are repetitions of childhood situations wherein sexual curiosity, anal or phallic erotic games, or strivings toward sexual contact with parents were met with real or imagined threats, teasing, punishment or ridicule. In the symbolic repetition, the child (masochist) succeeds in seducing the parent (sadist) into participating in a scene of sexual humiliation that contains a castration threat or the threat of annihilation (for females). This ritual becomes a veiled, incestuous gratification for both masochist and sadist, an overcoming of the castration threat, and is also viewed, on another level, as a kind of rite of passage to adulthood. However, it fails to bring about this passage to adulthood, as the enactment of these sado-masochistic games does not resolve the underlying conflicts, but rather reinforces them by gratifying the sexual fantasies.

Many sadomasochists practice their rituals with mutual consent. However, sadists with sociopathic personality features will prey on un-willing victims by sexually conquering and degrading them. Sadists with borderline, phallic–aggressive, or paranoid schizophrenic features may pick up passive or masochistic men or women and sexually tease, brutal-ize, and degrade them, exciting them while defiling them, often prevent-ing them from reaching orgasm or obtaining any satisfaction.

PEDOPHILIA

Pedophilia may involve a heterosexual or homosexual relationship and occurs most often among close associates, such as family members. It may contain physically or emotionally sexualized relationships. Often pe-dophiles are individuals who were themselves sexually molested or psy-chologically castrated as children. Male pedophiles act out castration fear by failing occupationally, socially, or sexually in the adult world and turning to a child for gratification, and female pedophiles act out penis envy by rejecting their husbands and having a seductive, though castrat-ing relationship with their sons or daughters. As with other forms of perversity, pedophilia has been primarily associated with men. However, if one includes in this category mothers who have emotionally incestuous and castrating relationships with their children, it is probable that there are an equal proportion of male and female pedophiles.

Socarides (1979), among others, posits a narcissistic element in pe-dophilia, in that the pedophile often chooses a child who becomes "the ideal representation of the self" (p. 186). The pedophile either treats this ideal child in the manner that he would like to have been treated, or in the opposite manner.

BEASTIALITY

Those who practice sexual acts with animals are rare, and are found among both males and females. Dogs, cats, sheep, goats, rabbits, cows and horses are the most popular sexual objects. Beastialists will engage in sexual intercourse with an animal, or train an animal, such as a dog, to lick their genitals. They are generally solitary individuals unable to form relationships with other human beings. Often they are the only child and have suffered from a great deal of deprivation during infancy. Subjective hate gets acted out through the complete avoidance, sexually, of the human race.

Krafft-Ebing (1932) describes a certain Persian woman "who showed herself in the sexual act with a trained bull-dog, to a secret circle of *roués*, at ten francs a head" (p. 562). Other women develop a fondness for horses, sometimes engaging in intercourse, but more often becoming sexually excited by riding them (like Lady Godiva). Men have been known to have intercourse with a variety of animals, but one of the strangest cases related by Krafft-Ebing was of a man of high social position who had intercourse with chickens. When a number of them died and neighbors became suspicious, the police were called in. The man said he had done it because his penis was too small for human females. Upon examination it was found that he indeed had an extremely small penis.

RAPISM

Rape is the most hateful form of perversion, an extreme, sociopathic brand of sexual sadism. Groth (1979), in a large-scale investigation of the psychology of rape, found that most rapists reported having been molested or abused in their childhoods. Lindner (1955), focusing on the background of an individual rapist and murderer, discovered that his father had abandoned the family when the child was 4, after which he was given up for adoption by his mother. From then on he had a sporadic and tantalizing relationship with his mother; she would visit him for an hour or so at the orphanage or reform school where he was at, and once when he stayed with her for a weekend she slept with him (nonsexually). Meanwhile, he was abused at one school after another, until his rage spilled over in the rape and murder of a young woman.

Female "rapists" use their sexuality to seduce and then psychically rape their victims. Often borderlines, they can be hypnotically charming and then suddenly turn into witchlike figures, smiling viciously at their prey when they know, and he knows, he has been had. I once had a female patient who was skilled at psychic rape, and openly boasted of her prowess. This woman, as a child had been sexually abused by both her mother and father. She described how her father would give her enemas until she was 9 or 10, forcing her to lie on a table naked, while her mother watched. These enemas were rapes, in that they were given as punishment when whe was bad. As an adult, she went after older men who reminded her of her father. She would pick up at a bar the angriest-looking one (whom she decided was a misogynist), take him home to bed, and then at the last minute stop him and disparage his sexual performance.

"I love to see their eyes when they know they've been had," she told me. "You can see everything in their eyes, see their little male egos jumping up and down like rabbits, trying to find a way out. It destroys their sense of themselves." She liked it best when they tried to fight back, and she had already taken several men to court for "date rape." During her brief therapy, she frequently made sexual overtures toward me, and I am sure I would have been a feather in her cap, had she been able to get me to make a move—and then pin a malpractice suit on me. Unable to accomplish this, she soon became bored with therapy and quit.

Unfortunately, while male rapists can be prosecuted, female rapists—who are probably just as numerous, and whose impact is probably just as devastating to the ego—are generally never even questioned about their behavior.

CONCLUSION

My own work with perverse types has confirmed strong fixations in the anal-rapprochement stage, although, as Fenichel (1942) noted, the seeds for a perversion may be laid earlier in infancy, in the form of an oral-dependent, overly gratifying relationship with the mother. Hence, the typical mother of a pervert babies her child on the one hand and sexually rejects him or her on the other. The pervert often remains adolescent in appearance.

As with characterological types, perverse types are often mixed. A homosexual may also be a pedophile with a sadistic bent, for whom the child becomes a sort of fetish. A fetishist may also be a transvestite, voyeur, and exhibitionist. A sadist may also be a pedophile and a beastialist. At any rate, this list shows the range of perversity and provides an idea of how it develops and how it becomes a deviation from normal sexuality that then breeds on itself. Because these acts are symbolic enactments of subjective hate in the sexual sphere, those who practice them cannot achieve optimal bonding.

Therapy with perverts requires an understanding of this subjective hate as it manifests itself in the transference. It also requires a redefinition of perversions that considers the perverse—although socially accepted—aspects of female sexuality and behavior, and the hate that underpins it.

5

Political Forms
of Hate

The most clever forms of hate are found in politics. Here hate is almost always disguised behind high principles and great causes, and the recipient of hate is the enemy of these causes.

Each political party regards itself as right and good, while looking upon the opposition as wrong and bad. People tend to associate themselves with one party or another, or with one political philosophy or another, and their outlook on life is often wedded to this political philosophy or party. Political groups and political ideologies often serve to gratify not only our most basic, but also our most neurotic and narcissistic needs; they are a secondary form of bonding.

One of the basic needs they satisfy is the need to belong to a group. Human beings, according to Freud (1921), are horde animals. They have an innate need to belong to a horde. He deliberately made a distinction between horde and herd, noting that humans were aggressive animals who, upon banding together in groups, tended to regress to a state of primitive mental activity and impulsivity, "of just such a sort as is ascribed to the primal horde" (p. 125). He envisioned a horde similar to those of sea lion colonies, in which the strongest males take over hordes of females. Human beings also band together in hordes, but it is not only a strong leader who influences the horde, according to Freud, but also the psychological processes of hypnosis and identification. Members of groups show the same compliance and the same absence of criticism toward the leader of their group, or toward the idea which the group represents, as a hypnotized subject does to a hypnotist or a lover does toward a loved one. "A primary group is a number of individuals who have put the same object in the place of their ego ideal and have consequently identified themselves with one another in their ego" (p. 116).

Groups such as political parties are, on the one hand, extended families that offer opportunities for group bonding and identification around a leader or an ideology, and on the other hand, as both Hoffer (1951), a sociologist, and Kardiner (1954) have noted, they also serve to channel and justify aggression. By joining a group, the individuals feel more powerful, are more susceptible to suggestion, and are carried away by aggressive impulses that they would normally restrain. People in groups do not want to listen to objective feedback from those outside the group, and they rationalize through group consensus their acting out of irrational anger. Hoffer observes that it is chiefly "unreasonable hatreds" that drive people to merge with others who hate as they do and which meld into the "kind of hatred that serves as one of the most effective cementing agents" (p. 98).

Kardiner makes the point that mass movements offer individuals a chance to evade responsibility for themselves, since the leaders of such movements invariably tap into their constituents' misery and suggest that they are suffering through no fault of their own but are being victimized by something or somebody else. "This elevates fallen pride and mobilizes aggression, which in itself brings relief, because it implies hope and action. . . . Hatred is a powerful solvent for conscience, and that is why, in an atmosphere of universal rage, acts of injustice are committed with more or less good conscience. Aggression is enlisted in the aid of justified self-defense" (pp. 180–181).

W. Reich (1933) invented the term "emotional plague" to represent the type of mass acting out to which groups are prone, a type of behavior in which destructiveness is condoned by group consensus, as exemplified during the Christian Crusades or the Nazi empire in Germany. Reich was also the first to write about political characters psychologically, but it was his student, Baker (1967), who provided the most in-depth analysis of how the various political groups of the left and right do their acting out.

Baker contends that healthy individuals do not belong to any prefabricated political position but stay more or less in the center, deciding each issue on its own particular merits—a view with which I wholeheartedly agree. Below I have attempted an extension of Reich's and Baker's work.

THE LIBERAL PERSONALITY

Liberalism developed as a reaction to the repression and mysticism of the Dark Ages. Liberals sought mastery through knowledge, and they strove for freedom from authority. However, as Baker (1967) notes, this freedom caused anxiety and guilt. "Thus, his intellect, as well as being an outlet for expression, began to take on a defensive function against emotional release" (p. 165).

Today's liberals are cut off from their feelings and enmeshed in words and ideas. Out of touch with their core, they feel incomplete, and politicize their feelings, looking to an outside source to provide them with security. They demand that their views be applied to all of society, and they compensate for emotional detachment through declarations of brotherhood with people they have never met, trying to solve their personal conflicts by curing the ills of the world. They tend to be educated, rather than working-class people. They are drawn to passive rather than active pursuits.

Liberals can range from reasonably healthy individuals who are open to reason, to those who find it difficult to tolerate any criticism of their beliefs. More disturbed liberals are dogmatically wedded to liberal ideologies. In general they defend the underdog and are against authority. This defense of the underdog is often justified by a modified form of humanism, an overconcern with individual rights and the plight of the "common man" or the "victim," which loses sight of what is really best for society. Levine (1979) alludes to this overconcern with individual rights in the case of liberal pressure to have society accept homosexuality as normal, noting that the humanistic tenet of egalitarianism has been stretched by liberals to a point where it may be harmful. "The humanist ideology has thus taken on a relativistic emphasis, with questionable consequences ensuing in regard to the public's understanding of homosexuality" (p. 330). Kardiner (1954) echoes Levine's sentiments, warning that liberal social values have brought about an erosion of male-female relations and of the family. "This is the form that the anarchy latent in liberalism takes today," he asserts. "The struggle for subsistence and prestige is eroding the cohesion of the family" (p. 228).

Genesis

Liberals are usually from educated, urban families in which the mother is the dominant force, and in which permissiveness is the predominant theme of child-rearing. Mothers of liberals view themselves as underdogs, victims, or martyrs. Fathers of liberals tend to be passive types who hide behind intellectual ideals. Baker (1967) states that liberals are "secretly rebellious against the father." They identify with the mother and with underdogs in general (who are symbolically associated with the mother), and they oppose all authority (which represents the father). "Subversively defiant, he [the liberal] dare not show any open aggression, so great is the fear of the father and so intense the guilt.... He can allow himself to be aggressive only in causes and abstractions" (p. 171).

Having been overindulged and pampered as a child, the liberal becomes an adult who is forever demanding more and more rights from the world. Parents of liberals spoil their children and indoctrinate them with liberal ideas while accusing them of mother-bashing if they criticize the mother; hence their aggression gets diverted toward the father (who is generally a weaker figure), men, and conservatives (who represent the discipline of a traditional father). However, the liberals' rebellion against the father is at the same time a plea for a father who will stand up to them.

There is an emphasis in liberal families on intellectual pursuits at the expense of emotional well-being and balance. They indulge and pamper their children, but deprive them emotionally. They encourage educational achievement while deploring competitive sports which they feel bring out the evil in man. Hence, as adults liberals are often so intellectual that their sexuality becomes mechanized and passionless, and their intellectuality becomes a way of competing without acknowledging it.

Liberal Hate

In general liberals express subjective hate by denying their own aggression and projecting it onto those whom they deem to be unenlightened. Liberals are generally passive-aggressive. They are masters at provoking aggression from others in order to make their enemies look bad and themselves look good.

Typical of the liberal process of acting out hate is their way of dealing with racial or sexual questions. Whenever there is a conflict between blacks and whites or men and women, the liberal will take the side of the "underdog," no matter what the particular issues of the situation are. In doing so, the liberal can take out his anger on white Southerners, the conservatives, or on "old boys" who supposedly run the world, who are viewed by him as evil, while to African-Americans, women, and the liberal community he is seen as a hero.

Because of their guilt at being indulged and pampered as children, liberals have a need to prove that they are defenders of the less privileged. Burnham (1964) writes that "The guilt of the liberal causes him to feel obligated to try to *do something* about any and every social problem, to cure every social evil... even if he has no knowledge of the suitable medicine, or for that matter, of the nature of the disease; he must *do something* about the social problems even when there is no objective reason to believe that what he does can solve the problem—when, in fact, it may well aggravate the problem instead of solving it" (p. 195). Burnham's comments apply to the liberal's attempt to help African-Americans. By continually taking their side, liberals keep blacks dependent upon whites, encourage them to think of themselves as victims, fan the flames of racial discontent, and foster the very cycle of black poverty they purport to want to rectify. As long as African-Americans can get special treatment and sympathy by viewing themselves as hapless victims of discrimination, their victimhood will be reinforced. Hence liberals, while seeming to help blacks, are in actuality behaving in a subtly hateful way that keeps blacks dependent and poor. This allows liberals to play the role of the champions of civil rights. Out of a fear of being seen as prejudiced, they deny any negative feelings they might have toward blacks in general or toward individual blacks; that is, they develop a reaction-formation toward them, compensating for forbidden thoughts of superiority by manifesting the opposite attitude of overconcern and admiration for blacks. Hence their relations with blacks are unreal.

Their unreal view of African-Americans also prevents them from properly assessing the black situation. Their unconscious aversion to blacks, individually, causes them to guiltily and hastily conclude that blacks suffer from poverty, criminality, and mental illness because of racial discrimination. This guilt also causes them to want to diminish all distinctions between races, ethnic groups, or the sexes in order to pretend that all people are identical and equal. But blacks are different from whites, and one main difference is that blacks score much lower on I.Q. tests than whites (and whites score lower than Asians). Liberals try to dismiss I.Q. scores by contending that I.Q. tests are culturally biased against blacks. But what about Asians, who do best of all? Why do liberals not contend that these tests are culturally biased against Asians?

The Liberal attitude toward South Africa is also unreal. There has been a massive hue and cry by liberals against the South African government for keeping blacks and whites separate. Indeed, liberals have stirred up the world community against South Africa, demanding that the South African government end apartheid immediately, treating the South African government as if it were the worst kind of villain. Liberals do not understand the evolutionary process in Africa. When the Dutch settled there in the eighteenth century, blacks in the region were primitive tribes, similar to the American Indians. As the years went on and blacks became more civilized, the South African government began making more changes. But these changes were never fast enough for liberals, who used the South African situation to expiate their guilt and act out hate against the South African government (the father).

In contrast, there has not been nearly the same kind of protests by liberals about human rights' violations in Cuba, where millions were killed, tortured, and deported or exiled to America, where Castro's dictatorship rules supreme and eliminates all opposition. Liberals have not protested these abominations because Cuba, whose entire populace has been kept virtually imprisoned for years, pretends to be a collectivist state where all citizens have equal rights and competition is eliminated.

It should also be pointed out that the natural inclination of people is to live in separate communities—such as blacks in New York's Harlem and Chinese in Chinatown. The liberal pressure for integration represents an attempt to force nature to become egalitarian when, in fact, nature is nature—a myriad of species and ethnic groups with distinctive differences, where strife and inequality and the survival of the fittest are the rules of life.

Liberals are prone to twisting statistics in order to advance their causes. With respect to African-Americans or, more recently, with respect to women, liberals will cite statistics showing a low percentage of blacks and women in government, in the executive ranks of business, in law, and the like. This, they say, is evidence of discrimination. Or they will point out that there is a higher proportion of blacks in prison than whites, and cite this as evidence of discrimination against blacks. However, if one counters that there is a much higher proportion of men then women in prison, or that, in proportion to their percentage of population, blacks hold more governmental positions than whites, liberals will quickly come up with justifiable reasons for these disparities. It will also be noted that liberals do not defend other minority groups, such as Koreans, who are equally unrepresented in high places, and who could no doubt also make claims about all kinds of discrimination against them as a group, if they had a mind to do so. Koreans, like African-Americans, have been enslaved and ruled over by various peoples during their history, but liberals have never championed the Korean cause; hence Koreans have shaken off the yoke of victimhood at home and abroad. Those who have immigrated to the United States have quietly and stoically done what they had to do in order to work their way up in our society and become responsible citizens.

Liberals proclaim themselves to be for the rights of women, but in actuality they are only for the rights of some women—women who follow the liberal philosophy. Liberals do not support the rights of women who oppose abortions, who are critical of feminism, or who espouse conservative values such as being housewives or devoting themselves to full-time mothering. On the contrary, they often ridicule, ostracize and stigmatize such women. While they continually speak of human rights, they are not at all concerned about the rights of fathers to decide whether or not to have a child, or to visit their child after a divorce. Nor do they ever ask children what they want when they blissfully toss them into daycare centers. They will condemn men who "womanize," but not women who "manize" or homosexual men who are promiscuous. Only heterosexual men are villainized for sexual excesses.

Liberals use their facility with words, as well as a self-righteous and sarcastic tone of voice, to defeat and destroy opponents. They fling around words like "bigot," "sexist," "racist," and "homophobic" in order to shame and silence detractors, and they address them in a tone of voice that suggests that the opponent is evil for even thinking, much less saying things that go against the liberal ideology. The more psychologically disturbed liberals are, the more they cling to the notion that liberalism represents all that is progressive and good and right, and can never be questioned; indeed, for some, liberalism becomes sacrosanct, and all who question it are seen as threats to their sanctity. Baker (1967) notes that this pathological form of liberalism "represents a misfired solution to the problem of guilt and anxiety: the anxiety gets bound up in political attitudes and ties, fixed to a specific characteristic ideology. These 'self-evident' truths the modern liberal sees as unshakable and unarguable, since any attempt to challenge them shakes the very core of his defenses and stirs up intolerable anxiety" (p. 170). The result is that liberals themselves are often as bigoted as those whom they attack, but they will be incredulous if anybody says so.

Because of their permissive upbringings, in which they were appeased by their mothers whenever they behaved hatefully, and in which the father's attempt to institute discipline was undermined by the mother, the liberal in turn attempts to resolve any conflict by appeasing the person or group seen as the underdog (mother) while opposing the person or group seen as the topdog (father). Reich (1953) linked the phenomenon of liberal appeasement to the rise of Nazi Germany: "Weak in their guts with no prospect ahead of themselves, resting only on a once valid great doctrine of humanism, they delivered the German society to the Nazis" (p. 218). Liberals will invariably support the independence of underdeveloped countries and oppose the "tyranny" of colonial rule, whether or not a country is ready for independence or has the maturity to govern itself. They generally support all revolutions, even though such revolutions become tyrannies the moment they overthrow the existing government. They say they abhor war and violence, but will support the most violent revolutionaries and be blind to the atrocities they commit (for example, the liberal support for Stalin's communist revolution, despite ongoing reports of his slaughtering of millions of "counterrevolutionaries"). Because they are pampered as children and never learn to compete in a healthy way, they are against free enterprise and competition, athletic or otherwise, and favor socialism rather than capitalism. The conscious motive is to help the underdog (mother), while the unconscious motive is to topple the topdog (father). The liberal's opposition to all differences in social structure—as well as between the sexes or races—is also an expression of his or her unconscious desire to eliminate competition, assuage castration fear and penis envy, pull down the father, expiate feelings of inferiority and guilt, and compensate for a lack of normal self-assertion.

Malcolm Muggeridge (1965), a British literary critic, in an allusion to the liberal's narcissistic insistence on "life, liberty, and the pursuit of happiness," and denial of aggression, wrote that "Liberalism will be seen historically as the great destructive force of our time, much more so than communism, fascism, nazism or any of the other lunatic creeds which make such immediate havoc" (p. 27). In a sense Muggeridge may be right, insofar as societies generally start out conservative but become increasingly liberal as they decline.

Radical Hate

The hateful activities of radical liberals are well known. They are borderline or sociopathic characters who politicize their considerable rage and act it out against "The Establishment" through smear-tactics, terrorism, and revolution. Their childhoods have often been permissive to a severe degree, as their parents are totally inadequate in setting limits or modeling objective thinking and judgement. They suffer from political narcissism.

They have strong paranoid features in their personalities, and they experience any disagreement with their point of view as a threat to their existence; to be wrong, for a radical, is worse than death, and indeed many will sacrifice their lives to prove they are right. Like all borderlines, they are prone to splitting off their aggression, attributing it to others, and seeing the world in an extreme "good guys" and "bad guys" perspective. In their scheme of things, even moderate liberals who want to find ways to live in peace and harmony with conservatives, are to be distrusted. They measure people's worth by the extent of their radicalism.

Radicals such as Stalin in Russia, who had about 20 million "counterrevolutionaries" killed in death camps, justify their hate by preaching ideas about equality and collectivism for the common man and death to those who oppose the common man. They are absolutely closed to argument, and will distort the facts in such a way as to prove the righteousness of their cause, believing that anything that furthers their ideology or their sacred goal is justified.

THE CONSERVATIVE PERSONALITY

While Liberalism is a kind of psychological matriarchy, conservatism is basically an outgrowth of patriarchy. Conservatives tend to be from larger, father-dominated families, and they are often less well-educated than liberals. They are "feeling" people rather than intellectuals, and are drawn to physical rather than mental activities. (Baker comments that the gradual shift from conservatism to liberalism by psychoanalysts is evident in the trend towards deemphasizing the libido theory and emphasizing a more intellectual ego psychology.) While liberals define themselves through humanistic ideologies, conservatives identify themselves through their religions. They are cautious and slow to promote innovation, preferring evolutionary development to the liberal's revolutionary change. Indeed, the conservative does not adjust well to change at all. Whereas the liberal always supports the underdog (mother), the conservative will be just as dogmatic about supporting the topdog (father), or the status quo, in any situation.

Conservatives, like liberals, range from those who are fairly healthy to those who are quite disturbed. Conservatives of the disturbed variety will be rigid, repressed, and pious. They will view those belonging to their religion or community as good, and all outsiders, particularly "heathens" (nonbelievers in Christianity) or secular humanists or liberals, as evil. They subscribe to a value system in which men are dominant and women are submissive, and in which a macho lifestyle is extolled and brutal aggression (such as the slaughter of 60 million buffalo during the nineteenth century) is extolled.

Genesis

Conservatives usually come from rural or suburban settings or blue collar backgrounds where "men are men," and where discipline and corporal punishment are staples of child-rearing. They identify with the father and learn to compete with him. Whereas in liberal families Mother is always right, in conservative families Father is always right. In addition, parents of conservatives have strong religious convictions, which they transmit to the child; these religious convictions, like the liberal's ideologies, become an extension of the family system—God being symbolic of the father (indeed, in Christianity, God is often called "God the Father"), somebody who must always be obeyed.

The conservative character is shaped primarily during the anal phase, when toilet training becomes the prototype of the conservative emphasis on the importance of obedience to the father and of discipline. Punishment is used freely in order to mold character. Religious instruction is also utilized in order to strike the fear of the Lord (the father) into the child and obtain obedience. The mother remains a passive, nurturing figure who stands behind the father.

As adults conservatives transfer their identification with the father to those who enforce law and order—the government, the army, and the police. Whereas liberals tend to side with the underdog and rebel against the topdog, conservatives always support the topdog in any situation, whether or not the topdog is in the right. They favor the use of force in order to "get it done." Because force and violence was administered to them during child-rearing, conservatives constantly fear violence being done to them; they are always ready for a fight, and are not hesitant to use force or violence when necessary in their personal lives or in the world—such as in quelling riots or fighting wars.

Conservative Hate

Conservatives range from those who are fairly healthy, in touch with their feelings, and truly committed to their families and to the preservation of the country and the species, to those whose fundamentalism and patriotism is carried to an extreme, who cannot tolerate a difference of opinion, and who become dogmatic bullies. An example of the former would be the character, Levin, in Tolstoy's *Anna Karenina*; an example of the latter would be Hitler.

In general conservatives act out hate in more overt ways than liberals do. They are at home with their aggression and feel morally justified in expressing it; but at the same time, they are apt to be more rigid about gratifying their sexuality, and therefore have a need to be devoutly and obsessively religious in order to maintain sexual restrictions. Baker (1967) explains, "Religion must be more devout to counteract the increased hate from his acutely rigid [defensive] armor" (p. 194). Conservatives impose strict limits on their own conduct, and they wish to do likewise with others. While liberals believe in freedom of personal expression and feel threatened by any attempt to limit this freedom, conservatives wish to squash personal freedom, particularly freedom of dress, speech, and sexuality. They emphasize conformity over individual expression, and traditional values. Women should wear dresses that cover their bodies rather than reveal them, and men should wear the pants.

In politics conservatives will act out hate by wasting taxpayer money on inordinately expensive and unnecessary defense programs, and they will persuade the public that these are required to maintain peace. For example, billions of dollars have been spent on a "star wars" project, which will supposedly prevent missiles from hitting the United States, but the reality is that by the time, many years from now, such a project is completed, other nations will have found a way to beat it, and it will become obsolete. Thus, conservative defensiveness and competitiveness leads to a greater and greater escalation of arms. At times firmness is necessary to bring a nation or a person to the peace table, but conservatives go to extremes in this direction. They will characterize liberals as "bleeding hearts" who wish to appease the enemy, and they will attempt to shame or bully them into silence through strong-arm tactics if liberals complain about defense spending. They generally respond to any conflict with a show of force, whether or not force is necessary.

Conservatives admire winners—the boxer who knocks out twenty opponents in a row, the businessman who scores big on the stock exchange, the general who defeats an enemy. Sometimes long after it is proven that an existing government is corrupt, loyalist conservatives will maintain their support for the old regime, even at the peril of their own lives. Because of their pent-up aggression and their envy of those who have had it easier, conservatives can be quite sadistic toward underdogs (losers), who threaten to displace them in the social scheme of things. Conservative whites have been known to brutalize African-Americans at various times and places—from the deep South to neighborhoods in New York City.

The more full of hate and envy they are, the more they will be full of self-righteousness and contempt for liberals, viewing them as selfish, hedonistic heathens, intellectual snobs, people who put on airs, or cancers to society who must be purged. They are also envious of liberals because liberals lavish themselves with rights and freedoms that conservatives cannot let themselves have. The conservative cannot think about such things, and considers all who do selfish. "He is still in contact with his core," Baker notes of the conservative, "but unable to express it naturally because of his rigidity. Instead, he expresses it compulsively through taboos against unnatural expression" (p. 194).

Conservatives have a deep fear of perversion and of all forms of sexual expression other than conventional male–female sexual intercourse. At the same time, they can be quite nasty to perverts, whom they see as a threat to their own psychic stability. The fear of homosexuality and perversion is linked to the infantile perverse impulses which are defended against through religious repression. Also, homosexuality goes against the conservative ego–ideal of the macho man.

Conservatives, like liberals, will also twist the facts to suit their purposes. Hence conservative businessmen who pollute our environment or chop down forests in order to build new housing projects will rationalize their destructive behavior by saying they are creating more jobs through these projects. They can be fierce and ruthless competitors; rather than rebel against their fathers, they wish to surpass them and become more powerful. At times they can be tyrannical to those below them. The punishment they received as children is internalized and then displaced onto their children, employees, or the world in general.

While liberals demand immediate social changes often before people are ready to handle them, conservatives, due to resentment about their restricted, punitive childhoods, will resist social changes, their retort being something like "Why should *they* have it easy when I had it so hard?" Hence conservatives will oppose government aid to the needy, which would provide people with benefits without their having to work for them.

The debate over abortion is a clear example of both liberal impetuosity and conservative rigidity. Liberals want any woman to be able to have an abortion "on demand," and believe it is solely the woman's right to decide whether to have an abortion, because the fetus is viewed as part of her body. This position represents an acting out of hate toward the symbolic father and against his attempt to enforce discipline and responsibility. In effect, liberals would make abortion a form of birth control, exclude the father from the decision-making process (although he is required to be financially responsible for the child should the mother decide to have it), and refuse to take into account the complicated circumstances that are associated with each individual abortion. On the other hand, conservatives who wish to ban abortion entirely are acting out hate toward the symbolic mother (liberalism symbolizing the mother–seductress whom conservatives fear, the Eve of the Bible who brought calamity to humankind). However, conservatives, like liberals, do not take into account that some abortions may be warranted and others ill-advised; nor do they properly consider the social difficulties that ensue when unwanted births occur, or the necessity for abortions on a universal scale in order to curb the population explosion.

China's population has skyrocketed well beyond a billion people now, and it is still soaring. Current birth control methods alone are not adequate to curb the explosion, but the widescale application of abortions has made inroads. If conservatives had their way, they would not only ban abortions, but also birth control. God, they believe, opposes any tampering with natural processes. Never mind that by not tampering with nature, human beings, left to their own impulses, would inundate our planet with human life and human waste beyond the capacity of its endurance. God, the conservatives seem to think, is not concerned about the extinction of the planet.

The religious fundamentalism of conservatives prevents them from being able to look at the big picture in other ways. At times they will not allow doctors to apply the latest techniques in medicine because it goes against "God's will." At other times they oppose social welfare programs because they say they violate the sanctity of the family. In places and times where religious fervor is at a high pitch, hate is directed at other religions through social ostracism and stigmatism. An extreme of this was the Spanish Inquisition, at which time thousands were burned at the stake for refusing to convert to Catholicism.

Baker (1967) notes:

> At his best he [the conservative] probably comes closest to health, at least in his social behavior, of any group in our sick society. At his worst, that is, the reactionary and fascist, he has been responsible for many of the horrors of the past: for example the Catholic Inquisition. He has persecuted or murdered nearly every great man who tried to help him, from Socrates and Christ to Freud. [p. 186]

However, Baker stresses that conservatives are more in touch with their feelings than liberals, and hence their hate is more out in the open. He makes the point that while liberals tend to embrace African-Americans and other underdeveloped groups as a whole, conservatives are more capable of relating to them on an individual basis, for they are more real about their feelings.

Reactionary Conservatism

Reactionary conservatives are sadomasochistic characters. They may be white or black supremists, male or female chauvinists, religious zealots, super patriots, or political terrorists. They usually have tyrannical fathers (Hitler's father reportedly beat him unmercifully as a child) and weak, masochistic mothers.

Reactionaries express subjective hate through mysticism and sadism. The mysticism often takes the form of a chauvinism with regard to their race, religion, country, or locality, and a feeling that they must remain pure of inferior elements that might threaten their sanctity (this impurity representing the hate projected onto the external environment). For example, Hitler and the Nazis in Germany extolled German racial purity and, in that spirit, attempted to eliminate all foreign elements, such as Jews, from German society. Sadism and brutality permeate the existence of reactionaries, but are most evident in their sexuality. Because of their brutal upbringings, they are quite sadomasochistic, and often they will seek out someone from an "inferior" race on whom to act out this sadism.

The more extreme a reactionary is, the more he or she demands absolute authoritarianism. Says Baker (1967), "He is the little man who grew up so inhibited and restricted and so dependent upon the father that he requires a father figure or the fatherland to continue to dictate his life and give him permission to express the brutality and hate he can no longer control" (p. 196).

CONCLUSION

Neither liberal nor conservative types are able to bond successfully. They cannot bond successfully in their personal lives because of characterological flaws associated with overpermissiveness or overpunitiveness. They cannot bond on a societal level because of an inability to empathize with "the other side." Unable to bond effectively, they attempt to manipulate or intimidate others into taking their side, but such bonding is not satisfactory. Another way of saying this is: the less an individual is able to love objectively, the more he or she will strive for power over others and, in extreme cases, for the power to destroy as many others as possible, as in a war.

As previously stated, centrism represents the healthiest political stance; a country without a strong center cannot endure any more than can a person without a strong ego. Indeed, I have suggested elsewhere (Schoenewolf 1989b) that there is a parallel between liberalism, centrism, and conservatism on the societal level, and the id, ego, and superego on the individual level. Just as an individual needs a strong ego to mediate between the impulses of the id and the threats of the superego, a country needs a strong center to mediate between the permissive tendencies of liberals and the punitive tendencies of conservatives.

Without a strong center, a country (or individual) gets polarized and pulled apart by conflicts. Each side—liberalism or conservatism—thinks that if it can completely dominate, everything will be all right. But this is an illusion. People need a balance of freedom and discipline, of risk and caution, of pleasure and pain. Children need such a balance in order to grow up well adjusted, and adults need it to live in harmony. When there is too much mother-domination or too much father-domination in child-rearing, this balance is thrown off as it is when there is too much liberalism or conservatism in a society.

6

Cultural Forms
of Hate

PREJUDICE AND PERSECUTION

Cultural hate generally takes the form of prejudice and persecution. However, the definition of prejudice and persecution depends upon the lens through which we view it. Complaints of prejudice and persecution are themselves acts of prejudice and persecution.

The term *prejudice* has come to mean an attitude against a group that is unwarranted by facts. Whites are said to be prejudiced against blacks solely on the basis of skin color; men are said to be biased against women strictly because of gender differences; Gentiles are said to be prejudiced against Jews only because of religious differences; and heterosexuals are said to be biased against homosexuals strictly because of the difference in sexual orientation. The prejudices of whites, men, Gentiles, and heterosexuals, moreover, are said to cause them to persecute blacks, women, Jews, and homosexuals. However, in actuality things are not so simple. There are extenuating circumstances.

In studying the various individual character types, I have found that those who have the severest inferiority complexes and are most masochistic and paranoid are the ones who are also most prone to complaining of prejudices and persecutory behavior toward them. For instance, a man who had an inferiority complex about his height—I will call him Dick—used to continually complain that women were prejudiced against him and persecuted him because he was short. Most of his therapy sessions were spent in lambasting women, whom he saw as spiteful, evil creatures out to keep him in his place. He would not listen to any attempts by me to point out other short men whom women found quite attractive.

"Yes, but he's a movie star," he would reply. Or, "Yes, but he's rich." Or, "Yes, but he's a manipulator."

Other men had advantages he did not have and were therefore not victimized on account of their height. Nor could I get him to analyze his behavior toward women or his attitude toward his height.

"I could tell from the moment I saw her she had a thing about my height," he said about one woman he met.

"What was her thing about your height?" I asked.

"She was contemptuous toward it."

"What made you think that?"

"The way she grinned at me. She had that superior grin women have when they feel sorry for you but want to hide it. She took one look at my height—looked me up and down—and decided I was a midget. From that time on she had that grin on her face. Like, we can be friends, but unfortunately you just don't cut it as a man."

"How do you know she was thinking that?"

"I just know."

"Are you sure?"

"I'm sure."

"Absolutely sure?'

"Absolutely."

All the calamities that besieged him in life were, in his opinion, because of his height. Once, when he was fired from a job, he spoke bitterly for months about suing his former employer for discrimination. "People don't realize how much discrimination there is against short people," he ranted on. "Big is beautiful, powerful, healthy; short is ugly, weak, unhealthy. The bigger you are, the more attention you get—that's all there is to it. If I'd been six feet tall, my employer would never have treated me that way." Because he had an inferiority complex about his height, he invariably behaved in such a way as to provoke others and call their attention to his height, which only served to confirm his suspicion that people were prejudiced.

He combed the news for instances of prejudice. Once when several nations came to the aid of a wayward whale stuck in the ice near Alaska, and were spending millions of dollars in time and technology to plow a path for the whale to get free and join his family in the ocean, Dick said, "See? Big is beautiful. Big is important. Look how much attention this whale gets! Do you think everybody'd get this concerned if a frog were stuck in the ice in Alaska?" On another occasion, when a popular song came out called, "Short People," which alleged, among other things, that short people were more vicious than tall people, he bristled. "You see? This is the very kind of prejudice and character assassination we shorties are up against."

His days were spent obsessing about the many examples of prejudice against short people in his present life and throughout history. Wherever he went, he was always looking, listening, and waiting for people to do something that revealed their "shortism," a term he invented to designate prejudice against short people. In the U.S. Army tall people were given priority for leadership positions over short people, he informed me, and his own informal study of corporations showed that the majority of corporate executives were above average in height, while another study of prisons showed that the majority of men who were incarcerated were below average in height. These studies proved to him that short people always got it worse than others.

His mission was to prove that his deluded view of things was correct, so that he could continue to excuse his failures in life as being due to his shortness (rather than due to a flaw in his character) and have reasons to act out hate toward all those whom he considered to be persecutors, primarily women.

During the course of several years of analysis, we were able to trace Dick's persecutory delusions to the inferiority complex about his height, to latent, ego-alien homosexual impulses, and to paranoia. Dick was an only child whose mother always compared him unfavorably with his father. His father, a successful businessman, was all-good, all-knowing, and all-powerful in her eyes. When he was in the phallic stage in which boys want to take their mother away from their father, and in which they take pride in exhibiting their penises and to showing what wonders they can perform, she became repulsed by him and by his penis. When he bragged that his penis was just as big as Dad's, she let him know that it was certainly not as big as Dad's, and he was being silly. When he said he would beat up Daddy and marry her, she said he was too little to marry her. Such remarks, combined with her revulsion toward his penis, and his own comparison of the size of his penis with that of his father's, became the core of his inferiority complex. Later, at the adolescent stage, when he stopped growing at 5 feet 5 inches, the inferiority complex centered on his height. He had hoped to grow taller than his father, who was 5 feet 10 inches, and who "belittled" his son; instead he remained shorter.

The close-binding but castrating relationship with his mother and competitive relationship with his father not only reinforced his feelings of inferiority (both the mother and father teased him about his height rather than providing him with the empathy that would have helped him overcome the complex), but also created a paranoid characterology, at the bottom of which was a fear of being homosexual (a fear of being castrated by the father) and a rage at his mother for leading him on, making him dependent on her, and then ridiculing him as a man "too little to marry her." However, due to his mother's pampering, he was unable to allow himself to feel this rage at her. He almost completely displaced it on other females, whom he experienced as being prejudiced against him for being too short.

Dick's case provides clues as to the meaning of prejudice and persecution in general. I have observed that all of my patients who felt that they were victims of prejudice and persecution—whether they were African-American or Jewish or homosexual or Hispanic or female—suffered from a similar combination of inferiority feelings, paranoia, or masochism. It is the most narcissistic, paranoid, or masochistic segment of a group—the chauvinistic African-American, the reactionary Jew, the militant homosexual or the radical woman—who complains most vociferously about prejudice and persecution. Like Dick, these individuals spend their daily lives obsessed with finding instances of prejudice. If a Jew is murdered in a temple, a black attacked in the subway, a woman raped on a back street, an Hispanic unfairly arrested by the police, a homosexual assaulted in a rough neighborhood, you can depend on it that the militants will come out in droves, hold as many press conferences as possible, and cite each such incident as proof that all Gentiles, all whites, all men, all heterosexuals, are evil, prejudiced monsters. This, of course, justifies the considerable, irrational, subjective hatred such militants feel toward those they dub as "the enemy," and their own enormous prejudice toward these groups. It is also, of course, a subtle form of psychological persecution of these groups.

What I am saying is that many of those who join in mass movements to proclaim themselves victims of prejudice are, like Dick, acting out the rage that is always associated with feelings of inferiority, paranoia, and masochism. For example, if all of the short people with inferiority complexes, such as Dick, joined together to form a movement, they would then find safety in numbers and a vehicle for expressing their rage and prejudice toward tall people or women in a socially acceptable form. As Kardiner (1954) notes,

> Rage requires only an avenue of discharge and a pretext to release it. In modern times the management and channelizing of mass rage has become very expert, due largely to media of communication. The trick is to create in those from whom you expect support the thought that they are suffering through no fault of their own, that someone else is creating the hardship and that the thing to do is to go after the real culprit. [p. 180]

In addition, by banding together in a mass movement, their combined rage has a considerable impact on society, particularly upon those segments of society which are most guilt-ridden about being overprivileged, such as liberals. Liberals will be quick to jump on the bandwagon and affirm that, yes, there is prejudice and persecution against short people. During times of war, whole nations become involved in this process, castigating enemy nations as evil persecutors in order to justify warfare. Healthy people see through such ploys and do not get swept up by such movements.

Erikson (1950) observes, The counterpart of intimacy is "distantiation":

> the readiness to isolate and, if necessary, to destroy those forces and people whose essence seems dangerous to one's own, and whose "territory" seems to encroach on the extent of one's intimate relations. Prejudices thus developed (and utilized and exploited in politics and in war) are a more mature outgrowth of the blinder repudiations which during the struggle for identity differentiate sharply and cruelly between the familiar and the foreign. [p. 264]

In Erikson's view, prejudices are an outgrowth of infantile identity confusion: the need to establish and identify with an ethnic group, a country, a religion, or a gender, stems from a deficient sense of personal identity. Various groups have been prone to this deficiency throughout history, and as soon as one group cries "Prejudice!" it invariably turns around and persecutes another, which will likewise cry "Prejudice!" Thus the Romans persecuted the Christians, crucifying them, feeding them to lions, and then the Christians turned around and persecuted the Romans (heathens), sending them to their deaths by various methods.

Does prejudice in fact really exist? Certainly there have been groups during the course of history that were discriminated against and persecuted. The question is, were they discriminated against and persecuted through no fault of their own? Was the persecution of Christians by Jews and Romans completely unprovoked, or did the defiant criticism of Jewish and Roman religious practices by Jesus Christ and his followers, along with their self-righteous proclamations about how only they knew the Messiah, and only they were saved and could count on an afterlife, while all others were heathens who would go to hell, have anything to do with their persecution?

This is not to say that prejudice and persecution do not exist, or that it is entirely in the eye of the beholder. Certainly there are those who truly discriminate against short people, and who will be unconsciously sadistic toward them. However, what is called prejudice and persecution is often the territorial aggression that is common to all species of the animal world, the "struggle for existence," as Darwin (1859) put it. One must carefully study those who level charges of prejudice and persecution to determine if they are also participating in that struggle and acting out aggression.

RELIGIOUS HATE

Religion is replete with martyrdom, which is a masochistic form of hate. Freud (1921) posited a primal guilt. He believed that religion began with the primal sin—that is, when the sons of the first primal horde banded together to kill and devour the father, and were then overtaken with remorse. This primal guilt, he believed, is what gave Christianity its great and long-lasting power over man, for Christianity is a religion that contains, in the crucifixion of Christ, a re-enactment of the primal parricide and its atonement. Kardiner (1954), however, disagrees with Freud's assumption of a primal guilt in man. "Guilt is not an inborn emotion like fear or rage; it is a cultivated emotion" (p. 118). Kardiner thinks martyr-dom is the result of situational stress, rather than from an innate primal guilt.

Menninger (1938) calls attention to the universality of religion and martyrdom as an expiation of guilt and an enactment of self-hate. He found it not only in Christianity but also among Mohammedans, Buddhists, Brahmans, and Hindus. "The Jews, the Greeks, the Romans and many others believed in sacrifice to forestall divine envy," he writes. "Juvenal describes how the expiatory rites of the worship of Isis aroused great enthusiasm in Rome; women broke the ice of the Tiber River on winter mornings to plunge three times into the water, or dragged themselves on bleeding knees around the field of Tarquin, or undertook long pilgrimages to Egypt to propitiate the goddess" (p. 104). He notes also that the theory that the body should be kept subordinate to the spirit by self-denial was also taught by pagan philosophers such as Plato and Cicero.

Menninger cites hateful ascetic practices of various religious groups throughout history. For example, the Filipovtsi were an eighteenth-century religious sect in Russia who barricaded their villages in order to starve themselves to death. The Mexican-American sect known as Los Hermanos Penitentes de Sangre de Cristo, in New Mexico and Colorado, used to practice public flagellation to appease the divine wrath of God. Hindu ascetics remain in immovable attitudes with their faces or their arms raised to heaven until the sinews shrink and the posture stiffens into rigidity; expose themselves to inclement weather while sitting nude; tear their bodies with knives; and feed on excrement.

One of the saddest and most haunting stories of religious martyr-dom was told by Menninger about Jeanne Le Ber, a modern saint who lived in Montreal. According to Menninger she was the only daughter of a rich merchant and his wife, who greatly overindulged her and lavished her with praise. The merchant continually gave parties for the distinguished visitors to Montreal, and presented his daughter to them, and they would shower her with gifts. However, from early on, the child disliked all this attention. While away at school, she gave away the boxes of sweets that were sent from home, and under the rich and beautiful gowns her father bought her she always wore a haircloth skirt. When she reached marriageable age, her father fixed a large dowry for her and many suitors came to call on her, but she begged to enter a convent instead. When her parents refused to allow her to do that, she obtained permission to go into retreat in her own house, taking a vow of chastity for five years. Her parents consented to this arrangement, hoping that the resolution of a 17-year-old girl would soon falter. It did not. She never spoke to them again, except when she stole out of the house to church. Her father, heart-broken, withdrew from society. Her mother's health faded, and on her deathbed she begged for Jeanne to come to her side, but Jeanne refused. When the five years were over, she renewed her vow. At the end of ten years she used her dowry to build a chapel, in which she had a cell constructed for herself behind the alter. The cell consisted of three tiers: a grill in the first floor that permitted her to be present, unseen, at mass, and had a window through which plain food was delivered to her. The second floor was a sleeping room, just large enough for a narrow bed where she slept without a heater. On the third floor she embroidered beautiful altar cloths and vestments, or spun yarn and knitted stockings for the poor. This narrow tower became her living tomb, from which she never again came forth.

Menninger sees in such martyrdom elements of aggression, self-punishment and denial of erotic impulses. Martyrs usually forgo any intimate or sexual relationship, usually as the result of a turning away from smothering, psychologically incestuous, or dominating parents. Their acts of suffering harken back to the tendency of children to hold their breath or refuse to eat unless their parents give in to their demands. Such acts always have an element of defiance or bribery to them and, in the case of death, an element of triumph, a victory through defeat. In Jeanne's case, it is obvious that she withdrew into asceticism and martyrdom in reaction to her smothering, narcissistic parents, and the fact that this was an act of defiance and spite was obvious when she refused to come to her mother's death bed. The nature of the martyr's aggression was captured in a poem by Clarence Day:

As The Worm Turns

When lovely woman weds a Tartar
And learns too late that love is grim,
How sedulously she plays the martyr,
And meanwhile makes one out of him.

(*The New Yorker*, March 2, 1935)

Religion is a culture of martyrdom; its basis is a narcissistic glorification of the victim and an indirect persecution of those experienced as persecutors. Hate is expressed not only against the self through self-denial and self-punishment, but also outwardly through masochistic provocation and the inducement of anger and remorse in others. Jesus, no doubt, knew what a commotion his death would cause, knew that his death would make his enemies—the Jews and Romans—look bad. Gandhi, through his brand of self-denying and provocative passivism, incited the wrath of the British in India and made them look like villains.

Religions have traditionally vied for influence over the minds and hearts of humans. In this sense they have taken a role in the historical bouts of territorial aggression. The Holy Roman Empire was a notable example of religious territoriality, and the Holy Crusades an example of how Catholicism expressed subjective hate toward those who did not accept its rule.

RACIAL AND ETHNIC HATE

To a certain extent racial and ethnic hate may be an aspect of the old adage, "Birds of a feather flock together." Ethologists Eibl-Eibsfeldt (1970) and Chauvin and Muckensturn-Chauvin (1977) support the notion of territoriality among human subgroups—of likes drawn to likes—and Lorenz (1963) goes so far as to posit an innate territorial drive similar to Eibl-Eibsfeldt's aggressive drive. It would appear that racial and ethnic hordes tend to flock together and defend their territory in whatever ways are necessary. New York City, for example, is full of ethnic and racial neighborhoods, from Chinatown to Black Harlem, and from Jamaica Heights, Queens (where Koreans have settled) to Williamsburg, Brooklyn (where a neighborhood of Hasidic Jews is located), and New York has a history of teenage gang wars between races, nationalities, and ethnic groups.

Baker (1967) believes that racial prejudice stems from primary process thinking (the kind of thinking, say, a 2-year-old would do). Thus, prejudiced whites see blacks in a symbolic way. "Psychologically, we shun black and associate it with evil, death, depression, and gloom" (p. 195). In dreams, the black man is seen as a phallic, animalistic creature, denoting "forbidden desires, particularly incest" (p. 195). On the other hand, prejudiced blacks see all whites as "white devils" who are out to exploit blacks. In either case, all that is repressed and split off in one's own personality (forbidden aggressive or sexual impulses) is projected onto members of the other race.

Each race or ethnic group has its own culture. The culture of a race or ethnic group contains its own endemic value system, and that value system depends on how evolved a particular race or ethnic group is. European-Americans, for example, are a very evolved ethnic group. Most tend to be educated, upper-middle-class people who have been raised in an indulgent environment. They have developed out of the Western civilizations of Greece and Rome and modern Europe. They are used to being in positions of power, and therefore they express their hate in subtle ways designed to keep them on top. They will be polite to "inferiors"—those beneath them in the social hierarchy—while casually snubbing them. They are careful not to speak ill of any race or group beneath them, for fear of sounding prejudiced.

On the other hand, racial or ethnic groups toward the bottom of the hierarchy tend to feel victimized and to speak openly of their hate of the European-American. Their culture will contain a value system that somehow excuses their being on the bottom (they are being kept down by European-Americans), and justifies blatant acting out of hate through sociopathic behavior such as rioting.

Racial and ethnic groups develop ill feelings about one another in the same ways that individuals do. Koreans harbor animosity toward the Japanese because Korea was conquered and occupied by Japan on several occasions. Individual families have also been known to carry on generation-to-generation feuds, such as those of the Hatfields and McCoys in the South, depicted in several movies in the 1950s. Indians and Pakistanis likewise do not like one another, due to a history of war between these countries, and Jews and Arabs hate each other for many reasons going far back into time. African-Americans and Jews do not particularly like one another either, not because of a shared history but because of a similar history of victimization. Victimized groups often feel competitive toward one another, each claiming the role of victim for themselves.

I have seen the same principle in operation during therapy groups, when individuals in the group will vie for who has the most to complain about and therefore deserves the most sympathy from other members of the group.

"Boy, I had a bad week," one individual will say.

"You think *you* had a bad week? Wait till you hear about mine!"

Or one individual will bemoan his parents. "My parents were both alcoholics."

"I wish I had parents who were alcoholics," another will say. "Mine both died of cancer."

"Yeah, well, if you'd had my parents," the first will reply, "you'd have *wished* they had died of cancer!"

In the same way races and ethnic groups also vie for the role of victim and the sympathy and special privileges that come with it. By claiming to be the victims of prejudice and persecution, they can often receive affirmative action in the form of preferential hiring for various government, educational, or corporate jobs. At the same time, they can express hate toward their victimizers through these claims, casting aspersions on them and putting them on the defensive. However, as previously stated, this form of group behavior will unfortunately keep the group at the bottom of the hierarchy. If you get rewarded for being a victim, you will stay a victim.

Cultural hate pervades all areas of society, but it is particularly prevalent in the media, through which cultural values are disseminated. Nearly everything which appears on television, radio, and newspapers, propagates a prevailing value system. Hence, on the heels of the recent upsurge of African-American complaints of victimization, we have been inundated with television series in which African-Americans are shown as leaders (to counteract stereotyping them as drug-pushers and the like), while whites are often shown in subservient roles to blacks. Such dramas bend reality in order to portray an idealization of the current "correct" value system. However, by bending reality, these programs are in fact expressing subjective hate, encouraging magical thinking, and avoiding focusing on life as it really is, in all its complexity, so that the real problems can be addressed.

Is it possible for various races and ethnic groups to bond with one another, or is there an innate drive, as some have intimated, causing humans to form into subgroups and remain in conflict with one another? Both questions can be answered in the affirmative. There is probably an innate tendency for races and ethnic groups to form subgroups, but it is also possible for them to bond collectively under a single authority. However, modern civilization, with its stress on individualism and on egalitarian principles, has tended to undermine authority.

Eibl-Eibsfeldt (1970) notes that the skeptical attitude of modern man, stemming from a liberal ethos that eschews traditional values, has resulted in his increased unwillingness to recognize authority and a propensity for choosing fanatics as leaders. This lack of leadership encourages anarchy and aggression. However, since people still need leaders, they seek "substitute authorities who are...as far away as possible, or already dead, and can therefore easily be idealized like Marx, Che Guevara, Ho Chi Minh" (pp. 232–233). They also choose leaders who, as Kardiner (1954) points out, cater to their need to believe that their suffering is from no fault of their own, certainly not from their own psychopathological values, but is caused by some external villain. In this way civilization breeds discontent, serves to aggravate racial and ethnic conflicts, and to accelerate the acting out of subjective hate.

NATIONAL AND GLOBAL HATE

The most obvious form of national hate is, of course, war. Human beings, according to ethologists, are the only species who habitually kill off their enemies, or who hunt and kill other species for sport (Chauvin and Muckensturn-Chauvin 1977, Darwin 1859, Eibl-Eibsfeldt 1970, Lorenz 1963). Animals of other species may battle for territory, but they seldom kill one another; oftentimes a frightening gesture is enough to vouchsafe a territorial boundary. Violence—whether between individuals or nations—is a human phenomenon and is the most blatant form of subjective hate.

To some extent nationalism and war represent the territorial strife inherent in all forms of life, but the intensity and violence of human nationalism and warfare go beyond the normal struggle for existence. Nations, like individuals, have their own particular personalities. Some nations are obsessive-compulsive (the Japanese are characteristically workaholic), some are passive (the Chinese are noted for their stoicism and patience), some are phallic-aggressive (the United States and the Soviet Union both want to prove they have the biggest national phallus), some are depressive (Sweden has the highest suicide rate), some are masochistic (Germany and Israel both have a history of provoking persecution), some are hysterical (Holland denies having any hate for anybody), and some are paranoid (Iranians think everybody is out to get them).

Hence strife between nations, like that between individuals, often involves such things as narcissism, sadomasochistic provocation, and sociopathic revenge (the Germans got beaten and humiliated after World War I, and, in response to feelings of low national self-esteem, developed a narcissistic characterology—"Deutschland über Alles"—with a sado-maschochistic component, which impelled them to provoke their persecutors into World War II). The United States, suffering defeat in the Viet Nam War (and a blow to its phallic-narcissism), subsequently invaded two small countries in the Caribbean and Central America to prove its might and regain a sense of worth in the world's eyes (while claiming to be saving these countries from dictatorships).

Aside from national characterology, there are other factors that contribute to both national and global hate.

Eibl-Eibsfeldt (1970), among others, suggests that overcrowding results in increased aggression. He cites experiments with tree shrews and rodents that have shown that once a certain population density is exceeded the animals irritate one another to a point where their hormones change and often produce death. With mild overpopulation a gland in the chins of tree shrews stops functioning; with greater stress the mammary glands atrophy; and as stress increases the gonads stop working, the animals lose weight, and die. "When we come to human adaptability we have no idea what its limits are" (p. 235). As the world has become more populated and nations have become more civilized, individuals have become more irritated, and they have developed more aggressive forms of killing. In cavemen days, clubbing an enemy sufficed; in today's overpopulated world, H-bombs are in order.

Chauvin and Muckensturn-Chauvin (1977) concur with this thesis, noting that primitive cultures are usually not violent, but become so when they reach a certain stage of civilization; they also note that in zoos, where animals are overcrowded, murder becomes frequent. "Could we not postulate, then, that what is engraved in the human genotype may be a certain genetic sensitivity to grouping?" (pp. 239–240).

Freud (1933) also believed that war was an inevitable reaction to civilization, which he saw as repressive to man's innate sexual and aggressive drives. "War is in the crassest opposition to the physical attitude imposed on us by the process of civilization, and for that reason we are bound to rebel against it . . ." (p. 216). From Freud's point of view, mankind's accelerating violence is related to the decrease, in civilized societies, of opportunities for humans to find socially acceptable outlets for sex and aggression.

The question is, if violence is directly related to overcrowding and the repressive force of civilization, why can we not curb our exploding population? Overpopulation itself would seem to be an expression of subjective hate, a form of aggression, that eventually leads to an outbreak of more aggression. Good bonding requires a certain amount of space, a certain amount of individuality.

Violence may also be related to other manifestations of global hate, such as the pollution of our atmosphere, the plowing of our forests, the extinction of other forms of animal life, and the corrosion of our ozone layer, all of which are affecting the balance of our eco-system and producing vast and unforeseen changes in our weather. We are being repeatedly warned by scientists about the peril to our planet presented by modern industrial society. Indeed, it now appears that from the time man first learned how to make fire, he began to pollute the planet, for scientists tell us that fire burns up oxygen and releases carbon dioxide and other gases into the air, and that too much of it over the years has itself contributed to air pollution and a decrease in oxygen; in other words, anything artificial and unnatural is toxic to the planet. Yet, human beings continue to populate, pollute, and destroy, paying only lip-service to the warnings of scientists.

Searles (1972a) is one of the few psychoanalysts who have looked at the psychoanalytic meaning of our environmental crisis. Noting the lack of interest by mental health professionals in this problem, Searles speculates that human beings are hampered by a severe and pervasive apathy, largely unconscious, and that this apathy has the mental health field, as well as the rest of the world, in its grip. He cites as additional evidence for this apathy the fact that the United States budget for 1971 (the time at which his paper was written) included only about one-seventieth as much for dealing with environmental pollution as for military purposes.

Searles lists many forms of planetary destruction, among them: we are dumping into the ocean as many as a half-million different pollutants, only a few of which have been studied for possible effects upon ecologically vital processes; we are burying and dumping radioactive waste from atomic reactors at an alarming rate in tank farms that will have to be guarded for 600 to 1000 years (several tanks have already leaked thousands of gallons into the soil, and one gallon is enough to poison a city's water supply); the world's population will double in less than thirty-seven years, and will double again in half that time, unless it is controlled. Since Searles's paper we have also learned that chemicals from industrial pollutants and from automobiles have burned holes in the ozone layer, poisoned our atmosphere as well as our rivers and lakes, changed our weather for the worse; and the clearing of tropical forests to establish ranches and condominiums is further changing the precarious balance of the ecosystem.

In explaining this destructive trend and man's apathy to it, Searles looks first at the fear, envy, and hatred "of formidable oedipal rivals" (p. 230) that lie at the root of the collective neurosis of mankind. Unconsciously we harbor the notion that since we do not immediately experience the ill-effects of pollution and the like, it will not happen to us, only to our oedipal rivals—our symbolic fathers and mothers, and siblings. In addition, Searles sees pregenital factors in this apathy. "Mankind is collectively reacting to the real and urgent danger from environmental pollution much as does the psychotically depressed patient bent upon suicide by self-neglect—the patient who, oblivious to any urgent physical hunger, lets himself starve to death or walks uncaring into the racing automobile traffic of a busy street" (p. 234). Finally, he speculates that our collective paranoia, stemming from unresolved fixations in earliest infancy, causes us to strive toward transcending our human state and attaining omniscience and omnipotence (common fantasies of infants) through more power over nature, more population, more industry, and more technology. This striving represents not only an enactment of infantile fantasies of omniscience and omnipotence, but also of infantile rage connected to feelings of powerlessness. The extreme of such infantile fantasies are connected with destroying everyone around, mother, father, siblings, and the whole world, in order to gain revenge and prove one's might.

While Freud viewed human aggression as innate, linked to an inexorable death instinct, and therefore inevitable, most other psychoanalysts have not shared that view. Menninger (1938), for example, argues that the therapeutic success of psychoanalysis itself disputes Freud's contention that it is useless to try to eliminate man's aggressive tendencies, stating that, "for if it be possible to change one individual, no matter how laboriously—if one person can be helped . . . to be less destructive—there is hope for the human race" (pp. 411–412). In view of Menninger and others, our self-destructive tendencies have largely been nurtured by our collective psychopathology; if we can understand and resolve this psychopathology, we can diminish the self-destructive tendencies.

In other words, our collective subjective hate is related to our collective inability to bond effectively. Global hate represents the accumulated, collective hate of each individual on the planet, directed outward at the planet. Each time we drive our cars, use an electric appliance, burn coal in our barbeque pits, throw toxic waste into our garbage, or smoke a cigarette, we are enacting hate for the planet (symbolic of the father, mother, sibling rivals, and of everything outside ourselves). It is the most convenient way to act out hate, for it is the most abstract of all. But it is also the most ultimately and irreversibly fatal.

Solving the problem of global hate will require a healthy global leadership that will firmly require that all of us take responsibility for understanding our own aggression and how it gets acted out on the world. Such leadership might come from the United Nations, from national governments, religions, or other organizations. Without such leadership, it seems impossible for us humans, driven by the horde instinct and possibly by a death wish as well, to control ourselves.

CONCLUSION

Cultural forms of hate grow out of the collective unconscious of each religious, racial, ethnic, or national group. They represent both innate and nutured processes—the innate tendency to join hordes of beings similar to ourselves and defend our territory, and the nurtured, psychopathic tendency to merge with groups in order to rationalize our individual conflicts and blame them on other groups. It is our nurtured psychopathology, however, that turns our aggression into a destructive, homicidal/suicidal drive. It is our subjective hate that represents an immediate threat to our planet and must be addressed.

Group narcissism—comprised of feelings of inferiority, masochism, and paranoia—lies at the root of our collective psychopathology. This narcissism causes us to see others as persecutors and ourselves as victims. Like all forms of subjective hate, it enables us to deny our own contribution to the problem. It fuels group-to-group hate as well as global hate, and is by far the most menacing form of subjective hate in existence.

7

Gender Hate

A legend from Greek mythology illustrates the age-old conflict between men and women. Zeus and Heras had a quarrel one day about which of them received more pleasure during love-making. Both contended that the other received more pleasure. Finally they called in Tiresias to render a judgment on the matter. After watching them make love, he declared that "Woman has nine times as much pleasure as man." Whereby Heras became so furious she blinded him.

The hate between men and women is the most primal of hates. Schopenhauer (1896) thought that the relation of the sexes is the "invisible central point" of all action and conduct, whether between women and women, women and men, or men and men. He believed sexual discord or harmony has a bearing on war and peace, and that it is the basis of all jests, the source of all wit, the key to all allusions, and the meaning of all hints. Sexual passion, according to Schopenhauer, is the most perfect manifestation of the will to live, while sexual discord is the cause of all misery. Schopenhauer's views more or less foreshadowed Freud's and bring us back again to the dual drives of bonding and aggression, this time as they relate to sphere of male-female relations.

Elsewhere I have written (Schoenewolf 1989b) extensively about gender hate—or sexual animosity—linking it to male and female narcissism. Since the subject is relevant to the theme of this book, I will recapitulate my views here. In general, gender narcissism denotes inferiority feelings about one's own gender and an aversion to the other gender. To the degree that one develops gender narcissism, one retreats from the opposite sex, and the sexual drive gets turned back onto the self—other objects serving merely as vehicles for self-stimulation.

Incidentally, I do not make a distinction, as others do (Freud 1914b, Kernberg 1976, Kohut 1971), between healthy and unhealthy narcissism; to me, narcissism is narcissism and, as I have previously noted (1990) what some call nonpathological narcissism is, in my opinion, simply healthy self-esteem. I think such distinctions (between healthy and pathological narcissism or between healthy and pathological masochism) complicate psychoanalytic theory rather than making it clearer and more precise.

MALE NARCISSISM

The male narcissist is a man who on some level feels his manhood has been insulted, questioned, or dismissed, and he reacts by overvaluing or retreating from masculinity, harboring either a depreciatory attitude toward it or a defensive bubble of pride and grandiosity. He fears and envies women and compensates for that fear and envy by withdrawing from them emotionally and sometimes sexually. The more narcissistic a man is, the less he will be able to achieve a sexual relationship with a woman. Those with less gender narcissism will be able to have heterosexual relations, but the sex will be hampered by their fear of, and rage against, women. Those with more gender narcissism will retreat from women entirely, becoming homosexual or expressing their sexuality in some other perverse form. In my opinion, gender narcissism is a component of all forms of psychopathology, from the neurotic to the psychotic.

Genesis

Winnicott (1965) noted that every man and every woman is born of WOMAN (Winnicott's term for the omniscient, omnipotent mother of early infantile fantasies), and that they retain a fear of WOMAN throughout their lives—a fear of re-engulfment by the all-powerful, all-knowing mother. Women are able to deal with this fear by identifying with WOMAN and actualizing their femininity; on some level they feel as though they are all mothers to all men. Men, on the other hand, in order to actualize their masculinity, must separate from mother and identify with father.

Anthropologist Margaret Mead (1935) recognized how important it was for men to separate from their mothers and from the influence of women, in order to develop masculinity. Studying several South Sea societies, she noticed how male separation from women was institutionalized, with men's houses and male initiation ceremonies created to foster the separation process. In one such rite, shrouded in mystery, adolescent boys were brought into a great womblike structure, maimed in the genitals—as if to provide them with symbolic vaginas—and were fed as if from a mother's breast. Such rituals seem designed to replicate the process of childbirth in order to help the boy work through his identification with his mother. Mead defines the central issue of every society: what to do with the men. Women fulfill their femininity simply by doing what comes naturally—giving birth to and suckling infants. Men must find other ways to define and assert their masculinity.

Male narcissism develops when a boy fails to separate from his mother and to establish a masculine identity with his father and with other men. The critical stage for the development of gender identity occurs when the boy is from 16 months to 3 years old (Khan 1979, Mahler 1968, Roiphe and Galenson 1981, Socarides 1979, Stoller 1968). At this stage the boy discovers the difference in sexual anatomy and, in a sense, seeks permission from his mother to be a male; that is, he seeks his mother's support for his separation from her both as an individual and as an individual who has a part of the anatomy she does not have.

According to researchers, when boys discover that they have penises and their mothers do not, their initial reaction is shock, disbelief, and denial. They do not want to believe that this towering, god-like being with whom they have identified until then does not have a penis. Along with this initial shock comes guilt about having something others do not have, and fear that it will be taken away from them (as they imagine it has been from others). Hence, the boy is smitten with phallic guilt, castration fear, and—particularly in cases where a boy has younger brothers or sisters—womb envy (envy of his mother's capacity to bear and suckle children).

The degree to which the boy develops gender narcissism depends on how narcissistic his parents are. A mother who has unresolved penis envy and animosity toward men will create in her boy a corresponding castration fear, phallic guilt, and womb envy. Unconsciously she will not want him to be a male or to separate from her (leave her sphere of influence). He will sense in her handling of him and in her attitude toward his penis, an aversion to his masculinity, and he will react in one way or another—sometimes by denying his masculinity, sometimes by overvaluing it, and sometimes by pretending to not be a man at all (as in the case of transsexuals and transvestites). If he is able to turn to a father who has a consolidated masculine identity, the boy can grab onto him as to a lifebuoy, and begin to establish an identity separate from mother. However, if the father has unresolved castration fear of his own, he will add to the boy's dilemma by rejecting or ridiculing the boy's questions about the difference in anatomy, being competitive with him, or in some other way behaving inappropriately. Roiphe and Galenson (1981) note that urination while standing with the father represents a turning point in his sexual development, a ceremony that serves to bolster his masculine self-esteem. When there is no father at all, the boy is all the more likely to develop gender narcissism.

The failure to separate from his mother, identify with his father, and resolve castration fear, phallic guilt, or womb envy, causes the boy to be emotionally bound to his mother as an adult and unable to give himself, sexually, to women. His mother's disparagement of masculinity and his father's inability to model healthy sexuality will leave him fixated at the stage of sexual discovery, forever attempting to find acceptance for his maleness. He will always be angry at his mother's repudiation and his father's distance. Masturbation (narcissistic self-love) will remain a primary sexual outlet, and he will not be able to bond effectively with women.

Male Narcissistic Hate

The narcissistic male expresses subjective hate by avoiding genuine bonding with women. He may appreciate them as ornaments, sexually exploit them, defeat them, degrade them, molest them, idealize them, emulate them, become one of them, murder them, acquiesce to them, or retreat from them entirely. But he will not give his heart to them. If he is able to form a sexual relationship with a woman, it will be hampered by impotence, premature or retarded ejaculation, or sadomasochistic elements. The more narcissistic he is, the more he will retreat from, or become aggressive toward, women. Castration fear will cause him to be either submissive or defiant toward them—submissive toward women who remind him of his mother (for example, phallic women) but defiant to other women.

Various character types will express male narcissism in their own particular ways. The phallic narcissist defends against castration fear by sexually conquering and degrading women; his motto might be, "Castrate them before they castrate you." The passive narcissist defends against castration fear and phallic guilt by withholding his emotions and sexuality from women and "yessing" them to distraction. His motto is, "I'll do and say whatever you want, but you'll never get to my real feelings." The anal narcissist defends against castration fear by dominating or submitting (and inducing guilt) in his relations with women. The oral narcissist defends against a general fear of WOMAN by being on the take—his addictions being more important than the woman. He defends against womb envy by allowing himself to be engulfed by women, becoming dependent on them for everything, like an infant, or by allowing women to become dependent on him and playing the mothering role himself. The sociopathic narcissist defends against castration fear and, when applicable, womb envy, by manipulating and exploiting women sexually and monetarily, and sometimes by physically abusing them. The psychotic narcissist defends against the fear of castration (re-engulfment by WOMAN) by withdrawing from women and people entirely.

Perverse narcissists defend against castration fear, phallic guilt, and womb envy by identifying with WOMAN and maintaining the illusion of a phallic mother; often they do not give up the unconscious infantile fantasy that their mother has a penis. Socarides (1979) suggests that perverse narcissists have a common "fear of fusion and merging with the mother, a tendency to lose ego boundaries, and a fear of loss of self or ego dissolution" (p. 183). Perverse narcissists will often be quite admiring toward women in public, but in private, among other men, they will viciously ridicule them, particularly their sexual anatomy. They will sometimes be outright hostile toward heterosexuals, men or women, who arouse their envy. Pregnant women stir up strong feelings of contempt (because such women put them in touch with feelings of inferiority, impotence, lack of virility, and womb envy).

Male narcissists tend to avoid real communication with women, always fearing that such communication will lead to castration—that is, to a re-arousal of the traumatic feelings and memories surrounding the original discovery of the difference between the sexes. They confirm the popular notion about men having weak egos: they really do have weak egos that need to be bolstered by a woman (a mother substitute), primarily because their mothers did not encourage the development of their egos and of independence in childhood, and they did not have a suitable male model to turn to.

Male narcissists will sometimes develop an exaggeratedly grandiose macho style to compensate for feelings of masculine inadequacy. Such men may earn a great deal of money or achieve fame in order to gain power and control over women. Homosexual men will express masculine grandiosity by extolling the achievements of gay writers, philosophers, artists, musicians, and the like: "Most of the great men were gay!" they will proclaim. Others male narcissists, who have strong reaction formations toward their mothers, will go to great lengths to prove their loyalty and understanding for women and women's causes (compensating for unconscious feelings of fear, resentment, and envy).

In general male narcissism has taken the form, throughout history, of a suppression and degradation of women. The mythical stories of Eve eating the apple and Pandora opening the box and bringing sin and misery to the world are expressions of a male narcissistic point of view, and are indications of how deep is the fear of WOMAN.

FEMALE NARCISSISM

The female narcissist is a woman who feels she has been cruelly betrayed and slighted by being born a female (which she regards as inferior to being male). She reacts by overvaluing her femininity, erecting a defensive bubble of female grandiosity and pride, or by retreating from it, assuming a masculine style, and harboring a depreciatory attitude toward femininity and all it entails, including motherhood. Because of her envy, fear, and resentment of men, she withdraws from men emotionally and/or sexually. The extent of the withdrawal ranges from those who can have sexual intercourse with men but experience orgasms only under special circumstances (such as when their clitoris is stimulated by hand), to those who cannot have orgasms at all or have vaginismus or other problems, to those who withdraw from men entirely and turn to women as a vehicle for self-stimulation, to those who withdraw from sexuality altogether.

Genesis

The genesis of female narcissism parallels that of male narcissism. As with males, the critical stage for the formation of female narcissism is the anal–rapprochement stage, from about 16 months to 3 years. It develops when a female fails to separate from her mother and to establish a healthy bond with her father, brothers, and other men. Typically, girls at this stage will react with shock and anger to the discovery that boys, their brothers, and their father, have penises and they do not. According to investigators (Mahler 1968, Roiphe and Galenson 1981) they often masturbate angrily after the discovery, then give it up altogether. Then they become obsessed with the subject of penises: who has them? why does she not have one? why does her mother not have one? when will she get one? In their fantasies female narcissists feel they have been castrated, cheated, betrayed, and they harbor hopes that someday their mother or father will give them a penis.

If during this stage the girl's mother, due to her own unresolved penis envy and female narcissism, reacts inappropriately to the little girl's shock and resentment about being deprived of an organ, or to her obsession with penises, or to her sexual curiosity about her father and other males, the girl will not be able to pass through this stage normally but will become fixated in it. (A mother with penis envy, for example, might refuse to answer questions about penises, belittle the girl's shock and resentment about not having one, or go to an extreme in explaining how great it is to be female and how unimportant it is to have a penis.) At the same time, due to her aversion to men, the mother will impede the girl's separation from her and interfere with her relationship with the father, wanting to retain the major influence over her and to prevent the father from bonding with her. Roiphe and Galenson (1981) document a number of cases in which girls with hostile mothers and distant fathers clung ever so tightly to their mothers. "In those girls with severe castration reactions, the hostile ambivalence to the mother becomes very intense, the maternal attachment is heightened, and the turn to the father does not occur" (p. 175).

Chasseguet-Smirgel (1970) emphasizes the father's role in this process. "It seems to me that one cannot base all female conflicts with the father and his penis on primitive conflicts with the mother and her breast; that would be short–circuiting the total transformation which occurs during the change of object inherent in the path to womanhood" (p. 133). Chasseguet-Smirgel has a valid point. The father delivers the decisive blow; if he reacts appropriately to the girl's infantile sexual curiosity toward him and his penis, and if he is strong enough to circumvent the mother's attempt to impede the girl's separation from her, he can help her work through her traumatic feelings, but if, due to his own male narcissism, he reacts inappropriately to her, he cements her fate.

The girl who cannot traverse this stage successfully remains embittered, always festering with the feeling that life has dealt her a terribly unfair blow; as an adult she may be continually depressed about it, or she may seek constantly to right this wrong. She will feel a phallic remorse (linked with an infantile notion that she must have been very bad to have had her penis taken away) and an envy of males for possessing something she lacks. She will also experience intense fears that her mother will abandon her. Gilligan (1982) makes the point that since males define their masculinity through their separation from mother and females define their femininity through their attachment to mother, "male gender identity is threatened by intimacy while female gender identity is threatened by separation" (p. 8).

Having failed to separate from her mother or to form a healthy relationship with her father, the female narcissist tends to form alliances with other women in an attempt to affirm her femininity and to retain mother's approval. Fearful of her mother's power and influenced by her mother's aversion to masculinity, as well as her resentment about her father's weakness, she displaces all of her anger and resentment onto men.

Female Narcissistic Hate

Female narcissists express subjective hate toward men by manipulating, depreciating, excluding, idealizing, suppressing, teasing, hiding from, submitting to, or psychologically castrating and torturing men. They are dedicated to avenging themselves on the male race for having been cheated out of a penis and the superiority they assume it stands for. The envy of the penis and resentment about not having one—having long been repressed—become transformed into a generalized envy and contempt for men.

Female narcissists understand on some level that they have a certain psychological and sexual power over men, and they use this power. A cross-cultural study of the sexual practices of 190 human societies as well as those of other species by anthropologists Ford and Beach (1951) provides evidence of this power. The study showed that females of all species of higher animals, including humans, give out signals of sexual receptivity through changes in body color, the emission of scents, or body language. In humans, the female makes all decisions in regard to sexual relations, indicating sexual receptivity through facial expressions, posture, and gestures, as well as verbally. Moreover, Ford and Beach found that in most societies men had to pay for sex either through a gift or a service. In the sexual sphere, men are almost always the petitioners.

The narcissistic female has an aversion toward men and their penises. Hence she often gives out mixed signals to men; with her body language she says "yes," but with her words she says "no." Those with mild narcissism are simply acting out an ambivalence without being aware of it, but those whose narcissism is more pronounced are consciously attempting to sexually tease, humiliate, and castrate what they view as the uppity male prick.

Various narcissistic character types have varying styles of hate. Phallic-aggressives defend against penis envy and phallic remorse by conquering the male with their intellectual phallus. Hysterics defend against penis envy, phallic remorse, and separation anxiety (toward mother) by seducing and abandoning men. Anal narcissists defend against penis envy and separation anxiety through domination of or submission to men. Oral narcissists defend against penis envy and fear of abandonment by either becoming passively dependent on a man or infantalizing a man and making him dependent on themselves. Homosexual narcissists defend against penis envy and fear of annihilation (by Mother) by withdrawing from men and aligning themselves with other women. Borderline narcissists defend against penis envy and fear of annihilation through sexual subterfuge. Psychotic narcissists defend against penis envy and fear of annihilation through complete withdrawal.

All female narcissists have feelings of inferiority about their femininity and defend against them by projecting them onto men and erecting an armor of female grandiosity. They then make men the scapegoats for their inner conflicts about their femininity. It is men, they think, who judge them and their femininity to be inferior; therefore they will prove to all men that they are not only their equals but their superiors. The need to constantly prove female superiority is one of the primary symptoms of narcissism and penis envy.

Another symptom of both penis envy and phallic remorse is an attitude of self-righteous and stubborn demandingness. Because they feel cheated and betrayed in early childhood (although they do not recall it as adults), female narcissists must constantly have their way with men, and they can never admit to any wrong-doing. It is as though they were saying, "You were given a penis and mine was taken away, so now I'm going to have it all!" They cannot tolerate being wrong because it arouses memories and feelings of the discovery of the difference in sexual anatomy, when little girls imagine they have been castrated for being bad, without knowing exactly what they did wrong. Female narcissists are convinced that men are biased toward women, but they do not think women have any bias toward men other than that justified by male beastliness.

As male narcissists fear women, female narcissists fear men, but for a different reason. Their fear usually centers on an obsession with rape. Since they consciously want to castrate men, they naturally fear that men will also want to castrate them by raping them. Susan Brownmiller's (1975) introduction to *Against Our Will* illustrates the irrationality of this fear. "Man's discovery that his genitalia would serve as a weapon to generate fear must rank as one of the most important discoveries of prehistoric times," she writes, "along with the use of fire and the first crude stone axe. From prehistoric times to the present . . . *all men* keep *all women* in a state of fear" (p. 5, Brownmiller's emphasis).

In this statement one can glean an ontogenetic reference to the infantile discovery of the difference in sexual anatomy. To a little girl who first discovers a penis, particularly a father's penis, it probably is a frightening event. One can also detect in Brownmiller's statement an obsession with rape, which is generalized to "all men," and an attempt to castigate men and attribute to them all gender hate. It is a typically narcissistic view of the penis as a vile weapon of fear, rather than as an instrument of pleasure and reproduction.

This attitude causes narcissistic women to make numerous false charges of rape against men, and of sexual molestation against fathers, which are quite destructive to men's lives. In general, it fosters a conception of male sexuality as evil, and of the male as a predator out to rape and molest women and children.

MASCULINISM AND FEMINISM

Masculinism and feminism are conduits through which male and female narcissists can act out collective hate toward the opposite sex, justifying the hate by making complaints of prejudice and persecution. Masculinists regard men as victims of women, feminists regard women as victims of men. By forming mass movements, they can use an ideology to justify and sometimes sanctify their hate, thereby avoiding taking responsibility for their inner conflicts and complexes. They shout slogans about equal rights and humanitarian aims, while branding the enemy in pejorative terms. Women who do not toe the masculinist line are called "man-haters," while men who do not take the correct feminist position are "sexists." These brands are used to control the opposite sex, the message being, "Either you behave as we want you to behave or you will be ostracized and stigmatized." Each side attempts to gain dominance through these and other tactics, creating a psychological warfare in which unreasonable hate is made to seem reasonable by sheer force of numbers.

Masculinism has only recently become a formal movement in the United States; however the masculinist attitude and philosophy has been informally practiced by certain societies throughout history. Clower (1979) provides some highlights: both the Christian myth of Adam and Eve and the Greek myth of Pandora make women responsible for the misery of the world; Muhammad of the Muslim faith was said to have asserted that when Eve was created, Satan rejoiced; St. Jerome of the Catholic Church purportedly claimed that woman was Satan, an enemy of peace, and cause of dissension; St. Augustine described woman as a temple built over a sewer; during the Middle Ages religious leaders debated over whether women had souls; and throughout the enlightenment of the eighteenth century and the empiricism of the nineteenth century, remnants of masculinism remained in the form of certain beliefs about female inferiority and restrictions on their rights to vote and participate fully in the democratic process.

Today's masculinist movement has become more moderate in its aims. Learning from feminists, masculinists use humanitarian slogans and claim to be fighting for equal rights for both men and women, and they come armed with grievances and statistics to prove that men are victimized by women. They point out that only men are required to register for the military draft, and only men are required to fight on the front lines during a war. In the legal arena, they claim women are given special treatment. A woman may, for example, engage in intercourse with a man and tell him she is using birth control when she is not. Should she get pregnant, she can decide to have or abort the fetus without consulting him and the court will require him to support the child, even though the conception was against his will. A recent newsletter of The National Center for Men states that men are 20 times as likely to go to prison as women, and that there is a double standard in the criminal courts; if a woman commits a crime against a man, she is usually found justified due to his bad character or her PMS (Pre-Menstrual Syndrome), but when a man commits a crime against a woman, he is entirely blamed for it, and no excuses are accepted. The newsletter also asserts that approximately 90 percent of all homeless people are male; 3 of 4 suicides are male; women outlive men by about 8 years; men are more prone to die early of heart attacks and strokes than women; and while there are numerous social service agencies for women, there are virtually none for men.

While some of these complaints have a certain validity to them, there is at the same time an angry underpinning to the masculinist movement, an attempt to blame women for men's misery and dump anger on them. On a psychological level they want to suppress the power of WOMAN, to assuage their castration fear, phallic guilt, and womb envy, and to compensate for feelings of inferiority by controlling and destroying women. Winnicott (1965) notes that the fear of WOMAN is "responsible for the immense amount of cruelty to women, which can be found in the customs that are accepted by almost all civilizations" (p. 164).

Meanwhile, waves of feminism have continually risen since ancient times. Feminism was evident during the waning years of both the Greek and Roman Empires, and it became a formal movement during the Victorian Era. A collection of writings by modern feminists (Tanner 1971) illustrates their narcissistic grandiosity with regard to femininity and the resentment and envy of the male. Linda Gordon claims that marriage is a form of oppression and slavery for women that has gone on for centuries, and accuses men of being tyrants; Ann Koedt claims that all heterosexual intercourse is a form of rape and exhorts women to become homosexual, proclaiming that the "clitoris...is the female equivalent of the penis" (p. 158); Betsy Warrior assails men for being the cause of all of women's and children's social problems, from psychosis to poverty; and Dana Densmore writes, "I control my own body, and I don't need any insolent male with an overbearing presumptuous prick to clean out my pipes" (p. 166).

These writings show evidence of female narcissism and sexual animosity. The portrayal of men as oppressors and tyrants is a way of destroying them through character assassination. Statements such as "I don't need any...overbearing presumptuous prick" and the "clitoris ...is the equivalent of the penis" harken to fixations in the anal-rapprochement stage of development. These statements reveal an aversion to the male and a desire to merge with other women in a homosexual alliance (a symbolic merger with Mother) against men (symbolic of Father).

The feminist movement has its own slogans about equal rights for women, designed as a smokescreen and justification for the expression of gender hate. They say women do not have equal opportunities in government, business, and other professions, and quote the statistic that women make 62 cents to a man's dollar. They claim that women were persecuted and suppressed throughout history, and denied the vote until the early twentieth century, and that now they should receive affirmative action to make up for it. They say that men exploit women sexually and in other ways keep them in a subordinate position. Like the claims of masculinists, many feminist gripes seem valid, but there is always a substratum of bitterness and contempt underneath them.

Incidentally, many male narcissists become feminists rather than masculinists, particularly those with perverse inclinations, who defend against castration fear by appeasing female narcissists (i.e., their mothers); actually such males have the same antiheterosexual, antifamily bias as feminists.

Freud (1918b), observing the bitterness and contempt in the feminists of his time, was the first to link it to the envy of the penis: "Now, upon this penis envy follows that hostile embitterment displayed by women against men, never entirely absent in the relations between the sexes, the clearest indications of which are to be found in the writings and ambitions of 'emancipated' women" (p. 205). Not only the writings, but also the political activities of feminists serve as expressions of their hate, and they have succeeded in convincing many people that their hate is justified, that penis envy is no longer a valid concept, and that Freud was a sexist Victorian.

Over the last twenty-five years feminists have used their claim of being victims to demand that we change the way we talk, write, and behave. They have demanded that men become soft like women, curb their sexuality, and let women make all decisions about family planning. They have demanded that historians rewrite history and that social scientists revise theories pertaining to women so that they will be politically correct. They have demanded that schools teach children how women are victimized by men, that boys be indoctrinated about the beastliness of rape, and that boy children be encouraged to play with dolls and girl children to play with tractor trailers (despite their inclinations to the contrary). They have demanded sweeping changes in the roles men and women play in society, in business, and in government, so that now the two sexes compete with, rather than complement, one another. They have demanded that children be sent to daycare centers without bothering to ask children what they want or to ascertain the long-range effect of such demands. In my opinion, these expressions of subjective hate have won false victories for women while at the same time bringing about confusion, polarization of the sexes, an increase in perverse forms of sexuality, the disintegration of the family, and other social dilemmas.

CONCLUSION

Gender hate is perhaps the most significant form of subjective hate, since the relations of the sexes bear directly upon child-rearing and indirectly on all aspects of society. Men who disparage, suppress, or flee from women in order to defend against castration fear, and women who act out penis envy by disparaging men and running away from the responsibilities for child-rearing, are contributing to the many social problems of Western society. Indeed, the most prevalent and destructive disease in our society right now is not cancer or heart disease or AIDS, but gender narcissism.

Children need to have both a mother and father, and they need them to be loving parents. Parents who genuinely, objectively love each other, whose love is not marred by subjective hate, will be able to provide their children with a loving environment. Children who grow up in a loving environment, unpolluted by gender narcissism, will grow up to become healthy, objectively loving and hating adults who can form mature relationships and become productive members of society.

8

Parent–Child Hate

The most important, most difficult, and least-heralded occupation in the world is motherhood. Running not too far behind in importance is fatherhood. Mothers have virtually sole possession of an infant for the first two or three years—the most formative years—and therefore they must take most of the responsibility for child-rearing. Fathers become more important as the child begins to separate from the mother, and they take a role of equal importance during the phallic phase.

A. Freud and Burlingham underscored how difficult it is to raise children, noting their demanding and destructive natures. In a report about children being cared for at the Hampstead Nurseries in London, they wrote:

> Children between the ages of one and two, when put together in a play pen, will bite each other, pull each other's hair and rob each other's toys, without regard for the other child's unhappiness.... They will destroy their toys, pull off the arms and legs of their dolls or soldiers, puncture their balls, smash whatever is breakable and will only mind the result because complete destruction of the toys blocks further play .... Destructive and aggressive tendencies are still at work in children

in a manner in which they only occur in grown-up life when they are let loose for the purpose of war. [Menninger 1942, p. 11]

Mothers and fathers, as breeders of future generations, determine to a large extent the personalities of individuals and the collective personality of society. It is up to them to cope with the innate aggression and sexuality of children and socialize them. They have a major influence on whether children grow up healthy or sick, adjusted or maladjusted, motivated or delinquent, educated or ignorant, confident or bumbling, cooperative or rebellious, capable of loving others or of loving only themselves, subjectively hateful or able to express objective hate. As parents go, so goes the world.

The irony of it is that one does not need any qualifications whatsoever to be a parent. Anybody can become a parent, while in order to become a psychotherapist whose job it is to correct the mistakes of parents, one needs years of therapy, schooling, training, and supervision to obtain certification and licensure. Would it not be simpler if parents themselves were required to go through some training and therapy, and perhaps even be required to see a parent supervisor while they are raising children, to ensure that they are objective?

Practically all the problems that children develop are the result of their parents' conscious or unconscious expression of subjective love or subjective hate. Bear in mind that each family unit is a little kingdom, and the parents are the kings and queens of this kingdom; they may treat their children however they see fit. If the truth be known, the torture chambers of Nazi prison camps would pale in comparison to what goes on in millions of homes across the world every night. Children are completely at the mercy of their parents, and from that standpoint each of us knows what it is like to be a slave. Some slaves are treated well, while others are abused. So it is with children.

Menninger (1942), writing about his research with parents and children at the Menninger Clinic, observes that "the child often gets an insufficient amount of love and too great an amount of hate; and not only that, but in the lack of love, the neglect, the restrictions, sometimes even the attempts to be loving, there is an implicit element of hate which the child feels and reacts to" (p. 29). Menninger is describing both subjective love (attempts at being loving) and subjective hate. Indeed, subjective love is love marred by unconscious hate, and therefore it is itself a variety of subjective hate.

Parent—child hate is administered in various dosages from conception and throughout early childhood.

PRENATAL HATE

"I'm going to have the child, no matter what you say." This patient had come to me because the courts had mandated it. She cast a dark, forbidding glance in my direction, her eyes peering from behind her mussed-up hair, her legs displayed in denim shorts that had fashionable tears at the rear. "I'm going to have it, and that's that," she repeated, and she began to rock to and fro, as if to soothe herself. She had a history of drug-abuse and prostitution. Her first child was already being raised by her mother because she herself had neglected him. Now she was determined to have a second.

In vain, I tried some therapy with her.

"You seem to think I'm going to tell you not to have it," I said to her.

"Well, everybody else does. Why shouldn't you?"

"My job isn't to give you advice. My job is to help you understand your feelings so that you can make objective decisions."

"I've already decided."

"You're going to have it?"

"I'm going to have it. Nobody's going to tell me what to do with my body."

"Then what do you want from me?"

"I don't want anything from you. I'm here because they made me come."

She was having the baby out of spite. Her parents and practically all other authority figures in her life were against it, so she was for it. Having been smothered and deprived by her parents, she could not listen to anybody or be concerned about the new life growing inside her. After she left the consultation, she went on a several-week crack binge with her current boyfriend. She did not start therapy, but I was kept informed about her circumstances. The baby was born prematurely, underweight, and in other ways quite unhealthy, due to her mother's drug addiction, bad nutrition, and some strenuous activity (disco dancing) that immediately preceded the premature birth. The baby did not survive.

Any behavior by a pregnant mother which adversely affects her growing fetus is an act of subjective hate. A mother who smokes, drinks, or takes drugs or medication during pregnancy is acting out hate toward the unborn child, as is a mother who does not watch her diet, engages in risky activity, or otherwise behaves in a manner that may disturb the unborn child. Mothers under stress (due to a bad marriage, economic troubles, or psychological conflicts about motherhood), who feel anxious or depressed during pregnancy, may transmit this anxiety or depression to their baby, causing it to be born with a hyperactive temperament. Some abortions represent instances of acting out subjective hate, (as when a frivolous woman has numerous abortions simply because she is too irresponsible to use birth control) while others represent objective hate (as when a woman knows that her unborn child will be deformed or impaired, or that it will add unnecessarily to the world's overpopulation, and she therefore decides objectively to end its life for the sake of society).

Menolascino and Strider (1981) assert that "low birth weight and prematurity are often associated with the symptoms of mental retardation, epilepsy, and cerebral palsy," and that malnutrition during pregnancy "may cause infant death or permanent brain impairment." They also state that "excessive maternal alcohol consumption or drug use raise the risk of having an abnormal infant to almost 44 percent" (p. 615).

Hall and Mohr (1933) were among the first to document a link between a mother's emotional antagonism toward child-bearing and premature births. Greenacre (1941) noted a predisposition to anxiety in certain infants associated with intrauterine events, such as a pregnant mother's severe emotional distress. Montagu (1950) summarized the existing experimental literature that validated Greenacre's assumptions: stressful mothers have fetuses that show considerably increased activity.

Kolb (1977) notes that pregnancy itself may induce psychological or physical symptoms in the mother or father. "What her pregnancy unconsciously means to the mother is of significance, as is the birth of her child. Doubtless, it reanimates the patient's old attitudes toward her own mother and may revive old complexes of bodily harm or injury" (p. 180). Conflicts about marriage and motherhood may also result in a hostile attitude toward the growing fetus itself. Impending fatherhood may also induce symptoms of anxiety, related to unconscious fears of rivalry with the newborn child or abandonment by the mother; fathers may therefore fail to provide the supportive atmosphere their wives need. Quarreling, emotional upheavals, and violence between prospective parents will not provide a secure and peaceful milieu for the fetus. Kolb adds that in a few instances, schizophrenia and manic depression have been linked to prenatal causes. He concludes that prenatal factors must be "regarded as highly complex and as yet poorly understood" (p. 168).

As more research is completed, it is becoming apparent that the environment has an impact on the human embryo from conception. So-called predisposition to mental illness may turn out to be related not only to genetics but also to prenatal circumstances.

MOTHER HATE

Mother hate can range from mild and subtle forms such as a slight tendency to overprotect the child, to acts of infanticide by mothers suffering from postpartum depression. For the most part, however, mother hate has been shrouded in secrecy. There has long been a veil of sanctity surrounding motherhood, an idealization of "Mom" that tacitly prohibits looking objectively at how mothers relate to their children. This veil is in itself a form of subjective love and hate, since it prevents a deeper understanding of mothering that might lead to the elimination of subjective hate and improvements in mothering. Our aim is to break through this veil and look at mothering (and fathering) objectively.

Neurotic Mothering

Neurotic mothers raise neurotic children. They are generally overly anxious, guilt-ridden, and angry, and their anxiety, guilt, and anger cause them to be resistant to responding in a healthy way to the developmental needs of their children.

Winnicott (1965) observed that neurotic mothers were unable to develop what he called a "primary maternal preoccupation" with their infants. What is a primary maternal preoccupation? It is "the thing that gives the mother her special ability to do the right thing," due to an identification with the baby that brings about an "extraordinary condition which is almost like an illness, though it is very much a sign of health" (p. 15). Such a mother, Winnicott notes, "recovers her self-interest" at the rate at which her infant can allow her to do so, and in the process weans the infant at the right time. He details two kinds of mothers who diverge from this norm: at one extreme is the mother, usually a career woman, who cannot give up her self-interests, "fails to plunge" into the state of primary maternal preoccupation, and does not really wean the child; the other plunges into it in a pathological way, prolongs her identification with the baby for too long, and tends to wean suddenly, "without regard for the gradually developing need of the infant to be weaned" (p. 16).

It is during the later stages—the anal, phallic, and adolescent stages—that a neurotic mother's hate becomes most manifest. The hallmark of the neurotic mother is an unwillingness to allow her children to grow as they will. They cling, suffocate, induce guilt and intrude on their relationship with their children. Suffering from anxiety and guilt, they compensate for these feelings by being overconcerned or overbearing. Much of the anxiety and guilt is connected with conflicts about motherhood and femininity. Their female narcissism makes them overvalue the traditional male role (earning money in a career outside the home) and devalue the traditional female role (mothering and nurturing children). Their children bear the brunt of this conflict.

Many children do not see their mothers often, and when they do see them for a brief time in the evenings or the weekends, they are too tired from work to pay adequate attention to them. The neurotic mother will make a brave attempt to be everything for everybody—a dedicated careerwoman, a loving mother, and a loyal wife—but burn herself out doing so. Their neurotic guilt, anxiety, and female narcissism makes them persevere badly rather than admit that they simply cannot do it all. Ultimately, they become irritated with their husbands, their husbands become irritated with them, and they end up displacing much hate, often unconsciously, onto their children. It is even worse if the mother is a single woman.

Menninger (1942) asserts, "The women who must rear the children are themselves so thwarted and resentful that they tend to impose the same restrictions upon their children; and the children grow up and re-enact the same error" (p. 32).

Various neurotic types have their own particular styles of acting out subjective hate. The hysteric, due to her female narcissism and Oedipus complex, responds inappropriately to her children's sexual and emotional development. She will sexually tease or psychologically castrate her boy children, often by giving them the same kinds of double messages she gives to men, and when the boys make romantic advances toward her during the phallic stage, she spurns them, completely unaware of the sexual messages she has given out. To her girl children she will transmit verbally and through body language her penis envy, devaluation of her femininity, and animosity toward men. Anxious and self-righteous, she will stir up anxiety and guilt in her children, and deny the hateful meanings of her behavior. Whether she teases a child, favors one child over another, or is suffocating to a child, she will never acknowledge it, and the child will be left to repress his feelings and to doubt his perception.

Obsessive-compulsives act out subjective hate to both boy and girl children through an overbearing obsession with their cleanliness, orderliness, and the like, which robs the children of spontaneity. During toilet-training they make children feel that their feces or urine is obscene (which makes children feel dirty and unacceptable). Often obsessive mothers become enraged if a boy forgets to lift the lid when he urinates. During the phallic phase they induce guilt feelings about their children's sexual displays and curiosity. This leads to obsessive-compulsive guilt about sexuality and aggression, and inhibitions about expressing them.

Phallic-aggressive mothers are the type that Winnicott described as not being able to give up their self-absorption to become attuned to the baby during infancy. If they have a baby, it is generally in order to beat the biological clock; their career remains the top priority. Their hate of motherhood gets conveyed to their children as a hate of them for inconveniencing her. They will attempt to feminize their boys and make their girls into phallic-aggressives.

Passives will "yes" their children into a deep repression, wanting always to avoid any unpleasant confrontation. Hence, they indulge them on one hand, but deprive them on another—deprive them of their direct feelings of hate. They create an unreal, sugary atmosphere which sometimes fosters passivity in their children, and sometimes hyperactivity.

Deutsch (1944) postulated a normal masochism for women, suggesting that the woman who joyfully embraces the pain of defloration, penetration, menstruation, childbirth, and motherhood, is masochistic in a healthy way. Indeed, she felt that masochism, passivity, and narcissism were the three basic feminine traits. Meyers (1988) disagrees with Deutsch, viewing masochism as pathological, whether in women or men. This author agrees with Meyers, and sees nothing masochistic about a woman's acceptance of her femininity and all it entails.

Masochistic mothers cannot accept their femininity, and they often act out resentment by playing the martyr, viewing themselves as victims, usually with respect to the father. They get their children to side with them against Father and against men. They will be submissive or humiliating toward children—often alternatively—and breed in them a sado-masochistic character. Berliner (1956) describes a kind of masochistic situation (which he defines as moral masochism), in which a sadistically rejecting mother produces a son who grows up with a penchant for getting involved with rejecting women reminiscent of his mother in an effort to win love from a rejecting object; he ends up stuck in a repeating, masochistic pattern.

Narcissistic Mothering

Kohut (1971) traced the beginnings of narcissism to a narcissistic stage of development (roughly from 1 month to 6 months of age). During this stage, the child relates to the mother as though she were a part of himself, not a separate person or object. Kohut devised the term "selfobject" to describe this kind of relationship. Pathological narcissism, according to Kohut, is the result of failures of empathy and inadequate mirroring by the mother beginning in this narcissistic stage; that is, the mother does not value the child in a realistic way, but either idealizes or degrades the child through her expression or her general attitude.

When mothers idealize their children, the children's personalities become organized around a grandiose, exhibitionistic self, and they continue to need such idealization from people in later life lest they suffer narcissistic injuries (wounded pride). When mothers degrade their children and demand their idealization (the child is great because of his or her relationship with this great person, the mother), the children grow up to seek others to idealize in adult life. In either case, narcissistic children remain fixated at this stage, as they are not able to develop a self separate from Mother's, or as Kohut puts it, the "transmuting internalization" does not occur, and they never advance to a point of being able to relate to another person as a separate object.

Freud (1914b) describes narcissistic parenting as a sort of misguided pampering:

> The child shall have things better than his parents; he shall not be subject to the necessities which they have recognized as dominating life. Illness, death, renunciation of enjoyment, restrictions on his own will, are not to touch him; the laws of nature, like those of society, are to be abrogated in his favor; he is really to be the center and heart of crea-

tion, "His Majesty the Baby," as once we fancied ourselves to be. He is
to fulfill those dreams and wishes of his parents which they never carried out, to become a great man and a hero in his father's stead, or to
marry a prince as a tardy compensation to the mother. [pp. 48–49]

The narcissistic mother makes her child a narcissistic extension of
herself; her child becomes the admirer she always longed for, loyal only
to her, or lives out her dream. She does not allow the child to become
self-actualized, and so he or she becomes an adult whose self-esteem is
dependent on others, whose pride is fragile and who can be easily
wounded.

Borderline Mothering

Spitz (1965) writes of "deviant object relations" by mothers during a
baby's first year of life, and defines several styles of mothering that would
seem to fall under the borderline category. In general borderline mothers
are prone to severe anxiety and oscillations of loving and hating their
children. Spitz describes mothers who relate to their infant with "primary anxious overpermissiveness" and "hostility in the guise of anxiety."
In each of these instances, the mother is compensating for feelings of
hostility toward the child through an exaggerated anxiety and overconcern with the child's welfare. In observing 203 infants at an institution,
Spitz noted that about 15 percent developed eczema, and these had
mothers (usually teenage delinquents serving prison time) who were
overconcerned about, but at the same time did not enjoy touching, the
child. Other mothers, those who oscillated between pampering and being hostile, produced infants who tended to rock, as though to soothe
themselves.

Masterson (1981) believes that such mothers become most abusive
and abandoning during the rapprochement stage when the child is trying to separate from them. "Terrible tragedies are inflicted on many children during their early developmental years which plant time bombs
that go off later in life" (p. 187).

Perverse Mothering

Perverse mothers breed perversion and gender narcissism in their children through an unconscious transmission of a perverse attitude toward
sexuality. One of my male patients, a chronic masturbator and foot fet-

ishist, had an extremely dominating and sexually disapproving mother who, during his early childhood, would slap his hand and frown if she saw him playing with himself, become furious if he forgot to lift the lid when he urinated, and generally make him feel ashamed of his penis and its products. Once she and his older brother shamed him endlessly because he put his underwear on backwards.

McDougall (1970) describes a perverse and hostile mother who demanded complete allegiance from her daughter and required that she renounce all involvement with her father. "A devouring love for the mother and a phobic clinging to her in childhood is paralleled by unconscious wishes for her death" (p. 210). This unconscious anger toward the mother is displaced onto the father, who is weaker than the mother, and later onto all men.

Stoller (1968) describes perverse mothers as women who have an unusually strong envy of males which expresses itself in a need to "damage" their boys by making them hate their masculinity. Writing about mothers of transvestites, he states, "There are rare mothers who kill their sons, there are many more who in their hatred of their sons help produce many different neurotic and occasionally psychotic states, and there are some who produce passivity and ineffectualness. The mother of the transvestite... makes a little 'girl' of him" (p. 183).

Psychotic Mothering

Spitz (1965) details cases of "primary active rejection" by mothers of their infants, due to a "global rejection of motherhood." One case is about a 16-year-old unmarried girl who was seduced by the son of her employer. When the baby was born, the mother, a devout Catholic who felt guilty about her pregnancy, took no interest in feeding the child and could produce no milk. "During nursing the mother behaved as if her infant were completely alien to her and not a living being at all," Spitz notes. "Her behavior consisted in a withdrawing from the baby, her body, hands, and face rigid and tense" (p. 211). The baby sank into a stuporous, semicomatose state and almost died. Spitz describes other cases in which infants died as the result of maternal rejection following on the heels of what is now referred to as postpartum depression, and still other cases of mothers trying to kill their infants. Those children who survive such early deprivation end up as isolated, depressed adults, forever looking for an infantile kind of bonding.

Lidz, Fleck, and Cornelison (1965), as well as Laing and Esterson (1964), did in-depth studies of schizophrenic families and found a consistent theme of disturbed family relations. Lidz and colleagues posited a "schizophrenogenic mother"—a mother whose behavior toward a particular child is so twisted that it drives the child crazy. Mahler (1968) describes the mother of an autistic child named Violet, who was herself deeply disturbed. This mother used to lock her infant daughter in her room all day while she and her husband practiced their music. The only contact she made with the daughter was to feed her several times a day; immediately afterwards she would put her back into her room and lock it. At first Violet kicked and screamed for attention, but when, day after day, her mother did not come, she fell into an autistic state. This mother would sometimes become violent; on one occasion, when she caught Violet playing with her feces, she beat the 1-year-old child, and subsequently the child mightily resisted toilet training. By the time she was brought to Mahler's clinic, Violet had stopped relating to other people, no longer looking directly at or speaking to anybody, although she was now over 3 years old.

FATHER HATE

Recently we have been inundated with reports of physical and sexual abuse by fathers. While it is true that some fathers, uncles, grandfathers, and the like, physically and sexually abuse children, they are exceptions—corresponding to that proportion of mothers who reject, physically assault, or psychologically damage or castrate their children. Most fathers are neither sexual nor physical abusers; they express subjective hate in much subtler ways, such as teasing, passivity, outright hostility, and indifference.

Neurotic Fathers

Neurotic fathers invariably pass on their neurotic traits to their children. When they are married to neurotic women (and most choose neurotics), they have almost as great an impact on their children as does the mother. This is because neurotic parents express hate most notably during the phallic stage, when the father's role takes on an importance equal to that of the mother's. Indeed, from the age of sexual discovery, at around the age of 2 or 3, a child's father becomes one of the corners of the oedipal triangle, with whom the boy competes for the mother's love, and to whom the girl turns in competition with the mother. Roiphe and Galenson (1981), in their empirical investigations of sexual identity development, noted that "the erotic turn to the father" during the phallic stage is crucial in a girl's development, while the father's availability and emotional involvement with his son during the same phase is equally significant to the boy's development. "The importance of paternal availability and support for the boy's growing sense of his male sexual identity during the second part of the second year of life cannot be too strongly stressed" (p. 274).

Fathers with phallic-aggressive characterology express subjective hate to their sons during this crucial phase by competing with them rather than supporting them. Such fathers must always be the winner in any competition for a woman, even if that woman is their own wife, and they feel threatened by their son's oedipal impulses. With their daughters, they are seductive and rejecting. When these fathers are the dominant parent in the household—and they often are—they tend to bind a favorite daughter to them and impede her separation in adolescence. This daughter will often marry a submissive man while maintaining a primary relationship with her father throughout her life; she will be unable to bond effectively to a man.

The obsessive-compulsive father is often hostile, indifferent, and driven by his work. He considers children a waste of his precious time. He comes home from work wanting to relax for an hour or so, watch television, get a little high, and retreat to his bedroom. Children of such fathers feel rejected and develop the unconscious notion that they are not interesting to be around. Another kind of obsessive-compulsive father sets himself up as an example for his children to follow: they must do things precisely his way or else they will fail. Many of my patients have reported a father who would embark on a project with them, then lose patience, take the project over himself, and say "Let me do it," implying that the child just did not have the right skills. Such fathers always have to know best.

Passive fathers may be the most numerous of all. They are usually neglectful of their children in subtle ways that the children cannot detect, which makes their expression of hate all the more devastating. Such fathers will cheerily seem to support their children, but at a crucial point they will not be there. One of my patients, for example, told me that as a child she would often complain to her father about her mother's abusive behavior, and the father would smile and hug her and tell her that the next time it happened, he would intervene; however, when the mother became abusive again, the father would stand at the mother's side, fearful of her wrath. Such fathers, always wanting to avoid confrontations, leave their daughters with a contempt for men and their sons with a legacy of passive hate.

Sadomasochistic fathers are sometimes strict disciplinarians who oversee all aspects of child-rearing, particularly toilet-training. Miller (1983) details how such fathers use the motto, "Spare the rod and spoil the child," as a justification for spankings and other forms of corporal punishment that go beyond the necessities of the moment. She describes how sadistically brutal and humiliating Hitler's father was, and how it led to Hitler's displacement of this sadistic rage onto the world. Fathers can also be masochistic, playing the martyr and allowing their wives and children to use them as doormats, in which case they can achieve a moral victory, inducing guilt and feeling morally superior to their victimizers (children).

Narcissistic Fathering

Narcissistic fathers express subjective hate by relating to their children as selfobjects (Kohut 1971), exploiting them for the fulfillment of their own needs. If there are several children, such fathers pick one as a favorite, pamper him or her, and in return expect that child to idealize him. Sometimes the father will see himself as a great man with special insights into things (even though, realistically, he may be doing poorly in his marriage, his job, or other aspects in his life), and he will expect this chosen child to support this ideal image of himself. At other times he will demand that this chosen child be his representative in the world and fulfill his frustrated dreams, preventing the child from attaining self-actualization. Meanwhile, he will disregard his other children, viewing them as deficient and therefore of no value to him (i.e., they cannot help him bolster his lagging self-esteem, since he does not see them as special and therefore their opinions cannot matter to him).

Borderline Fathering

The borderline or sociopathic father is the one who is most prone to sexually or physically abusing his children. Kernberg (1975) writes that borderlines tend to relate to all people, including their children, in typical ways that reflect their inability to trust, to tolerate ambivalent feelings toward the same person (the person must be either good or bad, not both), and to control their rage. "The presence of generalized splitting ... the persistent primitivization and aggressive infiltration of interpersonal relationships, the emotional turmoil, the characteristic overinvolvement as well as withdrawal and protective shallowness, all reflect the generally serious pathology... of patients with borderline personality organization" (p. 144).

They are impulsive, excitable, and alternately sentimental and violent with their children. Fearing abandonment (Masterson 1981), they often run away from the responsibilities of fatherhood, leaving their children to fend for themselves. A patient with multiple personalities reported having a father who used to rape her in front of her brothers and sisters whenever he felt she had done something bad. "You're getting just what you deserve," he would tell her as the family looked on. On other occasions, this same daughter was the one he turned to for comfort when he quarreled with his alcoholic wife. Fathers of this type can be extremely confusing; they will win their children's trust by playing on their sympathies or promising them anything they want, but then turn on them when they shift from an all-good to an all-bad view of them.

Perverse Fathering

Stoller (1968), writing about how transvestites develop, refers to fathers of tranvestites as "co-conspirators." "It is astonishing to discover how often the fathers, knowing that their wives are dressing their sons in girls' clothes, do not put a stop to it. These men are usually hardly members of the family in that they are scarcely ever home, or if they are home, they are silent and passive" (p. 184). Stoller describes other fathers who punish their sons for dressing in girls' clothes by making them dress in an even more feminine way; such a punishment only makes the transvestite want to wear dresses even more, to spite the father and later other men.

The perverse father is generally perverted himself, either in an actualized or latent way. Homosexual fathers who marry and have children will sometimes be sexually rejecting toward their daughters while being overaccepting, and sometimes seductive, toward their sons. Likewise, fetishists, exhibitionists, voyeurs, and pedophiles will also respond in a perverse manner to their children's sexual strivings.

Fathers who are pedophiles may lure a daughter into a perverse, incestuous relationship that can go on for years right in front of their wives (in which case the wife becomes a co-conspirator). McDougall (1970) asserts that fathers of girls who become homosexual are often passive and rejecting, allowing the mother to dominate the daughter. Such fathers, having strong homosexual and antifeminine features in their personalities, ridicule their daughter's phallic-erotic advances.

Psychotic Fathering

Schizophrenics fathers as well as mothers are generally quite disturbed. Laing and Esterson (1964) describe an interview with a father, a mother, and schizophrenic daughter during which the father and mother repeatedly winked at one another. When the interviewer asked the father why he was winking at the mother, he denied he had been winking. At other points during the interview the father likewise denied saying things that he had just said a moment before. Laing and Esterson conclude that parents of schizophrenics communicate with their children in pathological ways, inducing confusion, identity disturbances, defects in reality testing, and thought disorders.

Often fathers of schizophrenics maintain a "folie à deux" relationship with their wives: they are both deluded in the same way and support each other's delusion. In such cases the father, once again, becomes a co-conspirator in an unconscious alliance with the mother against the child.

DIVORCED-PARENT HATE

The divorce rate has risen dramatically in the past century, and this rise may be seen as an indication of social sickness. Sometimes a divorce, like an abortion, is necessary, but more often it is not only an expression of subjective hate by husbands and wives—a way of acting out rather than verbalizing and resolving resistances to bonding—but also an expression of hate towards children.

Dicks (1967) citing a 3,350 percent increase in the divorce rate in England and Wales from 1910 to 1953, calls the rash of divorces in Western society a disquieting social epidemic.

If disintegration of the cells of the social organism is growing at this rate, what chain reactions will it bring in its train for our future community?... A marked and rising proportion of broken or grossly disturbed marriages is bound to swell the numbers of conflict-torn, potentially destructive offspring to whom the world, its culture and its institutions are the enemy. [p. 5]

Dicks sees a progression in Western history, from the large family units and networks of medieval times to the single-parent units of modern times. "The constriction and atomization of the modern family ... have intensified the mutual reliance on its members to yield all the satisfactions for relational security and other needs previously met by a more diversified and structured family milieu buttressed by social and religious sanctions" (p. 26). He sees urbanization, industrialization, and the changing roles of men and women as underlying sociological causes of this breakdown of the family.

Dicks links the psychological cause of failed marriages to the denial of hate by the two partners. "By denying the reality of the ambivalent hate or anger... one or both spouses attribute to the partner those bad feelings they must not own themselves, or else make the partner all-good and exalted while themselves taking on the guilt and the badness" (p. 43). This denied hate leads to marital discord and divorce.

Children of divorced parents often become sacrificial pawns in a chess match between parents over custody, child-support, alimony, or visitation rights. Each parent has a need to prove the other parent is at fault, in order to get the child to take his or her side. Children of divorced parents are often shuttled back and forth from one parent to another, afraid to form a bond with either out of fear of rejection by the other. In some instances, when parents compete for a child's favor by bestowing gifts and in other ways trying to win the child's favor, the child learns to play the parents against one another and grows up with a cynical, "on-the-take" attitude toward people.

SINGLE-PARENT HATE

No matter how healthy single parents are, they cannot give their child what all children need: a mother and father. Hence, to be a single parent is in itself an act of subjective hate. Often a single woman or man will have a child in order to make themselves less lonely and to have somebody around on whom they can take out their frustrations. Such women and men are usually not able to establish a stable relationship with the opposite sex for various reasons having to do with fear of dependence, gender narcissism, or fear of abandonment. They give birth to or adopt a child for the wrong reasons, and transmit their alienated way of functioning to their child.

Roiphe and Galenson (1981) document the father's importance to a family. In those households without a father figure, both girls and boys tend to form pathological relationships with their mothers. To a girl, a father's love and respect are crucial for her development of healthy feelings about her sexuality, menstruation, and motherhood. To a boy, a father's love and companionship paves the way for his masculine identity development.

STEPFAMILY HATE

The children's story "Cinderella" is an illustration of one way subjective hate can be expressed in a stepfamily. In this story, Cinderella's father marries a woman with two daughters of her own. While the father is alive, Cinderella remains his favorite; in fact, he favors her not only over his two stepdaughters, but also over his new wife, enacting subjective hate in this manner. However, when he dies, Cinderella encounters a backlash in the form of the built-up resentment and jealousy of the two stepsisters as well as of her stepmother, all of whom ridicule her and force her to become virtually a household slave. Such are the politics of stepfamily life.

Haley (1976) recounts a case of a woman with several children marrying in order to have a man's help in raising the children. However, when the new husband tries to discipline the children or show affection, she pushes him away, saying that they are not really his children and he does not understand them. Hence a conflict ensues over who has authority over the children, or who is allowed to be close to them, and the children become mediators or holders of marital tensions. "Many problems between a couple that cannot be dealt with directly may be communicated about in terms of—and therefore through—the child" (p. 116).

A stepfamily has all the problems of a regular family, along with the added complications stemming from the nature of the stepfamily: that is, each stepfamily is formed as the result of the rupture of a previous family unit. This rupture will leave deep wounds in children that must be reckoned with in the new family. However, all too often the stepparent seeks to brush aside a child's feelings about this rupture, as it arouses jealousy and fear of rejection, and the child's feelings never get properly soothed and resolved.

Another complication in step families is sibling rivalry. This exists in regular families in proportion to the discord between parents. In stepfamilies, sibling rivalry is even greater. Usually the children of one parent will be jealous of, contemptuous toward, and competitive with the children of the other parent. What often develops is a hierarchy of hate, with the youngest children often bearing the brunt of the family's conflicts.

INSTITUTIONAL AND FOSTER-PARENT HATE

An increasing number of children are sent off to day-care centers where they must compete for the attention of disgruntled attendants, for whom they are not much more than customers, and where at times they become victims of physical or sexual abuse. They are left with a succession of baby-sitters who come and go, leaving behind a multitude of unredressed frustrations relating to emotional deprivation and abandonment. They are given up for adoption by foster parents whose reasons for adopting a child are often the wrong ones, having to do with fulfilling narcissistic needs. They are sent to orphanages where sometime hateful behavior by nuns, priests, social workers, and attendants is often the rule rather than the exception, and hate among fellow orphans is rife.

Spitz (1965) believes that the decay of patriarchal authority and the mother's absenteeism have combined to "set the stage for a rapid disintegration of the traditional form of the family in our Western Society" (p. 299). He calls the orphanages, foster homes, baby-sitters, day-care centers, and other cultural institutions devised to treat the disturbances caused by civilization, "palliative measures" that do not go to the source of the evil. "The evil is the rapid deterioration of those conditions which are indispensable for the normal development of earliest object relations" (p. 299).

THE CULTIVATION OF HATE IN CHILDREN

Most of this chapter has concerned ways in which parents unconsciously cultivate hate in their children. However, in some instances parents deliberately cultivate hate. Chagnon (1968), an anthropologist, provides one of the more striking examples of this. He studied a tribe in the jungles of Brazil called the Yanamamö—the fierce people—in which children were reared to become fierce, hateful head-hunters and cannibals. This tribe was so fierce, it even ate the ashes of its own dead. Men and women walked about trying always to look as mean and repulsive as possible: for example, they took pride in having snot hanging out of their noses and sticking half-inch bamboo shoots through their earlobes.

Chagnon details how young boys were encouraged by their father to be vicious. Writing about a typical father and son he notes: "Kaobawä, for example, lets Ariwari beat him on the face and head and express his anger and temper, laughing and commenting on his ferocity" (p. 84). Men and boys were described as blissful batterers of mothers and girls, and mothers were said to be equally ruthless with daughters. According to Yanamamö mythology, children were the primary targets of hate in the form of sorcery by other tribes, who were out to magically attack and devour the vulnerable portion of the children's souls. Such myths, told to children repeatedly, served to terrorize them and induce ever greater hate and violence toward people in other tribes. The Yanamamö were justifiably known as the most fearsome people in Brazil.

CONCLUSION

From the societal perspective, disturbed parent–child relations—be they neurotic, narcissistic, borderline, perverse, or psychotic—have consequences that threaten the foundation of our community, our society, and our world. If children begin life in an atmosphere of subjective hate, they will be unable to trust, relate, care about themselves or others, or preserve the species. To bring a child into a world of subjective hate is to produce an emotional cripple. The greater the expression of parental hate, the more socially crippled the child will become.

Spitz observes that individuals who suffer the consequences of disturbed family relations are unable to understand or participate in the more advanced kinds of social bonding. "The relations they are able to form barely reach the level of identification and hardly go beyond, because they have never been able to achieve the earliest, the most elementary one, the anaclitic relation with the mother." He warns that "the only path which remains open to them is the destruction of a social order of which they are the victims" (p. 300).

Eibl-Eibsfeldt takes a more optimistic view. "What has to be done is to strengthen our trust in fellow men who are not known to us, and this happens on the family level. Only in this way can we evolve the social responsibility which is a prerequisite for a peaceful communal existence, probably indeed for any further existence at all as a species" (p. 245).

Menninger (1938) also more optimistic, notes that in "the analysis of the origins and manipulations of the destructive tendencies, one may expect to find the key to the salvation of mankind" (p. 408).

We have analyzed the origins and manipulations of the destructive tendencies—the various forms of subjective hating—and now we will propose ways of countering that subjective hate with objective hate. Now we are ready for a detailed study of the art of hating.

9

The Art of Hating in Therapy

Hating is an art, and it may be one of the most difficult of arts. It is much less threatening and more immediately satisfying to express hate subjectively than objectively. To master the art of expressing hate objectively requires:

1. *An understanding of others* that enables you to know when a person or group is expressing subjective hate, how they are expressing it, and what kind of objective hate will be required to counter their hate, handle it, or resolve it. This understanding also enables you to distinguish between those situations that can be handled, those that can be resolved, and those which cannot be handled or resolved, and must be avoided if possible (such as instances of violence).
2. *An understanding of yourself* that enables you to know when you are feeling hate, why you are feeling it, and who is making you feel it. Also an ability to distinguish between your own subjective and objective feelings of hate and the capacity to control the former and use and express the latter.
3. *The courage* to do what is necessary in order to counter, handle, or resolve subjective hate, even though it may put you in a petty, angry,

unfair, mean, or ridiculous light, and even though it may make you vulnerable, idealized, or unpopular.

Obviously, most people do not have this kind of understanding, self-awareness, and courage, otherwise the world would be in better shape. A minority of individuals who have had a fairly healthy upbringing will have it; the rest of us must study and practice the art—usually arduously and at length—before we can develop these abilities. To begin with, we must study how the art of hating has been perfected by psychotherapists and others over the years.

HISTORICAL PRECEDENTS FOR THE USE OF HATE IN THERAPY

In ancient times "madness" was often countered with crude forms of hating. The first psychiatrists, the cave men, used a technique similar to lobotomy. From studying the skulls of cave men, scientists have found that some had holes pierced through them, and it has been speculated that this hole was made so that the patient's evil spirits could leave the brain.

During the Dark Ages those seen as mad were considered possessed by the devil (most primitive tribes shared similar beliefs). One way of testing whether people were bewitched or not was to tie them up and throw them, naked, into the water; if they floated it meant they were possessed; if they sank, they were innocent. (Often, the innocent ended up drowning.) Priests used various methods of torture such as flogging— referred to as exorcisms—to scare the devil out of possessed persons. When all else failed, they were burned at the stake. It is estimated that 150,000 to 6 million people, mostly hysterics, were brought, naked, to trial, had all their hair shaved, were beaten or maimed, and then burned to ashes in public spectacles (Roback and Kiernan 1969). Joan of Arc was the most famous woman to be burned as a witch; at 17 years of age she led the French army to victory, but when she revealed that she had heard "voices" she was brought to trial and executed.

The attempts by early psychiatrists to confront madness were not much better. In Bedlam, one of the first mental hospitals in England, patients were kept confined in kennel-like rooms, chained and handcuffed, naked except for a blanket to cover them. Methods used to counter the madness of the inmates included the "hunger cure" in which they were tied in a basket and raised above the dinner table each meal to watch other inmates eat; "water cures" in which fifty to a hundred pails of ice-cold water were poured on a patient or he was forced to sit in a tub of ice; "whirling bed cures," in which patients were chained to a whirling bed capable of a hundred turns a minute; the "standing up cure," which harnessed patients into a standing position for days; the "blindfold cure," strapping inmates to a chair and covering their faces with a box so that they could not see; "bleeding cures" that had leeches sucking their blood; "purging cures" utilizing forced enemas; and the "padded cell," a form of isolation still used today.

In the modern era of psychiatry, new methods of psychiatric hate emerged such as electro-shock and insulin-shock treatments, lobotomies, and drugs which pacify a patient's madness but do not cure it. Even today many psychiatrists still prefer to use drugs rather than psychother-apy, despite the knowledge that both are often necessary in treating psychotics—drugs to stabilize the patient and psychotherapy to produce characterological change.

The advent of psychoanalysis marked the beginning of the scien-tific perfection of the art of objective hating. Josef Breuer conducted the first psychoanalysis in 1890, but he became frightened by the powerful feelings "the talking cure" evoked and retired. It was up to Freud and his followers to come to grips with such feelings.

THE EARLY PSYCHOANALYSTS

Freud mainly utilized passive forms of objective hating. Observing that patients had a compulsion to repeat infantile forms of behavior and to act out hate in habitual ways in the transference relationship, he coun-tered by frustrating them. Essentially he played a waiting game, holding himself back until such time as the patient became honest. During this time he remained a blank screen (refusing to reveal himself or answer personal questions), was abstinent (refusing to gratify them or respond to their attempts to seduce or provoke him) and gave them interpretations about their acting out. Those who practice classical psychoanalysis or ego psychology still continue to limit their expressions of objective hate to these methods.

For example, it took the Rat Man, a 30-year-old obsessive-compul-sive, several months to develop a transference neurosis toward Freud during which, according to Freud (1909), "in his waking phantasies, and his associations, he began heaping the grossest and filthiest abuse upon me and my family" (p. 206). Freud never revealed his own emotional response to the Rat Man's personal assault, but calmly brought this hate to his attention and traced it to its real source, his parents. One day the Rat Man told Freud he dreamed that Freud's mother had died and that he was anxious to offer Freud his condolences, but he was afraid that in doing so he might break into an impertinent laugh. Freud, having determined that this dream was an expression of transferred hate, interpreted that the mother in the dream was really the Rat Man's mother, and that he wished her death. The Rat Man bristled at this suggestion and angrily accused Freud of taking revenge on him with such interpretations. (Freud viewed such an angry reaction as a sign that the interpretation was correct.)

As the Rat Man stepped up the pace of his attacks and Freud refused to respond to his provocations, the Rat Man began feeling guilty. "How can a gentleman like you, sir, let yourself be abused in this way by a low, good-for-nothing wretch like me? You ought to turn me out: that's all I deserve" (Freud 1909, p. 206). Freud remained blank, neutral, unwavering in his interpretations. The Rat Man grew more agitated. Now, following verbal attacks on Freud, he began burying his head or jumping up from the couch and roaming around the room. Freud asked him what his behavior meant. All at once the Rat Man got in touch with the feelings he had been transferring: "I'm afraid you'll give me a beating" (p. 206). His father, he recalled, had had a nasty temper and had not known when to stop. Being able to understand that he was responding to Freud as though Freud were his father was a turning point in the treatment. Freud's objective expression of hate—his frustrating of the Rat Man's attempts to provoke him into a hostile father-son relationship such as the Rat Man had experienced with his father, and his continuous stream of interpretations forcing the Rat Man to reckon with his negative feelings—became the antidote to the Rat Man's subjective hate.

Ferenczi was one of the first analysts to break away from standard technique and experiment with other forms of objective hating. One of his early patients was a young woman who used to lie on his couch and tell him, over and over, that she was in love with him. Occasionally, while she was in the midst of professing her love, she would remark, as an aside, that saying such things brought forth feelings "down there." Ferenczi then noticed that she always lay with her legs crossed. "This led us—not for the first time—to the subject of onanism, an act performed by girls and women for preference by pressing the thighs together" (1919, p. 190). Ferenczi forbade her to lie cross-legged, explaining that she was acting out her impulses rather than verbalizing them. In the weeks that followed, she thrashed around on the couch, spewing out fantasies in a delirious manner and recalling important events from her childhood which provided clues to the traumatic roots of her illness. Ferenczi's intervention of forbidding her to lie cross-legged was just the active expression of objective hate needed to get her to stop acting out and to start verbalizing.

Ferenczi was also one of the first analysts to understand that certain patients—such as narcissistic, borderline, or schizophrenic types—cannot tolerate complete abstinence or a blank screen. In order to work with such patients, he contended, the therapist had to gratify them at times with "almost inexhaustible patience, understanding, good will, and kindness" (1931, p. 132). Yet the therapist also had to be genuine; if the patient was acting out subjective hate, it would be an error for the therapist to respond with kindness. "It is better to admit honestly that we find the patient's behavior unpleasant, but we feel it our duty to control ourselves" (p. 133).

W. Reich was more aggressively active than Ferenczi. A pugnacious individual who was eventually ousted from the psychoanalytic community, as well as from practically all other communities or countries in which he tried to live, Reich (1933) developed an elaborate technique of cracking a patient's "defensive armor." For example, in working with a man he refers to as a masochistic character, he used mockery to force him out of his "masochistic bog" of martyrdom. When the man arrived at his door each day "with a sullen, pain-distorted, spongy face, the epitome of a bundle of misery" (p. 244), Reich himself would put on the same face. When the patient, behaving like a 2-year-old, would blurt out, "No, I won't! No, I won't! No, I won't!" each time Reich made a suggestion, Reich would again mock him, echoing the patient with a "No, I won't! No, I won't! No, I won't!" of his own. Still later, when the patient began kicking and screaming on the couch, Reich lay on the floor beside him and kicked and screamed. Soon the patient had given up his "woe-is-me" stance and had become openly hateful toward Reich. They were then able to proceed with the analysis of the patient's hate and trace it to a point, at the age of 5, when he had been severely humiliated by his father.

When a masochist plays his victim game, those around him often respond by attempting to reassure him or assuage his anger or resentment. This, of course, never works, for deep down he does not really want reassurance. He is looking for opportunities to act out his resentment, and the best way to do that is to provoke people into being sadistic to him. Some people do respond sadistically, giving the masochist what he unconsciously wants, but they are responding with subjective sadism: they really want to injure the masochist. Reich was responding sadistically to his masochistic patient by mocking him, but his aim was not really to injure the patient, but to force him out of the victim stance and get his anger into the open; as soon as that was done, Reich retreated to analytic neutrality and standard procedure. His sadism was objective hate.

Winnicott stresses throughout his writings how important it is for therapists (and mothers) to simply tolerate their patients' (and children's) hate. In Winnicott's view, children often get derailed from normal development when their innate aggression and destructiveness is not accepted by their mothers. It is normal for infants to want to destroy the mother's breast, once they are first made aware, through frustration, that the mother and her breast are separate from them and not always at their command. Hence, they bite down fiercely on the breast. If a mother, due to unconscious feelings of neglect and unresolved hate, gets angry at the infant, yells at it, slaps it, or in some other way retaliates, she proves that she cannot survive, be strong for the infant, and accept all of its feelings. Hence, the infant will continue to attempt to destroy the mother and indeed will become even more destructive in an attempt to get the appropriate response from the mother. If the mother continues to retaliate, a vicious circle ensues, and the child becomes entrenched in this destructive behavior. Mothers should hate their infants, Winnicott asserts, without retaliating; that is, the hate should be objectified and expressed in some way that does not interfere with the infant's development, such as by showing the infant that they can take anything it can deliver, by verbalizing the hate to another person, or by singing songs like "Rockabye Baby" to the infant, which express metaphorically their desire to retaliate.

This theme occurs again and again in Winnicott's case histories. For example, in one case (Winnicott 1971, pp. 48–50) a mother brought her 6-month-old little girl to his clinic because she was suffering from infective gastroenteritis and constipation. She brought the child back again at 7 months because she had begun to lie awake crying, and to throw up after eating. At 9 months she had begun to have occasional fits. By 11 months the fits had become frequent. They usually lasted five minutes or longer, and during them she sometimes bit her tongue or wet the bed. The mother tried to handle her fits by distracting the child. By 1 year the child was having four or five fits a day, and crying for the rest of the day.

During one of the sessions Winnicott took the child on his knee and allowed her to bite his knuckle. He said nothing. A few days later she sat on his knee and bit his knuckle three times so severely that she almost tore the skin. He said nothing. She then began playing a game of throwing spatulas on the floor, all the while crying. Two days later she sat on his knee again and bit his knuckle, to which Winnicott again did not respond. Then she played a game of biting and throwing away spatulas, and then she began playing with her toes. Now she had stopped crying and had become completely absorbed in her play. Four days later the mother reported that her child had not had any more fits and was a different child. Sometimes, as in this case, objective hate is expressed passively by the therapist, the message being, "I can take anything you can dish out. You can't destroy me. I am stronger than you. I can tolerate your hate and still survive, still retain the capacity to love you."

THE LATER PSYCHOANALYSTS

While the early psychoanalysts limited themselves for the most part to the treatment of neurotics, later psychoanalysts found themselves dealing with an increasing array of perverse, sociopathic, borderline, narcissistic, and psychotic patients, whose expressions of hate were much more intense and more difficult to deal with. Such patients usually required active, rather than passive expressions of objective hate as well as active expressions of objective love.

Jacobson (1971) noted that psychotically depressed patients need "a sufficient amount of spontaneity and flexible adjustment to their mood level, warm understanding, and especially unwavering respect—attitudes that must not be confused with overkindness, sympathy, reassurance" (p. 299). At crucial moments during the treatment of her own patients, she asserted, she had to be prepared to express hate—that is, to respond with spontaneous expressions of anger, so as to help them through dangerous depressive phases.

Greenson (1974) tells of a middle-aged patient who had spent a good part of her four years of analysis complaining, fault-finding, and in general showing contempt for his skills as a therapist. He frequently tried interpreting her hostility to him, her unconscious envy, her defense against her loving feelings, and her wish to provoke a sadistic response from him—but to no avail. One day she paused and unexpectedly remarked that she supposed she was not a pleasure to work with. Greenson's initial reaction was subjective:

> I felt a sudden urge to blast her with some sarcastic remark like, "You ain't just awhistlin' Dixie," but restrained myself by forcibly bringing into focus that she was a patient, not a friend, not a relative. I eventually replied: "Yes, these hours of nagging complaining and nagging and complaining are a pain." I should add, this was said with some intensity, but controlled. [p. 509]

The patient at first responded with horror and anger, telling him that what he had just done was not therapeutic and that she felt insulted. He pointed out that he had not meant to insult her, but that he only wanted to confirm her statement that she was no pleasure to work with, to give her a piece of reality she needed, therapeutically. The patient cried and suddenly realized she had never let herself think of his feelings, that she had been trying to wear him down without knowing she was doing it, and she could see that she was also that way with others. "Well, I want to thank you, God damn you, for opening my eyes," she said. "I'd rather hate you or detest you, but not be a nag." To which Greenson (1974) replied, "Hating one another brings people much closer" (p. 509).

Searles (1972b) describes the murderous feelings induced in him by one particularly disturbed schizophrenic woman. "There were times, particularly in unusually stormy sessions during the early years when I felt so threatened and enraged that I was seriously afraid lest I lose control of my own murderous feelings, and kill her" (p. 199). In one session, after she had been taunting him about being a "babyraper" and "Lucifer-Eternal Rest," he calculatedly told her, in so many words, "I feel sorry for Satan, for when you die and go to hell, as I'm sure you will, Satan will have to spend even more time with you than I have" (p. 220). He observed that in the following sessions she was more collaborative, explaining that she almost always thrived when he vented his harshest feeling about her.

Kernberg (1976) expresses objective hate by focusing on the minutest details of a patient's behavior and using it as an avenue for a controlled but unrelenting confrontation. One of his cases involved a narcissistic businessman in his middle thirties who filled his sessions with superficial chatter that wondered aimlessly from subject to subject, with little emotional depth. Although the man was successful in his career, it was apparent to Kernberg that he had managed only a "surface adaptation," and that he was unable to establish "meaningful, individualized relationships." Unconsciously, he expressed subjective hate by not letting anybody touch him emotionally. One day, as the patient was rambling from subject to subject in the usual indifferent monotone, an ironic smile appeared fleetingly on his face. He remarked, as an aside, that while he was lying on the couch he had the impression—a disgusting impression—that a spider was crawling across it. He added that he had not mentioned the fantasy when it happened because it seemed irrelevant and disagreeable, but then he thought that perhaps this was the kind of fantasy an analyst would be eager to hear. He then changed the subject and began talking about his business affairs.

Kernberg interrupted to ask about his smile: Why had he smiled while talking about the spider?

The patient replied, with some irritation, that he had already mentioned that this was "analyst's stuff," and that he was slightly amused by the thought that Kernberg would be eager to hear it.

Kernberg persisted, noting that most of the time the patient spoke in a monotonous tone, and that the smile seemed a significant change. He also observed that the smile was in contradiction to the feeling of disgust that had accompanied the fantasy of the spider.

The patient replied that he understood what Kernberg was saying, but he couldn't do anything more with it. He resumed talking about his business matters.

Kernberg interrupted again, wondering whether the patient was reluctant to explore the spider theme because it went against his self-image as somebody who was always relaxed, cool, elegant, and secure. He also wondered whether the fantasy of the spider might reflect his fear that disgusting thoughts or feelings or aspects of himself might come out during the session. After a short silence, the patient acknowledged that he had not mentioned all the details of his fantasy. Actually he had imagined that there were spiders coming out of his body and crawling all over the couch and the room, and he recalled having dreams along similar themes. He looked about the room anxiously for the first time, and began reflecting on the symbolic meaning of spiders, using psychoanalytic jargon.

Kernberg again interrupted him, suggesting that he was using psychoanalytic jargon to get away from his feelings and from the source of his fear and disgust. Eventually, assisted by Kernberg's bulldog determination, the patient got in touch with his fear that he himself was disgusting beneath his cool facade. He left the session visibly shaken for the first time.

Seinfeld (1990) utilizes a joining technique in which he plays whatever role a patient assigns to him in order to resolve their resistances. When Robert, a 9-year-old borderline Hispanic boy, first attempted to make direct contact with Seinfeld after several sessions, it was by making Seinfeld into his slave. He began by throwing a pillow at Seinfeld and then ordering Seinfeld to throw it back. When Seinfeld threw the pillow back, Robert was severely critical about the way Seinfeld had thrown it. He had Seinfeld throw it again and again, and Seinfeld could never quite do it well enough. "What's the matter with you?" Robert sneered. "Were you watching? Are you a retard? Do it right" (p. 150). In subsequent sessions, Robert became more and more belligerent and dictatorial, openly referring to Seinfeld as his slave. He would order him to retrieve a ball, move furniture out of the way, or perform some trick precisely as Robert did it. Robert might juggle a clay ball around one arm, then another, then behind his back, doing a clumsy job of it, then toss the ball to Seinfeld and expect him to do it precisely. If Seinfeld dropped the ball or did not do it precisely, Robert would accuse him of being stupid and inattentive. If Seinfeld got it right, Robert would tell him he was mistaken, he had done it wrong, and he would ask for the ball back and add a new twist to the trick.

Then Robert began having Seinfeld do exercises during each session. He would command him to do 50 army push-ups. Seinfeld would do as many as he could without straining himself, and Robert would call him a sissy. Next Robert would command him to do 100 sit-ups, and again Seinfeld did as many as he could. If Seinfeld tried to rest, Robert told him he was lazy and weak. When he asked Seinfeld to do a push-up on one arm, Seinfeld tried it and demonstrated that it could not be done. Robert threatened to break a pencil if Seinfeld did not do it.

After a year the boy's attitude changed. He would sometimes begin to scold Seinfeld for not doing something right, and then become concerned that he had hurt Seinfeld's feelings—the first sign of the development of empathy. Ultimately Robert stopped ordering Seinfeld around and the two of them would simply play catch or Robert would practice his tricks while Seinfeld looked on. If Robert asked for a comment, Seinfeld would say, "You did fine." Seinfeld notes that most therapists become exasperated, angry, and defiant when asked to be such a slave; Seinfeld was able to overcome his subjective hate and to play the role assigned to him, but in a limited way. If Robert asked him to pick up a ball, he would be like an automaton, doing only what the patient asked for, no more and no less. "I do not have to artificially remind the youngster that we are only playing or that I am only assuming a role, because the fact that I enact the role in the precise words and tone of the youngster's directions keeps our interaction in the realm of the transitional play space. By acting as if I am a puppet in the child's play, I serve as an extension of the child's self" (Seinfeld 1990, p. 298). Had Seinfeld refused to do as the boy ordered, Seinfeld would have become a rejecting, and then a rejected parental figure. By doing it as an automaton, Seinfeld acted out objective hate in a passive way, by going along with the boy to a point while frustrating the boy's attempt to provoke him to anger and holding back any real communication with him until the boy actually asked for it.

Spotnitz, perhaps more than any other psychoanalyst, has perfected the art of objective hating. Expanding on Escalona's (1953) concept of emotional contagion—the theory that mothers can unconsciously (or consciously) infect children with emotions such as hate—Spotnitz built a theory of psychotherapy placing emotional contagion and "the toxoid response" (see Chapter 1) at its center. This theory, which also echoes W. Reich's (1933) notion of the emotional plague, is not new. "In the past emotional contagion was linked with the black arts of witchcraft; in our age, the phenomenon is primarily associated with the spread of antisocial attitudes, disordered behavior, and mental illnesses" (Spotnitz and Meadow 1976, p. 76). The theory holds that severe forms of narcissism are the result of emotional contagion in early childhood. "A mother who feels hatred for the father tends to carry over the same attitude to the child and act it out with him even though she feels great love for the child. The child, under the influence of this non-verbalized hatred, behaves very negativistically. The phenomena is encountered repeatedly—a Medea complex" (p. 80). Unlike other psychoanalysts, Spotnitz does not focus on the particulars of relationships between parents and children; rather he takes an overall view, asserting that the bottom line is the emotional contagion—stemming from unconscious parental hate—that damages children and denies them the maturational responses they need in order to develop normally.

Over the years Spotnitz has devised an elaborate array of techniques for dealing with the emotional contagion of narcissistic, borderline, sociopathic, and schizophrenic patients. Schizophrenics, for example, tend to distance their therapists in the early stages of therapy through a posture Spotnitz calls "rage withdrawal"; he uses paradoxical joining techniques to maneuver them into a "rage-combat" position.

Often schizophrenics and other severely narcissistic individuals will induce rage in the therapist by making disguised threats and preventing the therapist from doing anything about it. For example, one of Spotnitz's patients used to continually talk about wanting to commit suicide. Such threats, when heard week after week in a whining, self-pitying voice, arouse intense feelings of hate in a therapist, because they keep the therapist constantly on edge, while rendering him impotent, therapeutically. Underneath the patient's threat is a rage that invariably goes back to infantile frustrations. In this case Spotnitz went after the rage through "ego-dystonic, negative mirroring"—his goal being to get the patient to express the rage at him directly so that he could deal with it.

When the patient was carrying on one day about hating herself and wanting to kill herself, Spotnitz (1985) replied that he hated himself too, and also felt like killing himself. The patient scoffed and told him he did not mean it. She asked why he would want to kill himself. "Do you think I like to sit in a dark room hour after hour listening to a hateful person like you?" (p. 269). This remark brought the patient to life, and she told him to go drown himself. He had succeeded momentarily in getting her out of her defensive posture and into a verbal exchange with him in which she expressed directly the rage she felt for him and for all authority figures. However, a few sessions later she went back to the self-hatred and suicide threats. Spotnitz returned to a variation of this technique:

"Sometimes," he said, "I hate you and would like to kill you."

"You wouldn't do it. You don't hate me."

"Why wouldn't I hate you? Why wouldn't I feel like killing you?"

"Maybe you do feel like killing me, but I'd rather do it myself."

"If your life really isn't worth living, why deprive me of the pleasure of putting you out of your misery? You're entitled to mercy killing." [p. 269]

Spotnitz went on about how he was a physician and explained that some physicians recommended euthanasia. The patient, initially intrigued, went along with him, asking how he would kill her. He said he would describe the many ways of doing it and she could take her pick. Suddenly the patient said, with increasing bewilderment and anger, that she thought he really would enjoy killing her. He asked why it would not give him immense pleasure. She told him to go to hell. "I'm not interested in giving you pleasure. I'd rather kill you first" (Spotnitz 1985, p. 270). Spotnitz had succeeded in getting her to verbalize her hateful feelings toward him, and in subsequent sessions he was able to draw her out more and more and help her work through the rage that had kept her immobilized for so long.

Spotnitz's method of dealing with a patient who acts out hate by canceling sessions is to mirror the patient's behavior by making himself less available. If a patient calls to say, "I'm canceling Wednesday's appointment," Spotnitz will reply, "Fine, call me at 10:30 next Monday and I'll let you know if I have an opening next week." If the patient does not call exactly at 10:30 the next Monday, Spotnitz tells him he already gave away his available hours, and reminds the patient that he was supposed to call exactly at 10:30. He suggests that he call again the following Monday at 10:30. When the patient calls exactly at 10:30, Spotnitz gives him another hour.

All Spotnitz's techniques are aimed at getting the patient to come out of his defensive posture and verbalize his feelings. "The patient's recovery requires an emotional relationship with an analyst who can at first appear to be like the extremists of the patient's childhood," Spotnitz notes. "Later the analyst presents himself as a moderating force" (Spotnitz 1985, p. 287).

OTHER SCHOOLS OF THERAPY

Followers of W. Reich have developed an unusual way of confronting an individual's subjective hate: through body contact. One of the most noted of Reich's followers, Baker, practices what he calls Orgone Therapy. His method is described in a book by Orson Bean, an actor and comedian, who went into therapy with Baker in the late 1960s. At the time, Bean was in a depression. His marriage of six years had broken up and he was given custody of his 1½-year-old daughter, Michelle. He was full of rage but not at all aware of it.

During the first session, Baker took a brief case history, then asked Bean to strip down to his underwear and lie on his back on a couch. Baker pulled a chair up to the couch and sat next to him. He began pressing very hard on knots of tension in Bean's jaw and neck. When Bean did not respond, Baker inquired if he was hurting him. Bean replied that it hurt a little. Only a little? Actually, it hurt like hell, Bean admitted. Then why had he not cried? "I'm a grown-up," was Bean's retort. Baker kept pressing, kept telling Bean to breathe, and kept encouraging him to cry or scream if he felt like it. When be began poking at Bean's ribs, Bean let out "a few pitiful cries." After working over Bean's chest, he had Bean turn over and pressed his fingers and elbows into Bean's shoulders, back, and legs. Then he had Bean turn around again, roll his eyes to the corners of the room, breathe deeply, and kick with his legs onto the sofa. "I felt transported and in the grip of something larger than me," Bean (1971) reports. "I was breathing more deeply than I ever had before and felt the sensation of each breath all the way down past my lungs and into my pelvis" (p. 35).

In subsequent sessions, Bean got ever more deeply in touch with the hate he had been blocking and acting out. He went through many sessions of angry crying. "The hard emotions have to come out first," Baker explained. "The rage and the fury and the hate. Only when they're released can you get through to the tender feelings—the love and longing and sadness" (Bean 1971, p. 66). Baker gradually resolved Bean's subjective hate by attacking knots of tension (hate) in Bean's body and commanding him to perform painful tasks.

Perls (1973), adapting Ferenczi's active therapy, invented Gestalt therapy, a directive approach that encourages an individual to focus intensely on the here-and-now. Although his followers usually blend Gestalt with other approaches in their individual practice, Perls himself would usually work with groups. He would keep the chair next to himself empty, referring to it as the "hot seat," and ask, "Who wants to work?" One by one, people from the group would volunteer to sit in the hot seat and be confronted by Perls, a rotund man with a long white beard, who would smile at them like a somewhat cynical Santa Claus. As they sat nervously before him, he would call their attention to details of their behavior: "What does that smile mean? Why did you wave your hand like that? Why do you keep looking away from me? How do you feel right now? Your head aches? Give your headache a voice, what would it say? Why do you keep clearing your throat like that? Do that even more."

Perls's confrontational and directive method would often get people's aggression out into the open, as when he was working with a couple named Bill and Ann. At a certain point Ann began to cry when she complained that Bill was not there when she needed him. Perls (1973) chimed in, "Now this is a very important form of manipulation. Playing the crybaby. I notice this is one of your favorite roles." Ann admitted that it was. He directed Ann to exaggerate her crying:

Perls: Crying is a very well known form of aggression. Look what you're doing to me, say this to him. Look what you're doing to me.
Ann   (to Bill): Look what you're doing to me.
Perls: Again.
Ann: Look what you're doing to me.
Perls: Louder.
Ann   (Crying): Look what you're doing to me [p. 151]

Perls turned to Bill and told him he was a naughty boy because he was not living up to Ann's expectations, which brought a laugh from the group. Here Perls expressed objective hate by exposing Ann's manipulation, ordering her to exaggerate it, and making fun of it. Such a technique can sometimes shock or shame a person out of a characterological stance. However, one shock will not be enough to bring about permanent change. She would have to receive numerous negative reinforcements over a period of time in order for that to happen.

One of the very best at the art of hating was Erikson, whose methods were reported and expanded by Haley (1973). Erikson, a sort of psychoanalytic shaman, used a paradoxical approach similar to Spotnitz's, but was not limited to it. Although he had not attended a psychoanalytic institute, he began his career by practicing analytic therapy, but soon shifted to a strategic therapy in which his focus was not on helping patients understand themselves (indeed, he believed self-understanding inhibits change), but on providing directives that cause change, often by communicating with patients through metaphor. He also utilized both formal and informal hypnosis, again breaking with psychoanalytic technique. He had no set plan for working with individuals or with different character types; rather he would improvise a new plan for each patient, sometimes on the spot. He was completely flexible in how he ran his practice, seeing patients in his place or theirs, for five minutes or three hours.

In one case he treated a young woman without her even knowing that he had done so. A mother came to Erikson to bemoan the fact that her 14-year-old daughter had not left the house for months because she felt self-conscious about her feet. She wouldn't go to school, to church, or on the street, and she became upset if her mother or anybody even brought up the subject of feet. When her mother suggested they go to see a doctor together, she absolutely refused.

Erikson arranged with the mother to pay a visit to their home under the pretext that he was coming to examine the mother to see if she had the flu. When he arrived, the mother was lying in bed. Erikson did an examination of her, still not having decided quite what he was going to do about her daughter. The daughter stood behind him, shy and furtive. He looked her over, saw that she was rather stoutly built and that her feet were not really large. "Finally, I hit upon a plan. . . . I was sitting on the bed talking to the mother, and I got up slowly and carefully and then stepped back awkwardly. I put my heel down squarely on the girl's toes. The girl, of course, squawked with pain. I turned on her and in a tone of absolutely fury said, 'If you would grow those things *large* enough for a man to see, I wouldn't be in this sort of situation!'" (Haley 1973, p. 198). The girl looked at Erikson, puzzled, as he continued to write out a prescription. Later that day she asked her mother if she could go out to a show, and the next day she returned to school. When Erikson checked back with the mother some time later, she reported that the girl had resumed a normal social life. Neither the mother nor the daughter knew exactly what Erikson had done.

In another case, Erikson worked with a son primarily through his mother. The mother, 27 years old, complained that her 8-year-old son had become unruly and defiant toward her ever since she had divorced his father some two years earlier. He had also become a problem in the neighborhood and at school. Her two daughters, both older than the boy, had also been a problem for a while, but she had managed to straighten them out through scoldings and spankings. Joe, meanwhile, stated that he would do whatever he pleased, and nothing would stop him. Erikson heard the woman out and then instructed her on a treatment plan. "Alone with the mother, I discussed a child's demand for a world in which he could be certain that there was someone stronger and more powerful than he. To date, her son had demonstrated with increasing desperation that the world was so insecure that the only strong person in it was himself, a little 8-year-old boy" (Haley 1973, p. 214). Erikson then gave the mother painstaking instructions on how to handle the boy for the next two days. The most significant part of the plan called for her to sit on her boy for as long as it took to "break him." During this time she was to show no pity for him, no matter whether he cried, made promises, or had tantrums. She was to tell him that she wanted to try to think of ways in which he could change his behavior, but was sure she would not be able to think of any, and so he would have to do so himself. Upon hearing this plan, the mother argued that she weighed 150 pounds and was afraid she would crush the boy, but Erikson assured her that the boy would let her know if she were crushing him. It took a great deal of convincing before the mother agreed to the plan.

The following day the mother had her grandparents pick up the two daughters, and while the boy demanded she make his breakfast, she brought sandwiches, fruit juice, coffee, and towels to the livingroom floor. Then she wrestled the boy to the floor and sat on him. For the rest of the morning and part of the afternoon he writhed and moaned and screamed and cried out. He threatened her, pleaded with her, and promised he would be good. He tried fiercely to buck her off. Nothing worked. She simply kept saying in a calm voice that she had to sit on him until she thought of a way he could change his behavior. However, she did not believe she could think of one herself. She believed he would have to think of a way to change his behavior. She could not for the life of her think of a way.

She poured herself coffee, drank juice, ate sandwiches, and called the grandparents to report to them that Joe was trying to think of ways to change his behavior (as Joe screamed in the background). After five hours, Joe surrendered, assuring her in a piteous voice he would do whatever she asked. She replied that her thinking had been in vain, for she did not know what to tell him to do. He burst into tears at this reply, but after a while he said he thought knew what to do. She replied that she was glad of this, but thought he had not had enough time to think about it. She suggested another hour of thinking about it. The boy silently waited as the hour passed. When it passed, the mother commented on the time but said she wanted to finish reading her chapter. The boy sobbed softly until she finished. (The mother later admitted to Erikson that it gave her an immense satisfaction to frustrate him the way he had for so long frustrated her.) Finally she got up.

By the second day, Joe had voluntarily cleaned up his room, had apologized to the neighbors for terrorizing them, and had told his mother that it would take a considerable amount of time to undo all the mischief he had done but he would do it. With a little further help from Erikson a few days later, at which point Erikson informally hypnotized the boy and became a model of a strong father-figure, Joe's behavior changed to that of a bright, cooperative boy with normally aggressive behavior.

These two cases show Erikson's approach to dealing with subjective hate. In the first instance, the young girl had turned her hate against herself, and it had gotten attached to a fixed idea about her feet being large, an idea which nobody could change. Her mother and everybody else had tried in vain to reassure her that her feet were not too large. Erikson not only did the opposite, he did it in a shocking way, giving the girl a negative reinforcement that would resolve both the fixed idea and the subjective hate that lay behind it. Joe's subjective hate was much more out in the open—enacted through defiance and other antisocial behavior. Erikson countered by having the mother, in effect, defy the boy. She defied him, first of all, by refusing to set him free despite his protests, controlling and frustrating him with her defiance just as he had for so long controlled and frustrated her. She also defied him by refusing to give him anything further to defy, insisting that he himself had to think of a way to change his behavior. If she had thought of a way and told him how to do it, he could have promised to do what she asked and then defied her. Erikson had, indeed, thought of everything.

The strategic and dynamic forms of therapy utilized by Erikson, Spotnitz, Perls, and others in private practice have also been tried, with some success, in mental hospitals. Rokeach (1964), a clinical psychologist, reports on one of the most unusual uses of a mirroring technique. At a mental hospital in Michigan, he was treating three paranoid schizophrenics each of whom believed he was Jesus Christ. Rokeach decided to put the three men into a room together and see what would happen. He hoped that "bringing together several persons who claimed the same identity would provide as untenable a human situation as is conceivable, and that in a controlled environment wherein escape was not possible, something would have to give" (p. 33). He had read about similar instances in which psychotics had been put together, and he wanted to test out the thesis that such mirroring actually worked.

When the three were confronted with one another, they immediately got into a debate over who was the real Christ.

"Did you say you are God?"

"That's right. God, Christ, and the Holy Spirit," [Leon said]. . . .

Clyde yelled: "Don't try to pull that on me because I will prove it to you!"

"I'm telling you I'm God!" Joseph was yelling, too.

"You're not!" Clyde shouted.

"I'm God, Jesus Christ and the Holy Ghost! I know what I am and I'm going to be what I am!"

"You're going to stay and do just what I want you to do!" Clyde said. [p. 7]

Eventually, after many months of haggling, Leon, the youngest of the three (he was in his forties) gave up his delusion, while Joseph, a man in his sixties, made a partial recovery. Clyde, who was in his seventies, continued to harbor the belief that he, and he alone, was Jesus Christ, son of God, come to save mankind from its sins. "Our evidence, while inconclusive," Rokeach (1964) notes, "gives weight to the common-sense conclusion that with increasing age the chances decrease that a patient will respond to social stimulation" (p. 334).

CONCLUSION

There are times when objective love will serve to resolve subjective hate and bring about healthier bonding. However, there are many cases when objective hate is necessary. Objective love only works with those individuals whose psychopathology is less severe.

The range of methods for dealing with and resolving subjective hate are numerous. Whether one uses standard analytic procedure, an active approach, body therapy, Gestalt, or paradoxical therapy, all are capable of achieving success. More and more, therapists are called upon to have an eclectic approach in treating today's patients. My own approach, described extensively elsewhere (Schoenewolf 1989a) utilizes all of the methods outlined in this chapter and more. Like W. Reich, I will sometimes mimic my patients, as when one of my female patients flashed a sadistic grin at me as she told me she never thought about me at all outside of her sessions, and I flashed back a similar grin and told her I never thought of her at all either. Like Seinfeld, I will sometimes play roles that a patient unconsciously or consciously assigns to me, and like Spotnitz and Erikson I will sometimes use a paradoxical approach, as when a patient kept telling me that he didn't care whether the therapy worked or not, and I told him that was splendid, that he should put all his heart and soul into not caring, day and night, and that I would assist him in not caring, to the best of my ability.

To reiterate what has been said in previous chapters, meeting hate with hate serves several purposes. As Erikson notes, acting out is often an attempt to test whether there is somebody stronger than one's self, and to feel the security of knowing there is. Objective hate demonstrates this kind of strength. As Spotnitz observes, objective hate insulates an individual's ego, demonstrating to him that his hate is not as destructive as he imagines, and that others (to whom he looks up) can be just as hateful as he. Finally, as both Spotnitz and Winnicott point out, objective hate provides a maturational response, a realness, that is necessary for an individual to move out of a fixation. At the same time, it allows therapists or other subjectively hated persons to vent the hate that is being induced in them so that they can continue to relate to the subjectively hating person without, as Winnicott puts it, "every now and then murdering him."

10

The Art of Hating
in Everyday Life

It would be nice if everybody in the world could express their hate in an objective way. Just imagine:

... You walk into a store and the clerk says, "You know, I have an impulse to be rude to you. I want to answer all your questions with sarcastic comments and make you feel like an idiot. I feel angry at the world today, and particularly angry at you because you look wealthy, which stirs up my envy. Anyway, my wife gave me a hard time before I left home today, and it would be gratifying to take it out on somebody."

"Thanks for telling me," you reply. Both you and the clerk feel better when you leave the store.

... You come home from work to find your wife sitting on the couch in a new set of lingerie, her hair tied in a pink ribbon, a smile on her face. "What's up?" you ask suspiciously. "Why aren't you sitting at the television set with a martini in your hand, ignoring me?"

"Because tonight I have something to tell you. Sit down."

"Sure." You sit next to her on the couch. She sidles up to you and smiles into your eyes very, very brightly.

"I've decided to tell you something I've never told you before, at least not directly."

"What's that."

"I've decided to tell you how much I despise you." Her bright smile became even brighter. "All these years I've despised you, resented you, envied you, and had contempt for you, but instead of telling you directly, I've been torturing you. I torture you with demands, I torture you by defying you, I torture you by rejecting you sexually, I torture you by putting you down as a man, I torture you by making you feel as though all my misery is your fault. The truth is that I'm full of envy and resentment and contempt for you and for all men. I hate your penis and your testicles. I hate the way you swagger around as though you own the world because you're a man and you've got a big cock. I hate the way you look at me when you think you're sexy. You remind me of my father, who used to walk around the house with the same swagger, his testicles hanging out of his jockey shorts. Mom always said to me, 'Men only want one thing. Their brains are in their dicks.' Sometimes I think she was right. All I know is I *do* hate you, and hate you with all my might. I was going to torture you again tonight, but instead, I thought I'd just tell you how I'd *like* to torture you, and how much I despise you. Well, what do you have to say about all of this?" she asks, smiling with all thirty-two of her teeth.

"I hate you too," you quickly reply, evenly, coolly. "I hate, despise and envy you. All these years I've hated you and tried in every way I could to defy you and spite you. I've had three affairs and I know now I was just doing it to spite you. You're just like my mother, always making demands, and nothing I do is ever good enough for you. I despise you and I'm disgusted by your vagina. I hate your constant guilt-tripping and sexual rejections. My father said, 'The only good broad is one who's flat on her back!' and I think he was right. I'll tell you what I think you need. You know what you need?" You grab her lustily and proceed to engage in some of the most hateful and gratifying love-making you have ever experienced in your life, tossing about on the couch for the rest of the night.

...You watch the news on television and are delighted to see a report that the automobile manufacturers of the world have gotten together and made a pact to immediately cease making gasoline-burning cars that pollute the world's atmosphere. "It is an act of greed and hate for us to continue to make such cars," the president of the association explains to reporters. "We can no longer deny the hate we are acting out toward the planet by making these cars. Starting next week, we will shift our attention to the manufacture of solar-energy cars. It doesn't matter how much money or how long it will take to perfect such cars, we must do this for the survival of our species and for the life of the planet."

Yes, just imagine. Sometimes such miraculous events do occur. But they mostly occur in dreams and fantasies. In reality, subjective hate generally rules supreme. Can the principles of objective hate that have been developed for resolving conflicts in therapy be applied to the conflicts that develop in everyday life? Can nontherapists master the art of hating? As I stated in Chapter 2, I believe that the art of hating can be applied to everyday life, and that nontherapists can master that art if they can meet the three requirements outlined at the beginning of the last chapter.

Essentially, objective hating involves truth—telling it, confronting it, or bringing about a moment of it. A word of caution might be in order, however. When dealing with situations of hate, one is dealing with a volatile truth. If you are not absolutely certain about what you are doing, or confident that you will be able to withstand an outburst of aggression from another person or group, you may cause yourself or another person harm. When you "take a bull by the horns," you may get gored yourself or you may make the bull even madder.

Following are a few ideas that can be used by therapists and nontherapists alike in dealing with common conflicts or impasses resulting from the acting out of subjective hate.

OBJECTIVE CHARACTEROLOGICAL HATING

Characterological hate is usually difficult to resolve, for it is deeply ingrained in one's character. Characters of all types act out rather than verbalize hate, not only because this is the way they have been brought up, but also by acting out rather than verbalizing hate they do not have to take responsibility for it. Moreover, situations of characterological hate tend to be ongoing and to involve collusions between two or more persons who are unconsciously devoted to perpetuating just such situations.

Impulsive Dyads

The most common impulsive characterological dyad is between the addictive and enabling personalities. The addict needs a person on whom to depend for his addictions. Usually, the other person is one who needs to have somebody dependent on him. The addictive person acts out hate by exploiting the dependable person, while withholding genuine feelings, particularly feelings of appreciation or love. The dependable person acts out hate by keeping the addictive person dependent on him, chastising him, and treating him like a child, which angers the addict and makes him want to defy the dependable person by taking more drugs, even after he says he will stop, and further exploit him. Either party in this dyad can resolve the situation by refusing to play his role and by being honest about how he feels. The addict can stop taking drugs or admit that he needs help in doing so. He can acknowledge that he hates himself for being dependent and his co-conspirator for cultivating that dependency. The dependable person can admit that he needs to assuage feelings of inferiority by keeping the addict dependent on him and immobilized by drugs, so that he can feel superior. If this does not work he can express objective hate by kicking the addict out of his life until the latter seeks professional help.

Phallic-Passive Dyads

Another hate dyad occurs between a phallic-aggressive/obsessive-compulsive boss and the passive-masochistic employee. This kind of boss always knows better and has little patience for those who do not do their work right or fast enough. Usually, however, this boss will in some way impede or sabotage the employee's capacity to do the job by not giving him proper instructions or tools. For example, he might give the employee a handful of keys and say, "Go unlock that chest of drawers and bring me a wrench." The employee stands before the chest of drawers trying out all the keys. He does not dare ask the boss which key, for then the boss will call him stupid for not knowing what key it is. After a while, the boss storms up and says, "Let me do it," yanking the keys out of his hands. With such a boss one cannot win, for he always puts the employee in a no-win situation in order to have an excuse to vent anger and feel superior. The employee perpetuates the situation by taking his time finding the right key. The more the boss puts him down, the less well or quickly he will do things, thereby passive-aggressively fueling the boss's discontent.

How can this situation be resolved? Again, either party may resolve the situation by expressing the hate objectively rather than subjectively. The boss, were he suddenly to become enlightened, could simply say to the employee, "You know, I hate it when you take so long to do things or do them badly."

This would then give the employee permission to say, "I hate it when you yell at me and treat me like I'm an idiot and don't really give me a chance to do things right."

Once the two can directly express their hate, the door is open for constructive communication. They are no longer trying to annoy one another; they are talking. The boss might say, "Well, I yell at you because you never do things right and you deliberately take too much time."

And the employee might say, "You're right, I do take too much time, because I don't like being yelled at."

This kind of communication may eventually lead to better understanding and a resolution of the characterological deadlock.

The Silent Treatment

Another destructive dyad involves two people not speaking to each other. Hysterics, borderlines, narcissists, and masochists who are prone to holding grudges will often reject people with whom they have a dispute and refuse to speak to or see them again. They will deny their own hate and, through the defense mechanisms of splitting or projection, see the other person as entirely wrong and bad. Not speaking to the other person serves partly to punish him and partly to protect the rejecting party from the truth—the truth being that he or she is also responsible. This kind of deadlock is very difficult to break, and can often go on for years.

One of my patients, who first came to me at the age of 28, had had a very abusive relationship with her father, was abandoned by her mother, and got along poorly with her brothers and sisters. She started and stopped therapy with me several times. She would quit suddenly and angrily, after a few months, without warning. I would call her and ask what was the matter, and she would reply that she did not want to speak to me anymore. A year or so later she would call me, desperately and fearfully, and only then could she tell me that I had made an interpretation she did not like, or had not responded with enough empathy to something she had said. After she had quit for the third time, I devised a new plan. When I received the invariable desperate call, I informed her that I would only take her back into therapy again if she paid in advance for six months. At first she angrily resisted this offer, but a few weeks later she agreed. Now she had no choice but to verbalize rather than act out her hate; to quit would have meant losing money to me, a notion she could not stand. For the first few months she spat out curses: I was a cruel, arrogant tyrant who abused my patients and she had a mind to report me to the American Psychological Association; I delighted in being sadistic to her; I got off on triumphing over her and bragging about it later with my colleagues. Once she began communicating her suspiciousness and anger, it became apparent to her that the feelings and impulses she attributed to me were in actuality related to her family. Not that I did not have such feelings; there were indeed times when I delighted in frustrating her, and I told her so. However, these were feelings she induced in me. I did not feel them for other patients. Having been raised in a family environment in which she was always made out to be the bad one, she had become an adult who wanted to do the same to others: now we were the bad ones, not she, and we would never, ever get her to admit she was bad. It took another year before she and I were able to completely resolve this pattern.

This kind of deadlock is much more difficult to resolve outside of therapy, particularly if both parties have the same characterological disposition to make the other bad and wrong. Neither party will be able to let go of this defensive posture, for it will feel as though they have given in. However, sometimes a third person can set it up so that they are compelled to talk about it. Indeed, at times both parties will try to convince a third party to take their side. This third party, be he a boss, a relative, or a friend, then has the leverage to communicate honestly with them, either separately or in a joint meeting. If nothing else works, the third party may have to use force: "Either the two of you talk to each other, or you're both fired." Unfortunately, some will maintain their defensive posture until they are on their death beds, when it is too late for change to make a difference in their lives.

Using Illness as a Weapon

There is another type of characterological deadlock in which one individual uses an illness to express hate and the other individual in turn acts out hate by behaving in a pseudo-caring, bossy way to the ill person. For example, I had a patient who moved far away from her mother because of her mother's constant demands and her tendency to induce guilt in her daughter. Soon after the daughter moved away, the mother became ill. For a year, every time the daughter called her, the mother would complain about a flu, a fever, arthritis, ulcers, headaches, or bad legs. She could not eat, walk, or leave the house to get supplies, and was developing bedsores. Nobody cared about her, especially the daughter. If the daughter really cared, she would not have moved away. Upon hearing such complaints, the daughter, who was in her late twenties, would castigate the mother for not taking better care of herself, tell her she was not going to the right doctors, and order her to do this and do that in the guise of being concerned about her—using the most contemptuous tone of voice she could muster. After a year the mother was totally bedridden, having developed several more illnesses. The daughter was finally forced to move back and take care of her mother, which she did with the utmost resentment—resentment she did not mind showing to the mother.

Resolving this situation required a lot of time and effort. I had to convince the daughter that she was keeping it going by being rejecting and reproachful to her mother. One day, after the mother had become completely bedridden and the daughter had been "forced" to nurse her for several months, she called me long-distance, complaining that she could not take her mother another minute, that she wanted to strangle her and end her mother's misery and her own. At last she was ready to listen to me. "Tell your mother that she's getting sick to spite you, and that unless she improves soon you'll leave, because you're not interested in helping her die." The patient was at first incredulous, but I had gotten her attention, and she soon saw that she would also get her mother's attention and cooperation through this tactic. I gave her detailed instructions, which included an analysis of the mother's possible responses and how she was to handle them.

When she told her mother what I had suggested, her mother was at first puzzled. "Where did you get such a notion?" Then she was angry. "If you want to leave, go ahead and leave, I'm not stopping you." The daughter calmly repeated that she would leave soon if the mother did not begin to improve, then sat silently at the mother's side. "Why don't you leave? I thought you were going to leave?" the mother kept saying. The daughter calmly repeated the same words. For several days the mother tried to induce guilt feelings by accusing the daughter of being selfish and mean. She sobbed, moaned, told her daughter to get out of her life, and requested that she not come to her funeral. At one point she asked the daughter if she wanted her to die, and the daughter calmly replied that sometimes she did feel like strangling her. The mother said she could not believe her ears. Slowly, begrudgingly, the mother improved. The anger she had been somatizing was now brimming to the surface. As she retained her health, she and the daughter began to speak honestly for the first time in a long while.

Victim-Victimizer Dyads

Hysterical, sadomasochistic, and depressed characters may act out hate and gain a secondary satisfaction and relief from being a victim. The hysterical kind of victim may be a wife who, due to her own insecurity as a woman and her need to prove that all men, including her husband, are untrustworthy, selfish, and mean, sets up situations in which her husband acts badly. For example, some wives push their husbands into having affairs by withholding themselves sexually and goading them with statements like, "That new secretary is quite attractive. Why don't you have an affair with her?" If the husband has the affair she has pushed him into, she can feel victimized, complain to her friends, get special attention and treatment due to her victimization, and achieve a moral victory over him. The husband in such a marriage has his own problems, having married this kind of woman because of fears of intimacy and a need for an excuse to act out sexually. Masochistic and depressive women will dramatize a more intense version of the victim game, in which they induce their husbands to become violent or to abandon them completely. The victim game can also be played by men who marry dominating women due to a characterological masochism or depression, and then live lives of 'quiet desperation,' sometimes drowning their sorrow in alcohol, never complaining about their rotten fate, but feeling an inner moral superiority.

The antidote is for either the victim or the victimizer to refuse to play his or her role. The husband of the wife who sexually deprives him and pushes him toward other women might respond by calmly calling her attention to what she is doing. "You're frustrating me sexually and pushing me toward other women. Do you realize that?" She will, of course, deny it at first, but if the man confronts her with all the situations that have frustrated him and all the times she had goaded him, after a while the evidence will be overwhelming, her denial will break down, and the underlying hate will come to the surface. Likewise a husband or wife of a masochistic or depressive spouse who induces feelings of violence should, if possible, simply verbalize these feelings and impulses rather than act them out. "You know, when you act like that, I feel like slapping you." The victim will probably challenge the potential victimizer to do just that. The spouse may then ask, "What would that do for you if I were to hit you?" Ultimately the victim's rage will become apparent. It is often more difficult for victims to turn their subjective hate into objective hate, since victims will cling tenaciously to the image of themselves as victimized, oppressed, or abused; but if they can direct their anger at the person originally responsible for cultivating their neurotic pattern, usually with the help of a therapist, they can begin to let go of it.

Suicide Threats

Borderline personalities will use suicide threats and the setting up of other crisis situations as a way of stirring up people around them, manipulating them, and making them share the misery from which they are trying to escape. The antidote for such expressions of hate is to remain calm throughout. When borderlines meet someone—a therapist or another—who can stand up to their turbulence without being stirred up, overpowered, enraged, or destroyed by it, they are forced to reintegrate their hate and work through it.

OBJECTIVE PERVERSE HATING

Perverted Marriages

When a perverted man marries a perversely castrating woman, his fear of castration and rage will cause him to feel inadequate sexually, which in turn will arouse her resentment. The woman will be even more castrating and contemptuous of him. The man will prefer his perversion to his wife; this may range from compulsive masturbation with a fetish, to fantasized or real experiences of homosexuality, exhibitionism, voyeurism, transvestism, sadomasochism, or the like. Such a man will often put his wife on a pedestal (as he does his mother), and will be unable to express his hate to her, much less acknowledge it to himself. Unconsciously he searches for a castrating woman like his mother, but one who, unlike his mother, will allow him to be a man. His wife is envious and resentful of men, having most likely had a mother who kept her away from her father, and a father who was too passive or perverted to stand up to the mother or to her. On one level the castrating woman wants to castrate men and feel superior to them, but on another she is looking for a strong father-figure who can stand up to her. The more the husband fails to do this, the more she wants to castrate him.

The man may resolve this situation by slowly and carefully revealing his feelings to her—telling her what bothers him. In little ways he must begin to assert himself by not always giving in to her demands. Also, he must eventually reveal his perversion to her—for as long as he keeps it to himself it is a protest against her and a barrier to communication. However, as he asserts himself and reveals more of himself, he should be prepared for an assault by her in the form of attacks on his character and threats to leave. In some cases she may actually leave, unable to tolerate a truthful and equal relationship, and the man has to decide whether to save the relationship by maintaining a dishonest form of communication or to let her go and start again with somebody else. However, if the wife can tolerate and accept his real self, their communication will become more honest, and it will be more possible for him to give her what she wants—sexual fulfillment.

The woman can resolve the situation by expressing directly her resentment and envy of the man, instead of attacking his character and castigating his sexual performance through subtle or not-so-subtle innuendos. She may tell him that she feels hurt and resentful that he ignores her sexually, or that he makes her feel like some kind of monster because he is always running from her and denying his anger to her. By bringing her feelings out into the open in a nonthreatening way, she then gives him permission to speak up as well. "Sometimes I do think you're a bitch," he may say, and the woman must be prepared to hear him out undefensively.

Homosexual Masochism

Another destructive dyad exists between a masochistic and a sadistic homosexual male. The masochistic homosexual male, because of hate for, and fear of castration by, the father, has a craving to be sodomized, humiliated, and dominated by a father-figure; it is his punishment for having taken his mother away from his father, and he regards it as his rite of passage into manhood. The sadistic homosexual defends against hate and fear of castration by identifying with the aggressor—the father—and punishing and humiliating another man who symbolizes himself. However, this homosexual, sadomasochistic ritual does not resolve the subjective hate or fear of castration, but perpetuates it. Indeed, gays of this sort are generally quite promiscuous; they are the ones who inhabit gay bars and go home with different men several times a week. They never really get to know the men they date, who merely serve as vehicles for the acting out of subjective hate. When their hate is severe, they have a strong unconscious death wish, which sometimes manifests itself in a reckless attitude about sex and today often results in their getting themselves infected with AIDS.

Individuals of this sort must be firmly and forcefully confronted. A friend or relative can do this by sitting down with them and saying, "You have got to stop. You're destroying yourself, and also hurting those around you."

This character type, like the impulsive, may appear to agree with you and to "see the light." "You're right, you're absolutely right," he may say, his eyes beaming with earnest remorse. "I'll stop immediately. I'm so sorry about everything. It's finished. Over. No more."

If you believe this, all will be lost. After a short attempt to reform, he will plunge right back into his destructive behavior.

Confronting him is only the first step. He must be given an ultimatum: "Either you seek treatment, or I don't want anything more to do with you." This may sound harsh, but it is exactly the expression of objective hate that is necessary to counter his intense addiction to acting out subjective hate. Indeed, the friend or relative who gives the ultimatum must be prepared to stand firmly behind it for the individual will put it to the test. He may start and stop therapy several times to see if the friend or relative really means it.

Eventually he will find out that his destructive ways hurt nobody but himself. Then he may stay in therapy long enough for it to be of help—that is, long enough for him to begin verbalizing what he has been living out—and his perverse lifestyle will begin to diminish.

Sociopathic Perversity

A rapist comes up behind you in the middle of the night, on a dark subway or street, with a knife or a gun pointed at your throat, and says, "Take off your clothes." What do you do?

Feminists advocate always fighting back. I disagree. So do many police officers. Fighting back is an expression of subjective hate; women who "lose their heads" when accosted by a sociopathic pervert are those who have the most animosity toward men. A rapist has been treated cruelly as a child and his need for vengeance thrives on victims who cringe or fight back. Part of the art of objective hating entails an ability to distinguish between those situations that can be handled or resolved, and those that cannot. In this case, you must determine, in a split second, how dangerous the pervert is, and how to communicate with him. Sometimes you may be able to run away or cry out for help. In some cases you may decide he has you cornered (in a subway, room, alley) and is so frantic, desperate, and enraged that submission is the only way out. In other cases, you may detect some kind of openness in his manner, and you may be able to talk with him, human to human. Fighting back should be the last resort, if your life is threatened.

Then again, if you have some acting ability and you want to try something a bit more daring, you may use the tactic I suggested to my own daughter as she was growing up: *act crazy!* If you begin smiling at him like an idiot, rolling your eyes around, drooling, quaking, or spouting out nonsensical statements about jellybeans or babies in space or thimble soup, he may shake his head and walk away.

OBJECTIVE POLITICAL HATING

Political characters and parties often regard their survival as dependent upon their ability to manufacture schemes for discrediting their opponents. The more psychopatholgical the individual or party, the more "dirty" he or it will fight, and the more they will insist on being right and on persecuting those who disagree.

Pathological Liberalism

Psychopathological liberals express subjective hate by championing human rights. Their cause allows them to prove how morally superior they are and how morally evil those opposing their cause—"bigots"—are. The writings and verbal arguments of such liberals are invariably laced with contempt.

To break through this hate, you must first of all be able to tolerate the hate and violence such liberals arouse. They meddle and agitate, speak in tones of self-righteous indignation, and use intellectual sophistry, sarcasm, and condescension to provoke a violent response from those deemed as bigots—in order to confirm their belief that bigots are violent people. If you can restrain yourself from strangling them, the next step is to stop them from talking in an abstract way. Baker (1967) notes that a liberal "will outargue the therapist and insist on everyone being what he terms 'reasonable,' although he himself is not open to genuine reason. In this respect he feels on safe ground, since one cannot argue against his high ideals even though his methods, motives, and general attitude toward these are irrational" (p. 186). Stopping liberals from talking is not easy. However, sooner or later if you disagree with them or they think you disagree, they will bring up racism, sexism, or one of their other isms. You may then go for the direct approach: "You know, I really resent it when you say or imply that I'm a racist because I disagree with you."

They will either deny accusing you of being a racist, or will begin a long-winded explanation that misses the point. In either case, you have now put them on the defensive and may be able to facilitate honest communication by expressing the hate they induce in you. "You know," you may say, "I hate it when you continually use words like racism and sexism to control and manipulate people." Again, they will deny doing this or start on another explanation. It may take a long time and a lot of patience to pin them down and get them to admit what they have said or implied. Less psychopathological liberals will eventually be able to do so, and they may retort with, "Well, I hate it when you say such and such." Now you have real communication.

These methods will not work with radical liberals. They are completely closed to therapy or to any feedback other than that which agrees with their radical stance. Only "counterrevolutionary" tactics can reach them.

Pathological Conservatism

While liberals hide behind their ideology, conservatives hide behind their religion. They need to feel that they, and only they, have real values, and their values come from their tried-and-true, down-to-earth, traditional beliefs in God, their country, and free enterprise. They tend to have obsessive-compulsive and paranoid features, insisting on law and order and fearing the worst, and they act out hate by forcing all around them to march to their beat.

To counter conservative hate, one has to come from a centrist position, as one has to do with liberals. If you are not a conservative, then you are one of those selfish kooks who wants to hand our country to the communists; if you are not a God-fearing man or woman, then you are one of those "secular-humanists" who have no morality and think that anything goes. If you do not believe in hard work, then you are a lazy hedonist. If you directly challenge any of the conservatives' beliefs, they may become red in the face and launch an angry sermon about traditional values. If you try to use words, they may become suspicious and grow silent. They attempt to intimidate through silence and moral sentimentality. However, according to Baker (1967), because conservatives are not intellectually defended, they can safely be allowed to talk through their resistance and are more open to having their defenses exposed. The primary difficulty is the breaking down of their fundamentalism or patriotism so that they will experience full contact and intimacy. "Why are you proud to be an American?" you may ask. The very question is likely to stir up anger. Eventually, if you keep probing them, less psychopathological conservatives will express their real feelings.

The reactionary conservative, like the radical liberal, is not open to therapy or outside feedback.

OBJECTIVE CULTURAL HATING

Subjective cultural hate has led to all the wars throughout history, to mass hysterias of various types, to air, land, and water pollution, and to the possible extinction of our planet. People have looked in vain for ways to counter subjective cultural hate. When Einstein and Freud exchanged letters in 1932 about how to prevent war, both agreed that war could only be prevented if we set up a central authority to handle all conflicts between nations. "There is no use in trying to get rid of men's aggressive inclinations," Freud stated (1933, p. 211), implying that cultural hate could not be resolved, merely regulated. Indeed, humans seem to require the existence of some higher power, whether it be a government, God, mystical force, patriarch, ideology, or advanced civilization from other worlds, to stay at peace with one another. Fighting subjective cultural hate is, therefore, an arduous task that sometimes requires one to assume the stance of a higher authority—or at least of a firm centrist—in order to be heard.

Racial, Ethnic, and Religious Conflicts

Conflicts between groups usually involve complaints and counter-complaints of persecution. A recent conflict between Jews and Catholics illustrates this point. Polish Catholics decided to use the site of a Nazi concentration camp in Poland as a retreat for nuns. The Jewish Anti-Defamation League saw this as an affront to Jews, and complained vigorously to a Polish cardinal, accusing him of disrespect toward the Jews killed at the camp and of anti-Semitism. The Polish Cardinal, for his part, accused the Jews of being pushy and demanding. The Jews reacted in horror to these accusations, viewing them as signs of anti-Semitism and comparing them to the kinds of statements Nazis were making about Jews before World War II.

When looked at objectively, there is no reason why the Jews should tell the Polish Catholic Church what it can or cannot do with real estate owned by the Polish government, nor to insult or call into question Polish morality. If the Jews wished to make a museum of this concentration camp, they could have directed their efforts toward obtaining it from the Polish government for that purpose.

There are many such instances of group conflict occurring throughout the world every day; on occasion they escalate into a war. It is one thing to make complaints about unfair treatment in the present and to do all one can to rectify that unfairness. It is another thing to resort to name-calling when another group does not give in to your group's demands, or to become obsessed with real or imagined unfair treatment in the past and use that as a reason to get special treatment in the present and to persecute others. These are the kinds of behaviors that escalate conflicts. The Japanese had every right to complain of victimization after World War II, when they were decimated by atomic bombs. However, they hardly complained at all; instead they went to work, and in a few decades they have become leaders of the capitalist world.

The antidote to this "victim game" is to stand firm from a neutral position: "Instead of complaining and demanding, get to work!" one might tell such a manipulative group. "Those who quietly, responsibly, and unsentimentally accept both their strengths and limitations, deal with the reality that life is not fair for anybody, put their aggression to productive use, and set about doing whatever they can do to make their own lives and the life of their group as successful as possible—they will reap the rewards."

Countering Global Hate

Many groups have sprung up, such as Greenpeace, which attempt to express objective hate toward the global enactment of subjective hate. The trouble is that sometimes such groups have a pious attitude which contaminates their efforts. This piety makes their hate less objective. What is required is for higher authorities to stand up, unequivocally, against pollution, deforestation, and other expressions of hate to our planet, and to use their powers to raise the collective consciousness of the world. It may also mean making decisions and getting laws passed that will anger people.

An example of this has happened with respect to cigarette smoking. Ever since the surgeon general of the United States came out unequivocally against smoking, it has declined considerably. His example also paved the way for others to speak out against the harmfulness of smoking, not only to smokers but also to those around them. Soon it became routine for nonsmokers to speak out against smokers in public who were polluting the atmosphere. This same thing could happen to car owners, if a member of the cabinet came out unequivocally against driving gasoline-fueled cars. Soon you might have people routinely speaking out against people who do not stop driving gasoline-fueled cars. "Hey, friend, would you mind not driving your car in my neighborhood? You're screwing up the air I breathe!" And the same process might be successful in fighting against the proliferation of nuclear reactors, the emission of toxic chemicals in the air by industry, and the cutting down of our tropical forests by real estate tycoons.

Naturally, just as cigarette smokers become furious when asked to stop polluting the atmosphere with their smoke, so also these actions will bring to the surface the unconscious hate that is being expressed indirectly by automobile owners, nuclear reactor builders, industrialists, and real estate tycoons. They will at first be furious, but eventually they will come around.

OBJECTIVE GENDER HATING

Subjective gender hate permeates all aspects of society; it is the age-old "battle of the sexes" that breaks up our homes, affects our job performances, and then contaminates our play.

Sexual Combat

The purpose of malicious flirting is to sexually conquer "the enemy," by giving out signals of availability and then, when the individual takes the bait, suddenly saying "buzz off." Those who take the bait, who respond to a malicious flirt, are generally masochistic, having their own unresolved gender animosity and looking for opportunities to be victimized and seek revenge. They will sometimes end up getting into an endless battle that may wind up with one or both parties taking the other to court, committing suicide, and sometimes murder.

How can a man best deal with an hysterical tease? How can a woman handle a phallic-aggressive sexual conquistador? Both types are outwardly flirtatious but inwardly cold and rejecting. If you pay attention to the feelings that are being aroused by them, you will detect a mixture of excitement and fear, which means you are being conned. (A sincere approach does not induce fear—although you might be afraid because of your own baggage.) They may come on strong, but if you look probingly into their eyes, you will see clues of their intentions. They will turn away, hiding their eyes, or keep their hands in their pockets (another sign of hiding something). They are masters of the indirect innuendo, but are vulnerable to directness. You might try, "You seem to be flirting with me, but I get the impression you're not really serious, or you won't be for long." The tease or sexual conquistador will usually give up the game when confronted in this way. Some men may lie in order to continue the seduction, but their lies will become more apparent.

It is more difficult for the tease or sexual conquistador to objectify their hate, since they are "on top" in this situation, and will be reluctant to give up their advantage.

Marital Hate

The usual motif in marriages is for each party to try to control or destroy the other, depending on the intensity of their gender animosity. Each will concentrate on the other's weaknesses. If one is domineering, the other will attack this domineering quality, and the dominant partner will become all the more domineering. If one is passive, the other will attack the other's passivity, and the passive partner will become even more passive. If the woman is frigid or the man impotent, they will attack each other's sexual inadequacy and their inadequacies will grow worse. When there are children, the battle lines are drawn around the children: who knows best, who will take charge, who will have the final say. If the mother clings to the children, the man will attack her for clinging and she will cling even more. If the man beats the children, the woman will attack him for beating the children or turn the children against him, and he will beat them even more. Obviously, there are a myriad of possibilities.

If one or both parties are to some degree enlightened and can listen to feedback from relatives, friends, or from their children, they can resolve these battles themselves. Again, it is a matter of both parties taking responsibility for their subjective hate and learning to verbalize it objectively. However, more often than not, married couples are too entangled in their subjective hate to make use of feedback, and only a trained therapist can help them do so.

Falling in Love

This is one of the most common ways men and women express subjective hate. It represents a sudden regression to a primitive, childlike trust for, dependence on, and idealization of the other (as a child relates to a mother) and is usually a reaction-formation defending against animosity. While they are in this state, lovers are completely out of touch with their hate, but at the first flicker of rejection both may suddenly flip into the most sordid acting out, involving name-calling, back-stabbing, betrayals, and counter-betrayals. The saying, "Everything is fair in love and war," describes the kind of warfare that goes on between ex-lovers of this type. The antidote? Do not fall in love. If somebody tries to fall in love with you, thank them and send them on their way. "Sorry, I'm just not into falling in love these days!" Objective love does not happen suddenly, but slowly, with a dash of hate.

Feminism and Masculinism

Imagine a college biology class. The teacher, a male, has begun to lecture about the difference in male and female sexuality. At a certain point he turns to a pretty female student in the front row and jokingly comments that his male sexuality is being aroused by her bare leg. Suddenly there is an irate female voice from the back of the room. "That's a sexist thing to say!" Then another voice, letting out a terrified cry: "I can't believe what just happened! This is sexual exploitation, clear and simple; he's using his position of authority to sexually exploit a female student!" More shouting erupts.

Instances of political gender hate can occur at any time. If the teacher is a masculinist, he will respond with subjective hate—for example, he might get into an argument or shouting match with them over what constitutes sexism, or he might tell them to stop getting hysterical (reacting to their name-calling with name-calling of his own), or he might appease them, apologize to them, and avoid the whole subject (identifying with the aggressors), which would be another form of subjective hate because he would be letting down other students who paid to hear the lecture. If he is healthy enough to objectify the feelings of hate such an outburst arouses, he may simply say, "You're entitled to your opinion, but for now I must ask you to either stop disrupting the class or leave. If you have any criticism of me or my teaching methods, you may come to me after class in a polite manner, or go to the authorities if you like, but disrupting the class is not okay with me." The teacher must be prepared to continue this fight all the way to the president's office, for to allow anybody, no matter what their cause, to disrupt the classroom or any public gathering is to give in to tyranny and invite it to stay.

Sometimes war is unavoidable, but it must be fought with objective, not subjective hate.

OBJECTIVE PARENT–CHILD HATING

Winnicott's work with the orphan boy, described in Chapter 1, and Erickson's treatment of Joe in the last chapter, are models of objective parent–child hating. If parents enact subjective hate toward their children, their children will respond likewise. It is up to the parents, as the adults in the relationship, to do whatever is necessary to resolve destructive communication. Below are some common ways children express subjective hate and how to deal with them.

Infant Crying and Clinging

Escalona (1953) and Spitz (1965) found that in cases when the infant continues to cry and cling even after feeding and rest and after being hugged and soothed by the mother, the infant is reacting to some unconscious hate being transmitted to the child. Therefore, mothers who find themselves having this problem with their babies need to closely examine their own feelings to become aware of any hate—in the form of anger at their spouse, resentment about women's roles, or anger at their parents—that is being unconsciously taken out on the child. Once they become aware of this hate, they may verbalize it to their husband or somebody else, or express it to the infant in an objective way. If this fails to resolve it, they may need to see a therapist.

Autism

The autistic child completely retreats from the mother and from all contact with people; when you are in the room with an autistic child, it is as though you are not there. Many psychiatrists and other professionals have concluded that autism is genetic. However, there is no conclusive proof of this. Mahler (1968) believed it might be genetic in some cases, but in other cases she found that such children had been stunted during the earliest phase of infancy—the first few weeks. This is a critical stage for infants; if they do not make contact with an empathic mother or mother surrogate at this point, they will withdraw and may never learn to relate. Mothers who suffer from postpartum depression and do not wish to pick up or care for their babies during the weeks immediately after they have given birth are most likely to produce autistic children. Later, they will not remember having rejected the child during this period, and exclaim to a physician, "I really don't know why the child acts this way; he has been this way since I brought him home from the hospital." The physician will, of course, be sympathetic to the mother.

In such cases, the father's role is vital. If a father sees that his wife is depressed after giving birth and not looking after the baby properly, it is his duty to intervene, and either nurse the baby himself or see to it that somebody else does. In this case, objective hate means doing what needs to be done, even if it hurts the mother's feelings.

Hyperactive Children

There was a case of a little boy who always said, "No!" No matter what his mother said to him, he would answer, "No!" Ever since his father had died, three years earlier, when he was 2 years old, he had said, "No!" If she wanted him to eat his dinner, he said "No!" If she wanted him to put on his clothes, he said "No!" If she wanted him to go to bed, he said "No!" If she wanted him to stop stomping on the floor, he said "No!" If she wanted him to stop drawing on the wall with crayons, he said "No!" His mother tried many things to get him to obey—spankings, scoldings, shaming him in front of others—but nothing worked. What to do?

First of all, the mother had to understand her feelings toward the boy. During the rapprochement stage children are noted for defiantly refusing to do anything their parents ask them to do, and for using the word, "No," on every possible occasion. This son was stuck in this stage, as a protest against his father's sudden death and his mother's refusal to allow him to talk about his father. She was furious at the father for dying, and she had blocked all the boy's efforts to verbalize his feelings about the father's death. Now she experienced each "No!" by the boy as an accusation and deliberate torture, which made her want to do whatever necessary to shut him up. In order to help her get a grip on her feelings, the mother confided the problem to a close friend, and the friend did what a good friend ought to do. She expressed objective hate to the mother, giving her a candid opinion of what she saw going on between her and her boy. "You're taking out your anger about your husband's death on your son," she told her in so many words. "You are what's making him hyperactive!" This mother was aware enough to hear her friend out. The fury she had been holding inside of her about her husband came gushing up. She ranted for a while, then fell sobbing on her bed. Afterward she was able to encourage the boy to talk about his father. From then on things got better.

Bed-wetting

Bed-wetting is a passive-aggressive form of defiance, a way of acting out the "No!" It may be linked to a wish by a child to punish the parents, a wish to exhibit, a wish to be picked up and held, a wish to experience the infantile freedom of wetting, the wish in boys for reassurance against castration anxiety, and the wish in girls to deny castration. Invariably there is a dominating parent in the picture.

Esman (1977) reports a mother bringing her 5½-year-old boy to him, complaining of nocturnal bed-wetting. The mother reported that she was disgusted with this habit, and she had tried corporal punishment, shaming, ignoring, and night waking as means of trying to combat the problem. Esman describes her as an "extremely tense woman" who had difficulty speaking and showed an enormous preoccupation with her son's bed-wetting. The mother had taken the son to a therapist, in the hopes that the therapist would straighten the boy out. Esman recommended that the mother take the boy out of therapy, for it served to emphasize his symptom and reinforce his image of himself as defective; at the same time, he recommended that she herself go into therapy. She admitted that many people had told her to go into therapy, but she had always resisted. He then suggested that she stop deprecating the boy and simply be loving and supportive in her attitude toward him, giving him the space to outgrow the bed-wetting.

When the boy was brought to Esman six months later, he was only wetting occasionally. The mother had become much less punitive and deprecatory, although she had still not gone into therapy herself. Esman apparently succeeded in getting the mother to curtail her expressions of subjective hate toward the boy, and this had improved their relationship. There was no further follow-up on the case, however, and one is left to wonder if the mother's refusal to go into therapy might portend that her subjective hate would find other avenues of expression later on that would lead to other conflicts with the boy. The fact that this mother resisted therapy despite the fact that numerous people had advised it shows a certain willfulness that could not help but affect her primary relationship.

The Exhibitionistic Child

A certain 3-year-old child liked to run around without any clothes on. She liked to finger her vagina and suck her thumb at the same time. She liked to run up to Mom and lift up her skirt. She liked to try to unzip Dad's fly. She liked to dance around in the nude and giggle. She liked to put things into her vagina—pencils, toothbrushes, jellybeans—and then into her mouth, and say, "Look Mom and Dad, look what I can do." She liked to urinate on the floor. Once she did it in front of her parents while they were watching television, smiling at them sheepishly. Her mother frowned, cleaned up the mess without a word, and continued watching television as if nothing had happened. When the child's behavior became more antisocial, the parents examined their feelings and realized they had been ignoring her, which was a subtle form of subjective hate. They agreed that it would be best to accept the child's feelings as normal for her stage, allowing her to act them out to an extent without responding to or rebuking her. However, the next time the girl urinated on the floor, her mother took her to the bathroom, without anger, and said firmly but lovingly, "You know you are supposed to go to the potty to do that." She expressed objective hate by disapproving of the girl's destructive behavior without disapproving of her normal exhibitionism.

The Shy, Backward Child

The play *The Glass Menagerie* offers an illustration of a kind of parent-child dyad that fosters a retarded emotional development in the child. The play is about an overprotective mother and a reclusive daughter who prefers relating to her menagerie of glass animals than to people. Throughout the play the mother expresses concern about the daughter's shyness, her marriage prospects, and her likelihood of becoming a spinster. She even has her son bring home a "gentleman caller" for the daughter. On the surface it would seem that the mother is behaving in a loving, caring way; but on a deeper level it is evident that she is actually reinforcing the daughter's backwardness and dependence on her. What the mother is enacting here are probably some kind of unconscious feelings of competition with the daughter, which may be a repeat of a relationship she had with one of her parents.

It is difficult for mothers and daughters caught up in such a destructive relationship to break out of it. The daughter would have to overcome her shyness (self-hate) enough to verbalize her resentment toward her mother. The mother would have to become aware of how she was acting hatefully toward the daughter. Usually it is the daughter in these cases who is more likely to break the deadlock. She might say to the mother, "I really hate it when you continually harp on my problems. And I hate it when you keep arranging things behind my back without asking me if I want it, like that gentleman caller!" The mother will at first be taken aback by such expressions, but if the daughter can persist, calmly and patiently, in making her mother aware of the underlying layer of her own thwarted hopes, which she defends herself from experiencing by focusing her attention on her daughter, she may begin the process of objective hating. Fathers, incidentally, can also have such relationships with their children.

Oedipal Situations

Some mothers will act out hate to their husbands by having a close relationship with one of their sons, in effect making the son the most intimate person in their lives. In other cases, a father will do the same thing with a daughter. When this happens, the children do not develop properly, but remain attached to the close-binding parent. Even if they marry, they remain closer to the parent than they do to their spouse, and their sexuality is often perverse.

The antidote to this problem is for one of the parties in the triangle to speak out about it. Usually the parent who is excluded is the one to do this, for he or she has the most motivation. It might begin with a simple statement like, "You're closer to our son (daughter) than you are to me. What's going on?" Such statements will be met with anger, dismay, or denial, and will have to be repeated many times, firmly but without malice, before they will lead to real communication. If this does not work, family therapy may be required.

Fathers and Daughters

Fathers and daughters often develop openly hostile relationships when the girl becomes an adolescent and begins to strive for independence. Such a daughter might have been sweet and obedient toward the father until that time, and then will suddenly begin defying the father and talking back to him. A power struggle ensues, and the father attempts various means to get the daughter to resume her former obedience—that is, to continue being "Daddy's girl." When nothing else works, the father will resort to violent, self-righteous outbursts.

Usually the girl is expressing subjective hate that has come to the surface with adolescence, but which originated during infancy, when she felt rejected by the father. She has repressed these feelings for a few years and "joined the enemy" by being obedient to him; adolescence then gave her the license to express the rage. The father will be surprised by this sudden change in the daughter, unaware of the subjective hate he expressed toward her during the phallic stage.

It is up to the father, as the adult in the relationship, to take responsibility for his behavior and find a way to reach the daughter. Punishment does not work in such cases; it only provokes more defiance. Basically, he needs to become aware of his own subjective hate, let go of it, and then get his daughter to talk to him. This is not easy. One father, an acquaintance of mine, broke through his daughter's barrier of defiance by using, on my advice, a joining technique. This daughter was given to hysterical fits during which she would destroy whatever was around her and throw things out of the window. The father would typically react by storming into the daughter's room, shouting at her to stop it, threatening her, and if that failed, slapping or shaking her. These scenes occurred again and again, with nothing ever being resolved. After having become enlightened about his contribution to the situation, the father planned out a new strategy.

When the girl had her next tantrum, the father peeped into the room and said, "That looks like fun. Do you mind if I join you?" To her amazement, he proceeded to do just as she was doing. When she pulled books out of her shelf and tossed them onto the floor, he did likewise, giggling with glee. When she picked up a pillow and tore it apart, sending feathers flying about the room, he picked up the other one and did the same with it. When she picked up a glass and threw it out the window, he did not pick up another glass; instead, he deliberately grabbed something he knew she valued—a statue that a boyfriend had won for her at a local carnival—and aimed it at the window.

"No!" she cried out. "Not that."

"Why?" he asked. "Isn't it fun to destroy things?"

"All right, I get the point. Please!"

He brought his arm back like a baseball pitcher and threw the statue out the window, where it shattered on the sidewalk. Then he stood facing her. Now, instead of assaulting her, it was she who assaulted him, rushing at him and pummelling him with her fists. He did not fight back, but merely covered himself.

"You bastard, you son-of-a-bitch, you asshole," she yelled at him, crying. "I hate you. You stupid, stupid, jerk, I hate your guts. . . ." He let her carry on until she had exhausted herself and fell sobbing onto the bed, then he sat beside her and waited.

"You're right," he said. "I have been a bastard at times. You should be angry at me."

After a while she looked up at him puzzled, angry, and forlorn. "That's right, I should and I am."

"Tell me about it," he said.

They began to talk.

The turning point in this instance was not only the joining itself, but the fact that the father did not spare his daughter's feelings when she begged him not to throw out her statue. He needed to defy her and cause her some pain—just as Joe's mother, in the previous chapter, needed to defy Joe—in order to make her truly feel her own cruelty and stop acting it out. This act of cruelty by the father, done objectively with a certain planned goal in mind, roused her from the acting-out mode and into the verbalizing mode. It also helped the father to release some of his anger at the daughter so that he could better stand up to her provocative behavior.

Teenagers and Drugs

Adolescents take drugs for various reasons, but whatever the reason, it indicates a need for a kind of attention they are not getting. Usually parents of adolescents who take drugs react with shock and horror, and take a condemnatory attitude. This only makes the teenager want to take even more drugs to spite them. Permissiveness or gentle persuasion does not work either. What works is a firm, nonmoralizing stand. The first step is to command them to go into Alcoholics Anonymous, a rehabilitation program, or therapy, "or else." The "or else" might be loss of allowance, loss of the use of the family car, or some harsher measure— whatever works. The second step is to begin communicating the hate that is being acted out in the family, perhaps with the aid of a therapist or other mediator.

Being Your Own Good Parent

One of my patients was a young woman who had been sexually abused when she was about a year old. She was a timid individual with a fear of men and a fear of sexuality. At a certain point in her life she began having nightmares and would wake up with bruises on her body. I asked if she were hurting herself at night, but she swore she was not. It appears that the nightmares themselves produced these physiological changes in her body. The nightmares were about being in her crib as an infant with her arms tied. A man stood before her, smiling. He masturbated and touched her genitals. She tried to scream "No!" but she could not yet talk, and anyway, she was gagged as well as tied. She wanted her mother, but her mother was nowhere around. She felt powerless, helpless.

This nightmare haunted her night and day. She became a recluse. She kept saying to me, "I wish these feelings would go away." I had her go through the nightmare again, and this time at a certain point I said to her, "What would you like to do to this man?"

"I'd like to kill him. But I'm too little."

"Go back and kill him now. Imagine yourself as your own mother, walking into the room to defend yourself."

"Really?"

She began to imagine it, but said it felt strange. She left the session smiling, and the next day she returned with an even broader smile. "I felt so excited to come here today," she exclaimed. Her entire body seemed to smile. "I feel so much joy. All last night I was going over the nightmare and killing the man. I never thought of it that way before. I never thought I could just kill him. I killed him all night. I can't believe it. I feel so light, so full of energy. I started a new painting today. I called a friend, we're going out tonight. I hope this feeling never goes away. I've never felt like this before."

The feeling did go away, but she never again felt so devastated by the nightmare. The subjective infantile hate that had for so long paralyzed her had been transformed into objective adult hate, and that had made a difference. Her nightmares were real enough to cause physiological changes, and now her murderous fantasies were equally effective. She had become her own good mother.

CONCLUSION

This list of situations in which the art of hating can be applied is not meant to be exhaustive, but merely to provide an introduction on how it is done. The basic premise is simple enough: get people to stop acting out and to verbalize their hate. However, sometimes the simplest things are the hardest to accomplish. It sometimes seems as though there is a world taboo against hating objectively. Such proverbs as "If you can't say something nice, don't say anything at all," and "You're over-reacting," and "You're so full of hate," serve to reinforce the repression and suppression of hate and encourage indirect expressions and somatizations. As I have previously pointed out, if we enact hate rather than verbalize it, we do not have to take responsibility for it. However, by not taking responsibility for it, we are creating all of the interpersonal, social, and global problems that beset us.

Not all problems can be resolved through objective hating. Kohut (1971) believed that certain personality types, such as narcissists, respond best to empathy, and therapists who practice supportive techniques find it helpful to say only what a patient wants to hear, particularly patients who are going through a crisis. Sometimes with higher-functioning individuals, a supportive comment or act of love is all that is needed to put him or her back on track. In other cases, a mixture of objective hating and loving is required.

Nor do I wish to mislead anyone into thinking that deeply ingrained, characterological styles of acting out or somatizing hate can be changed overnight. Turning points can be achieved when an individual begins to objectify hate, but sometimes it takes many years of painstaking work, during which there will be many relapses, before a destructive pattern is completely changed. Even then, there may still be occasional relapses, though not as frequent or as intense as before.

However, it is a myth that "love conquers all." Infatuation—what psychoanalysts call transference love—may conquer all temporarily, but only until reality sets in. The reality is that all human beings have both love and hate in them, and it is usually the hate that backs up the system.

11

The Future of Hate

THE FEASIBILITY OF OBJECTIVE HATING

We define hate as any resistance to genuine bonding, individually or collectively. It may take many forms—including characterological, perverse, political, cultural, sexual, and parental—and it may manifest itself in a range of emotions, attitudes or illnesses, including anger, envy, fear, disgust, shame, depression, ulcers, superiority, inferiority, dominance, submission, persecution, cancer, and martyrdom. It is both genetic and environmental in origin, and can be expressed subjectively or objectively. Subjective hate is a resistance to bonding that leads to the destruction of authentic communication and death. Objective hate is a healthy counterresistance that leads to resolution of subjective hate and genuine communication.

The qualities and techniques required for the practice of the art of hating are easy to describe, but not so easy to master. I have suggested that in order to practice this art, one must have an understanding of others, an understanding of yourself (which includes being in touch with your feelings and being able to distinguish between feelings of subjective and objective hate), and the courage to do what is necessary to counter-

191

act the subjective hate around you. The question is, can this art be learned by anyone, or does it require a special talent for hating?

In a recent psychoanalytic study of hatred, Galdston (1987) determined that hate is a skill that depends upon the maturity of an individual's ego. He divides people into three categories: those who cannot hate, those who hate but cannot stop hating, and those who can both hate and get over hating. Individuals in Galdston's first two categories would be prone to a form of subjective hating, while those in the last would seem to demonstrate the skills of objective hating. In his view, only therapy can enable those with deficient egos to reach a level of maturity in which they can effectively handle hate.

For the most part I agree with Galdston. While some higher-level neurotics may have the talent to master the art of hating on their own or with the aid of this book, most will need the help of an objective third person—friend, relative, or professional. Even those in the mental health field who have been practicing therapists for a number of years need weekly supervision and sometimes their own therapy in order to insure their objectivity. Talent alone is seldom enough for the mastery of any art.

On the other hand, many people will not want to master the art of hating; they derive so much secondary gain or convenience from their expression of subjective hate that they will not want to give it up. These include dominating, victimized, paranoid, or proud characterological types; extremist political types; feminist and masculinist gender types; militant ethnic or racial types; and the vast majority of people around the world who cannot stop killing our planet in one way or another.

However, for those who do have the motivation to learn the art of hating, there are several ways of going about it.

TRAINING FOR THE ART OF HATING

In a sense, all therapists must undergo training in the art of hating; that is, they must all go through their own therapy, supervised internships, and classwork so that they can learn the skills necessary to teach patients how to hate and how to love themselves and others. However, there is one school of therapy, the modern psychoanalytic school, which specifically trains students in the art of objective hating.

Trainees in modern psychoanalytic institutes are encouraged, throughout their coursework, to verbalize all their feelings—about the course, the teacher, the reading assignments, and other students. A class about the writings of Freud might be interrupted by a student's need to verbalize a feeling of envy about another student in the class which is preventing him from fully participating in the class. The teacher will ask the student to talk about this envy. In talking about it he may find out that the other student reminds him of his younger brother, and that the envy he feels toward the student and the coldness with which he was treating the student was unwarranted. Or he may find the other student is, indeed, behaving in a way that provokes envy, not only from this student but from other students in the class. The teacher may then ask the other student to talk about whether he is aware of wanting to be envied.

Hence, students in modern psychoanalytic institutes are constantly being trained to be aware of their feelings and to use them throughout their training. They call this an "emotional education."

Almost all training for the profession of psychotherapy involves a training therapy of some kind, as well as supervision, and if these are done correctly they will be emotional and they will require the trainees to become familiar with their hateful feelings. They will be forced, in their training, to understand the ways in which they act out or somatize hate rather than verbalizing it. They will be trained to tolerate all the feelings that are aroused in their training therapy or supervision without acting on them. They will be taught to distinguish between those feelings of subjective and objective hate (as well as between feelings of subjective and objective love). They will be shown techniques for using feelings to understand the emotional language of other people, and for expressing them objectively when necessary. They will be trained in when to use these feelings and how to use them most effectively.

One cannot master the art of hating without some kind of apprenticeship. However, formal training in a therapy institute is not the only path available. If one can find a friend or relative who is healthy and skilled in this art, who will serve as a mentor and unofficial supervisor, it is conceivable one could master the art this way. Most people discuss their problems with friends or relatives, but not the right friends or relatives. Often, people pick confidants who will say only what they want to hear, who have a point of view similar to their own. Confidants of this

sort cannot serve as mentors in the art of hating, for they will not challenge their student's point of view when it needs to be challenged.

A good marriage in which the husband and wife listen to, respect,
and take advice from each other, can serve that purpose, as well as a good
friendship. In such instances, each takes turns being mentor and student,
as the situation demands.

The main reason people need mentors or consultants in order to
learn to hate well is that it is impossible for them to see themselves objectively on their own. Nobody can do that. Freud, Jung, and other early
psychoanalysts tried to be their own analysts and failed to overcome
certain characterological traits, which inhibited their work; Freud did
not resolve his fear of competition with other men (his castration fear),
which caused him to be disinclined to work with more disturbed patients; Jung had strong schizoid features in his personality that limited
the scope of both his therapy and his writing. They went far, but could
have gone much further if they had had the benefit of a real
psychoanalysis.

Mentors are required to insure objectivity and train students in
understanding their feelings. Most people go through life not really paying very close attention to their feelings. They feel a bit depressed, a little
anxious, a tad "under the weather" but do not know why. For some
reason they cannot sleep. For some reason they get headaches, back-
aches, stomach aches. If somebody annoys them, they act reflexively
without stopping to understand what is going on. Most of the time they
do not even know that they are angry, much less how to distinguish
between subjective and objective anger. Mentors are needed to show
students how to recognize their feelings, tolerate them, understand them,
and use them.

There are other formal methods of becoming aware, such as medi-
tation with the spiritual guidance of a master. Buddhism and Hinduism
have such paths within their framework. There are also many "self-help"
organizations that provide guidance in this direction such as Alcoholics
Anonymous and its associated programs (in which you are assigned a
sponsor). All programs that strive for self-awareness are helpful.

Once people learn to tolerate and use their feelings to resolve
conflicts, life becomes more natural, peaceful, spontaneous, and full of
vitality. It is this goal that the sages of all times have had in mind.

FUTURE HATE

Will we, the people of the world, be able to overcome our blocks to objective hating collectively? Will we be able to learn to love objectively and to form healthy bonds? It seems conceivable that some people will be able to do so, but on a larger scale things do not seem very optimistic.

Subjective hate seems to be increasing as civilization becomes more crowded, technological, and free. Crowded conditions bombard the senses with stimuli and inundate us with stress. Technology has alienated us from one another and from the earth. We now have the power to push buttons and kill millions without actually experiencing what we are doing. Technology has made our lives easier and spoiled us to a point where we want more and more, where we have become addicted to ease and cannot do without it, even though it is destroying us. Individual freedom (human rights) has brought about a kind of anarchy, a battle over rights, values, and responsibilities that results in more crime, more perversion, and more social unrest. Like caged animals, we have become imprisoned by our civilizations and must struggle to find our identities; also like them, we have developed an increasing variety of mental and physical illnesses.

Human beings no longer have faith in the future, nor a convincing belief in a higher power. Both seem necessary for healthy bonding and social cohesion. History shows a progressive evolution from absolute rule by divine decree to partial rule by democratic process, from theism to atheism, from faith in an afterlife to resignation to this life, from a belief that we are the center of the universe to a recognition that we are but an infinitesimal microbe in that universe, from the assumption that we have free will to the acceptance that we have been genetically and environmentally programmed, from the belief that we are conscious of everything and masters of our fate, to the realization that we are mostly unconscious of what makes us tick and subject to the horde instinct, from an expectation that humanity will live on forever to the knowledge that the end may be nearer than we think, and that our world could be destroyed in an instant.

All of these contribute to a rise in stress and in the acting out of subjective hate. We are like a runaway adolescent who can no longer be reached. We drug ourselves, watch television, eat fast foods, drink soft drinks, avoid work, spurn knowledge, and try to suck as much superficial security as we can out of each day. Impulsive, proud, and sullen, we no longer heed the advice of scientists, religious leaders, or presidents.

No, things do not look too promising. Yet, there must be hope. Otherwise, why do people persist in writing books such as this one? Why does anybody bother to speak out at all? Because there is always the hope that people in general, and humankind as a whole, will one day achieve the maturity to tolerate feelings and thoughts without acting on them, to deal effectively with hate and to achieve lasting harmony and bonding through the application of the accumulated self-knowledge garnered over the centuries of existence.

A FINAL CONFESSION

This book is itself an act of hate—objective hate, I hope. By detailing the many ways people hate badly and providing techniques for productive hating, I am trying to jolt readers out of a subjective and into an objective mode of being. It may make some people angry, but I trust it will be the kind of anger that precedes growth. Perhaps it will encourage people to talk about feelings instead of ignoring them, or to look for new solutions to their present conflicts, or to seek professional help. To twist around an old proverb: "It is better to have hated well and lost, then to have never hated well at all."

References

Abraham, K. (1921). Contribution to the theory of the anal character. In *Selected Papers on Psycho-Analysis*, pp. 370–392. New York: Brunner Mazel, 1979.

Alexander, F. (1950). *Psychosomatic Medicine*. New York: Norton.

Baker, E. F. (1967). *Man in the Trap*. New York: Macmillan.

Bean, O. (1971). *Me and the Orgone*. New York: St. Martin's Press.

Berliner, B. (1956). The role of object relations in moral masochism. *Psychoanalytic Quarterly* 11:171–186.

Bieber, I., et al. (1988). *Homosexuality: A Psychoanalytic Study of Male Homosexuality*. Northvale, NJ: Jason Aronson.

Boesky, D. (1982). Acting out: a reconsideration of the concept. *International Journal of Psycho-Analysis* 63:39–55.

Bowlby, J. (1979). *The Making and Breaking of Affectional Bonds*. London: Tavistock Publications.

Breuer, J., and Freud, S. (1895). Studies in hysteria. *Standard Edition* 2.

Brody, S. (1964). *Passivity: A Study of Its Development and Expression in Boys*. New York: International Universities Press.

Brownmiller, S. (1975). *Against Our Will: Men, Women and Rape*. New York: Bantam Books, 1981.

Burnham, J. (1964). *Suicide of the West.* New York: John Day.

Bynner, W. (1944). *The Way of Life According to Lao Tsu.* New York: Capricorn Books, 1962.

Chagnon, N. A. (1968). *Yanamamö: The Fierce People.* New York: Holt, Rinehart and Winston.

Chasseguet-Smirgel, J. (1970). *Female Sexuality: New Psychoanalytic Views.* Ann Arbor, MI: University of Michigan.

Chauvin, R., and Muckensturn-Chauvin, B. (1977). *Behavioral Complexities.* New York: International Universities Press.

Clower, V. L. (1979). Feminism and the new psychology of women. In *Our Sexuality,* ed. T. B. Karasu and C. W. Socarides, pp. 279–316. New York: International Universities Press.

Coles, E. M. (1982). *Clinical Psychopathology: An Introduction.* London: Routledge & Kegan Paul.

Darwin, C. (1859). *The Origin of The Species.* London: John Murray.

Deutsch, H. (1944). *Psychology of Women.* New York: Straton.

Dicks, H. V. (1967). *Marital Tensions: Clinical Studies Towards a Psychological Theory of Interaction.* London: Routledge & Kegan Paul.

Eibl-Eibsfeldt, I. (1970). *Love and Hate: The Natural History of Behavior Patterns.* New York: Schocken Books, 1974.

Erikson, E. H. (1950). *Childhood and Society.* 2nd ed. New York: Norton.

Escalona, S. (1953). Emotional development in the first year of life. In *Problems of Infancy and Childhood,* ed. M. Senn. Ann Arbor, MI: Josiah Macy, Jr. Foundation.

Esman, A. H. (1977). Nocturnal enuresis: some current concepts. *Journal of the American Academy of Child Psychiatry* 16:150–158.

Fairbairn, W. R. D. (1941). A revised psychopathology of the psychoses and psychoneuroses. In *Essential Papers on Object Relations,* pp. 71–101. New York: New York University Press.

Fenichel, D. (1945). *The Psychoanalytic Theory of Neuroses.* New York: Norton.

Ferenczi, S. (1919). Technical difficulties in the analysis of a case of hysteria. In *Further Contributions to the Theory and Technique of Psycho-Analysis,* pp. 189–197. New York: Brunner Mazel, 1980.

——(1931). Child analysis in the analysis of adults. In *Further Contributions to the Theory and Technique of Psycho-Analysis,* pp. 126–147. New York: Brunner Mazel, 1980.

Ford, C. S., and Beach, F. A. (1951). *Patterns of Sexual Behavior.* New York: Harper & Row.

Freud, S. (1900). The interpretation of dreams. *Standard Edition* 4/5.

——(1905). Fragments of an analysis of a case of hysteria. In *Collected Papers of Sigmund Freud* 3:13–148. New York: Basic Books.

——(1909). Notes upon a case of obsessional neurosis. *Standard Edition* 10:155–237.

——(1910). Five lectures on psycho-analysis. *Standard Edition* 11:3–58.

——(1912). The dynamics of transference. *Standard Edition* 12:99–108.

——(1914a). Remembering, repeating, and working through. *Standard Edition* 12:147–156.

——(1914b). On narcissism. *Standard Edition* 14:67–104.

——(1918a). Psychoanalytic notes upon an autobiographical account of a case of paranoia (dementia paranoides). In *Collected Papers, vol. 3,* trans. A. and J. Strachey. New York: Basic Books.

——(1918b). The taboo of virginity. *Standard Edition* 11:192–208.

——(1920). The psychogenesis of a case of female homosexuality. *Standard Edition* 18:146–174.

——(1921). Group psychology and the analysis of the ego. *Standard Edition* 18:67–145.

——(1925). An autobiographical study. *Standard Edition* 20:3–74.

——(1930). Civilization and its discontent. *Standard Edition* 21:29–148.

——(1933). Letter to Einstein. *Standard Edition* 22:203–218.

——(1937). Analysis terminable and interminable. *Standard Edition* 23:216–253.

Fromm, E. (1956). *The Art of Loving.* New York: Harper and Row.

Galdston, R. (1987). The longest pleasure: a psychoanalytic study of hatred. *International Journal of Psycho-Analysis* 68:371–378.

Gillespie, W. H. (1956) The general theory of sexual perversions. *International Journal of Psycho-Analysis* 37:396–403.

Gilligan, C. (1982). *In a Different Voice.* Cambridge, MA: Harvard University Press.

Gitelson, M. (1952). The emotional position of the analyst in the psychoanalytic situation. *International Journal of Psycho-Analysis* 33:1–10.

Greenacre, P. (1941). The predisposition to anxiety. *Psychoanalytic Quarterly* 10:66–94, 610, 638.

Greenson, R. (1974). Loving, hating, and indifference toward the patient. *International Review of Psycho-Analysis* 1:259–266.

Groth, A. N. (1979). *Men Who Rape.* New York: Plenum.

Haley, J. (1973). *Uncommon Therapy.* New York: Norton.

——(1976). *Problem-Solving Therapy.* San Francisco: Jossey-Bass.

Hall, D. E., and Mohr, G. J. (1933). Prenatal attitudes of primaparae: a contribution to the mental hygiene of pregnancy. *Mental Hygiene* 17:226–234.

Harlow, H. F. (1958). The nature of love. *American Psychologist* 13:673–685.

Harlow, H. F., and Harlow, M. K. (1962). Social deprivation in monkeys. *Scientific American* 207:136–146.

Hoffer, E. (1951). *The True Believer*. New York: Time-Life Books, 1963.

Jacklin, C. N., Maccoby, E. E., and Doring, C. H. (1983). Neonatal sex steroid hormones and timidity in 6–18-month-old boys and girls. *Developmental Psychobiology* 16:163–168.

Jacobson, E. (1971). *Depression: Comparative Studies of Normal, Neurotic and Psychotic Conditions*. New York: International Universities Press.

Kaplan, H. S. (1979). *Disorders of Sexual Desire*. New York: Simon & Schuster.

Kardiner, A. (1954). *Sex and Morality*. New York: Bobbs Merrill.

Kernberg, O. (1975). *Borderline Conditions and Pathological Narcissism*. Northvale, NJ: Jason Aronson.

——(1976). *Object Relations Theory and Clinical Psychoanalysis*. Northvale, NJ: Jason Aronson.

Khan, M. M. R. (1979). *Alienation in the Perversions*. New York: International Universities Press.

Klein, M. (1932). *The Psycho-Analysis of Children*. Trans. Alix Strachey. New York: Delacorte Press, 1975.

Kohut, H. (1971). *The Analysis of the Self*. New York: International Universities Press.

Kolb, L. C. (1977). *Modern Clinical Psychiatry*. Philadelphia: W. B. Saunders.

Krafft-Ebing, R. V. (1932). *Psychopathia Sexualis*. New York: Paperback Library, 1965.

Laing, R. D., and Esterson, A. (1964). *Sanity, Madness and the Family*. New York: Basic Books.

Levine, R. (1979). Sexual deviance and society. In *On Sexuality*, ed. T. B. Karasu and C. W. Socarides. New York: International Universities Press.

Lidz, T., Fleck, S., and Cornelison, A. R. (1965). *Schizophrenia and the Family*. New York: International Universities Press.

Lindner, R. M. (1944). *Rebel without a Cause: The Story of a Clinical Psychopath*. New York: Grune and Stratton.

——(1955). *The Fifty-Minute Hour*. New York: Holt, Rinehart and Winston.

Little, M. (1951). Countertransference and the patient's response to it. *International Journal of Psycho-Analysis* 32:32–40.

Loewald, H. (1951). Ego and reality. In *Papers on Psychoanalysis*, pp. 3–20. New Haven: Yale University Press, 1980.

——(1973). Comments on some instinctual manifestations of superego formation. In *Papers on Psychoanalysis*, pp. 326–341. New Haven: Yale University Press, 1980.

Loewenstein, R. M. (1957). A contribution to the psychosomatic theory of masochism. *Journal of the American Psychoanalytic Association*. 5:197–234.

Lorenz, K. (1963). *On Aggression*. Trans. M. K. Wilson. New York: Harcourt, Brace & World.

Lowen, A. (1983). *Narcissism: Denial of the True Self*. New York: Macmillan.

Mahler, M. S. (1968). *On Human Symbiosis and the Vicissitudes of Individuation: Infantile Psychosis*. New York: International Universities Press.

Masterson, J. F. (1981). *The Narcissistic and Borderline Disorders: An Integrated Developmental Approach*. New York: Brunner Mazel.

McDougall, J. (1970). Homosexuality in women. In *Female Sexuality: New Psychoanalytic Views*, ed. J. Chasseguet-Sinergel, pp. 171–212. Ann Arbor, MI: University of Michigan Press.

Mead, M. (1935). *Sex and Temperament in Three Primitive Societies*. New York: William Morrow.

Melzach, R., and Scott, T. H. (1957). The effect of early experience on the response to pain. *Journal of Comparative Physiological Psychology* 50:155–161.

Meng, H., and Stern, E. (1955). Organ Psychosis. *Psychoanalytic Review* 42:428–434.

Menninger, K. (1938). *Man Against Himself*. New York: Harcourt, Brace & World.

——(1942). *Love Against Hate*. New York: Harcourt, Brace & World.

Menolascino, F. J., and Strider, F. D. (1981). Advances in the prevention and treatment of mental retardation. In *American Handbook of*

Psychiatry, vol. VII, ed. S. Arieti, pp. 614–648. New York: Basic Books.

Meyer, W., and Chesser, E. S. (1970). *Behaviour Therapy in Clinical Practice*. Harmondsworth, England: Penguin Books.

Meyers, H. (1988). A consideration of treatment techniques in relation to the functions of masochism. In *Masochism, Current Psychoanalytic Perspectives*, pp. 175–189. Hillsdale, NJ: The Analytic Press.

Miller, A. (1981). *Drama of the Gifted Child*. New York: Farrar, Straus & Giroux.

——(1983). *For Your Own Good: Hidden Cruelty in Childhood and The Roots of Violence*. New York: Farrar, Straus, Giroux.

Mintz, I. L. (1980). Multideterminism in asthmatic disease. *International Journal of Psychoanalytic Psychotherapy* 8:593–600.

Monro, A. (1972). Psychosomatic Medicine: I. The Psychosomatic Approach. *The Practitioner* 208:162–168.

Montagu, A. (1950). Constitutional and prenatal factors in infant and child health. In *Symposium of the Healthy Personality*, ed. M. Seen, pp. 148–175. New York: Josiah Macy, Jr. Foundation.

Muggeridge, M. (1965). A review of *The Liberal Establishment* by M. S. Evans in *Esquire*, Sept. 1965.

O'Regan, B. (1985). Multiple personality—mirrors of a new model of the mind. *Investigations* 1:1–2.

Panken, S. (1973). *The Joy of Suffering: Psychoanalytic Theory and Therapy of Masochism*. Northvale, NJ: Jason Aronson.

Perls, F. (1973). *The Gestalt Approach and Eye Witness to Therapy*. New York: Bantam Books, 1978.

Reich, A. (1950). Narcissistic object choice in Women. *Journal of the American Psychoanalytic Association* 1:22–44.

——(1966). On Countertransference. *International Journal of Psycho-Analysis* 32:25–31.

Reich, W. (1933). *Character Analysis*. New York: Touchstone, 1972.

——(1953). *The Murder of Christ*. New York: Orgone Institute Press.

Reik, T. (1941). *Masochism in Modern Man*. New York: Farrar, Straus, & Giroux.

Racker, H. (1968). *Transference and Countertransference*. New York: International Universities Press.

Robach, A. A., and Kiernan, T. (1969). *Pictorial History of Psychology and Psychiatry*. New York: Philosophical Library.

Roiphe, H., and Galenson, E. (1981). *Infantile Origins of Sexual Identity*. New York: International Universities Press.

Rokeach, M. (1964). *The Three Christs of Ypsilanti*. New York: Vintage.

Schoenewolf, G. (1989a). *101 Therapeutic Successes: Overcoming Transference and Resistance in Psychotherapy*. Northvale, NJ: Jason Aronson.

———(1989b). *Sexual Animosity between Men and Women*. Northvale, NJ: Jason Aronson.

———(1990). *Turning Points in Analytic Therapy: From Winnicott to Kernberg*. Northvale, NJ: Jason Aronson.

Schopenhauer, A. (1896). *The World as Will and Idea*. Trans. R. B. Haldane and J. Kemp. London: Kegan, Paul, Trench and Trubner.

Searles, H. F. (1958). The schizophrenic vulnerability to the therapist's unconscious processes. *Journal of Neuroses and Mental Disease* 127:247–262.

———(1972a). Unconscious processes in relation to the environment. *Psychoanalytic Review* 39:361–374.

———(1972b). The function of the patient's realistic perceptions of the analyst in delusional transference. In *Countertransference and Related Subjects*, pp. 197–223. New York: International Universities Press.

Seinfeld, J. (1990). *The Bad Object: Handling the Negative Therapeutic Reaction in Psychotherapy*. Northvale, NJ: Jason Aronson.

Shapiro, D. (1965). *Neurotic Styles*. New York: Basic Books.

Socarides, C. W. (1978). *Homosexuality*. Northvale, NJ: Jason Aronson.

———(1979). A unitary theory of sexual perversions. In *On Sexuality*, ed. T. B. Karasu and C. W. Socarides, pp. 161–188. New York: International Universities Press.

Spitz, R. (1965). *The First Year of Life*. New York: International Universities Press.

Spotnitz, H. (1976). *Psychotherapy of Preoedipal Conditions*. Northvale, NJ: Jason Aronson.

———(1985). *Modern Psychoanalysis of the Schizophrenic Patient*. New York: Human Sciences Press.

Spotnitz, H., and Meadows, P. (1976). *Treatment of the Narcissistic Neurosis*. New York: Manhattan Center for Modern Psychoanalytic Studies.

Stern, D. (1977). *The First Relationship: Infant and Mother*. Cambridge, MA: Harvard University Press.

Stoller, R. J. (1968). *Sex and Gender: The Development of Masculinity and Femininity*. London: H. Karnac, 1984.

Suttie, I. D. (1935). *The Origins of Love and Hate*. London: Free Association Books, 1988.

Tanner, L. B., ed. (1971). *Voices From Women's Liberation*. New York: Signet.

Wilson, P., and Mintz, G. L. (1989). *Psychosomatic Symptoms: Psychodynamic Treatment of the Underlying Personality*. Northvale, NJ: Jason Aronson.

Winnicott, D. W. (1949). Hate in the countertransference. In *Through Paediatrics to Psycho-Analysis*, pp. 194–203. New York: Basic Books.

——(1950). Aggression in relation to emotional development. In *Through Paediatrics to Psycho-Analysis*, pp. 204–218. Basic Books.

——(1953). Symptom tolerance in paediatrics. In *Through Paediatrics to Psycho-Analysis*, pp. 101–117. New York: Basic Books.

——(1965). *The Maturational Processes and the Facilitating Environment*. London: Hogarth Press.

——(1971). *Playing and Reality*. London: Tavistock Publications.

Index